Labor Relations in Japan Today

Tadashi Hanami

KODANSHA INTERNATIONAL LTD.
Tokyo, New York and San Francisco

Publication of this book was assisted by a grant from
the Japan Foundation.

Distributed in the United States by Kodansha Interna-
tional/USA Ltd. through Harper & Row, Publishers,
Inc., 10 East 53rd Street, New York, New York 10022.
Published by Kodansha International Ltd., 12-21 Otowa
2-chome, Bunkyo-ku, Tokyo 112 and Kodansha Inter-
national/USA Ltd., 10 East 53rd Street, New York,
New York 10022 and 44 Montgomery Street, San Fran-
cisco, California 94104. Copyright © 1979 by Kodansha
International Ltd. All rights reserved. Printed in Japan.
LCC 78-71313
ISBN 0-87011-492-1
JBC 1036-789776-2361
First paperback edition, 1981

CONTENTS

PREFACE

The remarkable economic growth in Japan during the last two decades has contributed to an increasing degree of attention and interest being given to the harmonious aspects of Japanese industrial relations. Japan's unique system of lifetime employment and enterprise unionism has led Westerners to believe that harmonious labor-management relations, obedience of employees toward employers and a cooperative union movement are the only distinguishing characteristics of Japanese industrial relations.

Certainly it is true that labor-management confrontation based on the Western model does not exist in Japan. It is also true that Japanese unions cooperate with management. The union's belief that their very existence depends on the company's survival and growth leads them to pay much attention to the welfare of the enterprise. However, industrial relations in Japan are not free from conflict and Japanese workers, as well as Western workers, can be dissatisfied with company policies.

There are two main reasons why Western observers have neglected to look into the question of conflicts and confrontation in Japanese industrial relations. First, most observers have been studying almost exclusively the larger enterprises where labor-management relations are better and where conflicts usually happen less often or are less serious than in smaller enterprises. The second and most important reason is that conflict in Japan manifests itself in a completely different way than it does in the West.

Because conflict is often implicit and its form of expression is more subtle, it is not always recognized as such by Western observers. Strikes rarely last longer than two or three days. What occurs is that, without engaging in an overt industrial action, the employees intentionally stop being cooperative. Since the criterion of conflict is the degree of cooperativeness given to the employer, it is very hard to tell when a dispute started or whether a dispute occurred at all. It is therefore evident that a slight decline in cooperativeness becomes a matter of serious concern because employee obedience and union cooperation have been a traditional pattern of industrial relations in Japan.

The very fact that conflict often remains under the surface also can lead to serious problems. Conflict is often allowed to proceed to an advanced stage without being recognized until it has become very difficult to handle. At that stage the matter no longer can be resolved without much friction. Thus, while disputes rarely occur in Japan, they are often of a serious nature and are hard to settle. One must also keep in mind that Japanese society frowns upon those who express their dissatisfaction or complain openly: individuals are expected to suffer in silence, which results in mental frustration. Should the informal, subtle and typically Japanese way of providing a harmonious solution to problems of human relationship fail, disputes all of a sudden tend to take a violent turn. In smaller firms such types of labor disputes are common today.

Thus the first purpose of this book is to inform Western readers of the fact that conflict does exist in Japanese industrial relations; that it takes a different form than in the West; and that it cannot be handled in the same way. The unique character of dispute settlement in Japan is the second main concern of this book.

In Japanese society, harmony is considered a basic social virtue, or norm, and conflict and personal confrontation a social evil. The goal of maintaining harmony in all aspects of human relationships is to be achieved by the practice of mutual understanding. Thus a person is expected to understand the problems and concerns of others and to behave in accordance with their wishes. However, this understanding of human relationships is not always present and friction sometimes does result. In such a case, the parties to the conflict do not rely on logic or on objective arguments as in the West. Rather they appeal to the emotions and sentiments of the parties. This method of dispute settlement is effective only where feelings of trust and the expectation of mutual understanding exist. Such feelings are naturally more prevalent in closed groups such as the family, the kinship group, or other communities of a similar kind.

Since the Japanese enterprise is a community which possesses some common characteristics with these tightly knit societies, the traditional way of resolving conflict can also be applied to industrial disputes. However, as discussed earlier, conflict is sometimes allowed to expand to such a degree that mutual trust and understanding between workers and management is destroyed. At that stage, resolution of conflict becomes very difficult because Japanese people are not used to solving industrial disputes logically by appealing to universal standards which are applicable beyond the limits of a closed society. The characteristics of industrial conflict and dispute settlement in Japan will be illustrated in this book by actual cases taken from contemporary Japanese industrial relations.

In recent years, labor management conflict in the Western world, and especially in Europe, has been directed to new issues. While in the past the workers were mostly concerned with economic problems, nowadays they demand that their social and psychological needs be satisfied. Because the collective bargaining system of the West evolved from the need to solve economic issues, it is less capable in dealing with the sociopsychological problems of workers in a post-industrial society. It is possible, therefore, that the unique aspects of Japanese dispute settlement could contribute to the search for new approaches in industrial relations by highly industrialized societies, thus leading us to the third objective of this book.

Japan is probably the only non-Western nation to have become a successful industrial country within the relatively short time of one

11

hundred years. Its most modern systems, including the legal system, were borrowed from Western countries. The introduction of Western culture, however, was not a simple process of imitation. The Japanese modified the Western model to adapt it to their own culture and, through this modification, the real nature of the Western model has sometimes changed into something entirely different. Inevitably, applying Western terminology to Japanese phenomena (often very different in nature from their Western counterparts) has led to confusion. Quite often the Japanese themselves are lured by the magic of terminology and are lost in a maze. This is especially true of intellectuals who received their higher education in Western institutions. The author of this book is no exception to the rule.

Japan's modern legal system was borrowed from the West in entirety. In particular, the labor law system is literally a fine patchwork of British, German and American systems. Until several years ago, my main effort as a scholar was to comprehend and to interpret Japanese labor law as systematically as possible in the light of my understanding of the original systems from which it was derived. From this understanding, I tried to interpret the law as it applied to actual labor relations. My basic approach has been to integrate the facts and precedents established in labor cases into a rational scheme—a scheme which corresponded to my image of an industrial relations system and, at the same time, took the Western model into consideration.

At some point, however, I began to doubt whether this approach could meaningfully be applied to Japanese industrial relations. This change in attitude can be attributed primarily to my experience as a member of the Tokyo Metropolitan Labor Relations Commission. During the ten years I was engaged in resolving labor disputes, presiding at hearings and issuing orders on unfair labor practice cases, I began to ponder more and more the differences between the Western concept of industrial relations and the Japanese reality. Many Japanese intellectuals, myself included, are uneasy and troubled by a sense of incongruity. This is especially true for those older scholars who have devoted themselves to

12

studying Western civilization simply because to them Westernization meant modernization. For these individuals the turning point came when the rapidly expanding Japanese economy reached the level of economic development in the West. Having accomplished this primary objective, we Japanese no longer have a clear goal to pursue and feel uneasy since we do not know where to go from here.

The original work on which this book is based was written in 1972 and published the following year by Nihon Keizai Shinbun Sha, under the title, *Rōdō Sōgi: Rōshi Kankei ni Miru Nihonteki Fūdo* (Labor Disputes: Industrial Relations in the Japanese Climate). During the process of translation into English, the text was changed and expanded substantially and the subject matter thoroughly reorganized to suit Western readers. Furthermore, I tried to improve the text by reexamining the problems, adding new material and referring to recent sources and theories which were not utilized in the original. Thus this study is a complete revision of the Japanese edition and might be considered a totally new book.

The intention of the original work was to describe the Japanese industrial relations system and to criticize its negative aspects in order to stimulate the rationalization of the system. However, in the process of preparing this text, I began to consider the problems that have arisen in Western societies in recent years. These problems are most dramatically exemplified by such occurrences as wildcat strikes affecting most industrialized European countries, the emergence of white-collar unions, the unsuccessful experiments with income policy, the stagnation of the traditional union movement and the apathy among union members since the 1950s.

In the present book, therefore, I have tried to analyze the malaise of the trade union movement as well as the industrial relations system as a whole in the light of the new developments in post-industrial society. These recent developments have been the object of many studies and numerous prescriptions have been offered to cope with the new problems. I shall approach the question from a different angle by dealing specifically with two points: first, the fact that the Japanese experience has failed to follow exactly the pattern of other industrialized societies and, secondly, the unique and unintentional successes which have resulted for Japan by not following that pattern.

During my work on the English version, my attention focused on two important academic problems, both related to anthropology rather than to the theory of industrial relations. First, American anthropologists have recently become aware of the fact that Western legal concepts, based on the principle of "reasonable man," do not always fit in different social systems. As a result of comparative studies on dispute settlement in several non-Western societies, they came to see the importance of negotiation as a step in the dispute settlement process as distinguished from adjudication. At the same time, they came to realize the similarities rather than the differences between these two modes of dispute settlement. Their research emphasizes that an adjudicator often becomes more of a mediator between the disputants than a decision-maker.[1] In 1965, a distinguished American anthropologist called attention to "the lack of mutual interest between those who study something called 'conflict resolution' and those who study 'legal procedure' and 'judicial process.' "[2] As a labor lawyer I have been concerned with both "conflict resolution" and "legal procedure." Thus, I hope that this work can throw some light on the questions raised by anthropologists. On the one hand, I shall attempt to analyze the nature of dispute settlement in the area of industrial relations where negotiation has always been considered one of the legitimate steps in the dispute settlement process.

On the other hand, Japan is one of the exceptional cases of a society where industrialization has been achieved successfully by applying a Western legal system without sacrificing traditional social values and culture at the same time. In Japan, an adjudicator always has been more of a mediator than a decision maker. We can consider the case of Japan, as well as that of China,[3] as interesting experiments in this respect. In both countries, the traditional preference for mediation over adjudication is based on fundamental societal values stressing harmony and compromise.

14

This preference has been successfully brought into play, perhaps intentionally in China and unconsciously in Japan, as a tool in the development of a new type of society and as a means of introducing norms different from the traditional ones.

The second problem which caught my attention while writing this book is one which is more elusive and at the same time more fundamental to comparative studies in general. I began to appreciate more and more the overwhelming difficulty of comparative studies and the reasons why the researcher is often driven to desperation and tempted to give up altogether. Scholars involved in comparative studies necessarily have certain ideas about the societies they study on which they build their hypotheses. However, these ideas are based on a limited knowledge of these societies. In the case of this book, I kept wondering whether my conception of Western industrial relations might not be drawn more from the literature on the subject than from the reality of the situation. Often what I have assumed to be uniquely Japanese can also be found in Western societies. In particular, the idea that Western society can be characterized as "rational" is not always reflected in reality. For example, one can easily find "irrational" phenomena in Western industrial relations as well as in business relationships. Thus, one can infer that the differences between East and West are simply a matter of degree and not of substance.

In recent publications, foreign observers have advanced the concept of "convergence," i.e., that the recent changes in Japanese industrial relations will result in the Japanese system becoming identical with the Western model.[4] In view of the fact that when changes take place certain fundamental characteristics of the Japanese society remain the same, I find myself unable to agree completely with this estimate.[5] However, it may be that the difference between the two theories is one of emphasis rather than substance. Probably the important question is to analyze "the complex relations between universal tendencies and national cultural differences, and the way in which change occurs."[6]

I am anxious, therefore, to continue the dialogue with observers engaged in studying the differences between East and West in every

15

field. I particularly appreciate the friendship of foreign friends and the valuable discussions we have had throughout the years. Especially, I would like to express my gratitude to those who have encouraged and helped me during the preparation of this edition, and without whose kindness this book would never have been published: Professor Robert E. Cole, University of Michigan; Father Robert J. Ballon, Sophia University and Professor Ehud Harari, University of Jerusalem. On the Japanese side, I am indebted to the late Professor Emeritus Ichirō Nakayama of the Japan Institute of Labor, who was a constant source of encouragement. I am also grateful to the Center for Japanese and Korean Studies of the University of California at Berkeley and the Ford Foundation, whose grants enabled me to work on the English edition of this book and to Mrs. Genévieve Jain and Mr. Paul Zito, whose painstaking editing is the only thing to have made this book somewhat presentable to English readers.

NOTES

1. P. H. Gulliver, "Case Studies of Law in Non-Western Societies," in *Law in Culture and Society*, ed. Laura Nadar (Chicago: Aldine Publishing Co., 1969), pp. 11–23.

2. Laura Nader, "Introduction," in *Law in Culture and Society*, p. 5.

3. Stanley Lubman, "Mao and Mediation: Politics and Dispute Resolution in Communist China," *California Law Review* 55 (1967): 1284–1359.

4. Bernard Karsh and Robert E. Cole, "Industrialization and the Convergence Hypothesis: Some Aspects of Contemporary Japan," *Journal of Social Issues* 24, no. 4 (1968): 45–64; Ronald P. Dore, *British Factory—Japanese Factory* (Berkeley and Los Angeles: University of California Press, 1973); Gertrude Horke, *Arbeiter unter der roten Sonne—Japans Unternehemensgenwerkshaften* (Vienna: Europaverlag, 1976).

5. See Part I, chapter 2.

6. Karsh and Cole, "Aspects of Contemporary Japan," p. 63.

Part I

Industrial Relations in Postwar Japan

1

TRADITION VERSUS MODERNIZATION

1. ESCAPE FROM FRUSTRATION AND DESPERATION

Japanese lawyers, and economists to some extent, occasionally despair when faced with the magnitude of the task of "rationalizing" and "modernizing" Japanese society. They usually assume that such rationalization and modernization are only possible through Westernization. Ever since the Meiji Restoration, the Japanese effort toward modernization has consistently followed the Western pattern, which was considered as the ideal model. Japan has introduced Western systems, especially the legal system, into almost every area of society without any major modifications. Intellectuals have adopted Western ideas and philosophy. Whenever they are faced with some gap or discrepancy between these imported systems and the ideas upon which these systems are based on the one hand, and the reality of the Japanese society on the other hand, they often conclude that the society has not progressed far enough along the path of modernization, in spite of a century of sincere efforts in that direction. From a "rational" viewpoint and on the basis of Western ideas, Japanese reality is always irrational and too emotional.

In the field of industrial relations as well, if one wishes to rationalize the Japanese system along Western lines, frustration and despair are inevitable. A distinguished labor lawyer, who has been involved in labor dispute settlements for many years, once acknowledged this fact by stating:

> Industrial relations are conducted without established rules; they are influenced by emotional factors and beset by treacherous antagonism and misunderstanding. This is particularly true in the case of the small and medium-size enterprises, but it also happens in larger enterprises when the disputes become disorderly. These characteristics obstruct dispute settlement by means of the unfair labor practice system. This system can function efficiently only when it is able to dispose of each case rapidly. Actually the parties do not expect the Labor Relations Commission to give a solution to specific problems. Rather they want the Commission to provide them with a panacea which will solve the problems which arise out of their impossible industrial relations system.[1]

Since the Japanese experience in industrial relations cannot provide valid guidelines for action, the Commission must find rules and norms for the way labor relations are practiced outside Japan. Such rules can only be derived from the Western model, which does not fit perfectly with the reality of Japanese industrial relations. Both types of industrial relations are based on different social and personal relationships: the independence of the individual and economic rationalism in the West and, in Japan, the existence of an emotional, perhaps sentimental, relationship between employer and employee within the enterprise. Although organizations systems, and activities such as unions, collective bargaining, work councils and disputes (including strikes) are based on the same concepts in Japan as in the West, their concrete manifestations are not identical.

As implied in the above quotation, those who have been deeply involved in the practice of dispute settlement have become aware of how deeply rooted are the "Japanese" characteristics in Japanese industrial relations. Secondly, they realize the futility of trying to introduce incompatible Western practices into the process. If we take the attitude that in order to catch up with Western levels we must imitate Western culture, frustration and despair are the unavoidable consequences. What good would it be to strive for a modernized Japan which could never be more than a poor imitation of the West?

Resistance to the Western model has come from two sources. The conservative viewpoint emphasizes the superiority of Japanese virtues over the qualities of the West and a more moderate view advocates blending modern and traditional values, according to the well-known slogan *wakon yōsai* or (Japanese spirit and Western technology). This slogan was launched at the time of the Meiji Restoration by Japanese intellectuals who welcomed the introduction of Western civilization but wished to preserve Japanese values. It is derived from an older slogan *wakon kansai* or (Japanese spirit and Chinese technology) which was used at the time of the introduction of the Chinese culture in the sixth century.

However, neither of these viewpoints helps to overcome the frustration of modern Japanese intellectuals. The conservative attitude cannot be sustained seriously because actual modernization has, in fact, closely followed the Western model. Similarly, those advocating compromise must acknowledge Western superiority, at least in the field of technology. In an attempt to find a way out of this philosophical labyrinth, the author has attempted to analyze the "desperate" state of Japanese industrial relations in the hope of discovering a new way to deal with labor problems and bring about a total change of attitude.

The objective of the Western industrial relations system has been to "organize" disputes, i.e., to provide dispute settlement machinery and to dispose of disputes rationally by assuming that labor relations are simply economic relationships. Until recently, this approach has been more or less successful. However, labor relations themselves are, by their very nature, more than mere economic exchanges of labor and wages: they are basically human relations. In the final analysis, labor disputes are "cultural" and informal (unorganized) rather than "economic" and formally organized.[2] Therefore, the Western methods of resolving conflict cannot work effectively in Japan. Moreover, the extent to which they are a failure is gradually becoming evident.

One also should note that the rights and obligations of the parties in labor relations are fluid and apt to be modified along with the development of their relationship. These rights and obligations are not as exact and clear-cut as those which govern economic relationships. Therefore, legal procedures are not suitable for the settlement of labor disputes since their function is to settle disputes by applying universal legal norms. The reality of labor dispute settlement in Japan is quite different from in the West, since the process has been adjusted to a particular Japanese situation. The courts deviate from the original functions of judicial institutions by playing the role of conciliator. They sometimes do not base their rulings on the universal legal norms but on "dynamic" norms which take into account the future development of the relations of the parties to the dispute. The role of the Labor Relations Commission is also apt to make rulings which have the force of law on subjects on which the labor code is silent, a role perhaps not desirable from the standpoint of the principle of autonomy of the parties.

In most Western countries, the autonomy of labor and management has been considered essential and government or court intervention, when permitted, has been looked upon as a necessary evil. However, a transformation in the functions of the courts and of conciliation bodies is taking place in Western countries as well. For some time now, the labor courts have been unable to limit their role to that of neutral bodies and limit the role of conciliators to that of simple helpers in the bargaining process.[3] The reluctance of Westerners to acknowledge that the reality differs from the model is the result of their ideological commitment to the principle of autonomy. This principle is based on the belief that the parties in industrial relations, especially the labor unions, are the instruments of progress. However, as pointed out by John Kenneth Galbraith, in Western societies unions are no longer thought of as the harbingers of the future.[4]

In Japanese society, unions have not contributed so much to the development of human rights and human welfare as they have to economic growth.[5] The author does not think that economic growth, industrialization, or even the growth of the G.N.P. are synonymous with "progress." If we understood progress in these terms, Japanese industrial relations would be considered more "progressive" when compared to the West. It is quite understandable that Western countries, in which the existing system is now facing an impasse, have become interested in the unique Japanese system, which appears to be in the privileged position of avoiding this impasse while maintaining the pace of tremendous economic growth. Some of the peculiar features of the Japanese industrial relations system, such as enterprise unionism or the unique methods of dispute settlement, might be more advanced than Western practices. Masao Maruyama has ironically pointed out that the "old stratum" of Japanese culture might have made modern Japan the most advanced country in the world, in part due to the confusion and stagnation of the West.[6] This is perhaps true also in industrial relations.

In general, Japanese people tend to believe in the uniqueness of Japanese culture and emphasize its differences from Western culture. Foreign observers also are struck by these differences when they first encounter Japanese society and culture. In recent years, however, a number of Westerners have put forward the notion of "convergence" of the two cultures. In the field of industrial relations, Kerr, Dunlop, Harbison and Meyers's classical work has had a tremendous impact.[7] According to them, the "logic of industrialism" leads to a convergence which cuts through and undermines "tradition," irrespective of the main features of culture and history, and the values which are peculiar to the society engaged in the industrialization process. This hypothesis is rejected by the so-called "culturalists." One of their spokesmen, James Abegglen, points out that the differences between the two cultures persist in spite of some modifications necessitated by the advanced degree of industrialization.[8] Having examined these two theories, Robert E. Cole proposes a third possible approach: the "functional alternatives" hypothesis. This approach is based on the viewpoint that "there are limited sets of functional alternatives which are

23

compatible with the requirements of operating advanced technologies."[9]

It is certainly true that the "culturalists" ignore some fundamental similarities which are found between two cultures resulting from the process of industrialization. Furthermore, this approach denies the possibility of cultural change and development. The culturalist theory, with its emphasis on Japanese uniqueness, tends to be fatalistic and leads to pessimism. On the other hand, the "convergence" theory neglects the differences which exist in spite of the trend toward uniformity. In fact, the difficulties encountered by many developing countries engaged in the process of industrialization can be attributed to an exclusive reliance on the theory of "convergence." Similarly, the narrow viewpoint of Westerners engaged in development programs is partly responsible for the failure of these programs in developing countries. Therefore, there are compelling reasons for examining the Japanese model in order to evaluate and analyze the meaning of the cultural uniqueness and the extent to which it has persisted as a "functional alternative" throughout the process of industrialization. In other words, it is worth finding out why and to what extent Japanese uniqueness has survived and whether its survival has facilitated or impeded industrial development in Japan.

A good starting point for this inquiry would be to study the lifetime employment system in Japan, to which both Cole and Abegglen have paid a great deal of attention. Since the publication of their studies a number of works dealing with the Japanese employment system have been published in English.[10] In the following sections, we shall discuss the scope of the lifetime employment system (in particular the question of the often-neglected nonpermanent labor force) and the significant changes which have affected the system as a whole since the early 1950s. These two aspects of the question must be taken into account if we are to understand the meaning of the lifetime employment system and to predict the possibility and the extent of future changes in the system. The impact of the permanent employment system on the personal relationships between employees and employer will also

24

be discussed since the nature of this relationship has a direct bearing on the nature of labor disputes in Japan, which is the main subject of this book.

2. LIFETIME EMPLOYMENT AND SENIORITY WAGE

The labor force in Japanese enterprises is divided into two categories: regular employees and temporary employees. Although figures on the respective percentages of the two categories of employees are not available, it is generally accepted that regular employees largely outnumber temporary employees in most enterprises, except perhaps in very small ones. Some idea of the numbers can be derived from statistics concerning newly hired workers. For the last several years, temporary workers have amounted to less than 20 percent of the total (19.4% in 1970; 17% in 1970; and 19.5% in 1973).[11]

Each enterprise recruits most of its regular employees in April right after graduation from high school or college. There is no legal obligation for employees to stay in a particular enterprise longer than one year. Article 14 of the Labor Standards Law of 1947 provides: "Labor contracts, with the exception of those without any set period, shall not be concluded for a period longer than one year, except in the case of those requiring a definite period for the completion of a project." Nor does the employer have a legal obligation to keep his workers: employees may be dismissed with or without notice, depending on the reason for the dismissal. According to Article 20 of the Labor Standards Law, the employer must give at least a thirty days' advance notice before dismissal or pay a compensation amounting to thirty days' average wage, "except when the continuance of the enterprise is made impossible by reason of some natural calamity or other inevitable cause, or when the dismissal is caused by the employee's own behavior."

Usually, after a period of probation, ranging from fourteen days to six months depending on the enterprise, workers gain the status

25

of regular employees. Thereafter they are expected to stay in the particular enterprise until they reach the retirement age prescribed in the work rules of the enterprise, normally between fifty-five and sixty years of age. Employers are not expected to dismiss regular employees. Dismissal is largely the result of grave misconduct on the part of an employee or of an unusual decline in business. In order to cope with normal business fluctuations, however, Japanese enterprises make use of temporary workers. Temporary workers are employed for a certain period, most of the time one or two weeks but sometimes one or two months. As long as business is booming their contracts are renewed. On the other hand, when the enterprise considers it necessary to cut its manpower, it simply refuses to renew the contracts of the temporary employees. In other words, the temporary employees are the shock absorbers of business fluctuations in a lifetime employment system.

Under this system, regular employees receive annual wage increments which are given automatically with each year of service. Thus the total income of each employee increases in accordance with the length of time he has worked in the enterprise. In addition to monthly wages, most Japanese enterprises pay yearly bonuses, which range from three to six times the average monthly wage, depending on the business situation of the company. Retirement allowances, paid in a lump sum, also depend on the length of service. The allowances paid to employees retiring at the prescribed retirement age are particularly generous, thus encouraging regular employees to stay with the company. As a result of such a "seniority" wage system, the wages of employees of the same age and with the same educational background tend to be the same. Some important exceptions will be discussed later.

At this point, however, an important question arises. Since dismissal is an exceptional procedure, what makes the individual employee work so hard in a system under which he could work less but still expect to keep his job and to enjoy wage increases every year? Why are Japanese workers so industrious? It is true that payment based on results exists in Japan and that certain segments of the paycheck are linked with the worker's efficiency. But these are not the main factors which motivate Japanese employees to work as hard as they do.

One of the key clues to the mystery of Japanese efficiency is the promotion system. Although wages basically depend upon a worker's educational background and length of service, when chances for promotion to responsible positions arise after a few years of employment, differences do become apparent. Only some of the employees recruited in a given year can immediately reach higher positions. Others have to wait longer before being promoted and some never rise beyond a certain level. As time passes the differences become more pronounced.

Since workers expect to stay in the same enterprise for their entire working lives, those recruited in the same year compete fiercely with each other. The anxiety and frustration prevailing among employees at the time of yearly personnel changes is well described by Thomas P. Rohlen.[12] A blue-collar worker may become head of a plant or may end up as *kachō* (chief of a section). A university graduate may become president of the company, while most of his colleagues might still be *buchō* (chief of a department) when they retire. These differences in rank and status result in substantial differences in total wages and in retirement benefits among workers of the same age group with the same educational background (see Table 1).

Table 1
Wage Differences among Employees of Same Age and Educational Background

	Middle School Graduate		High School Graduate		University Graduate	
Age	Minimum	Maximum	Minimum	Maximum	Minimum	Maximum
18	100	121	117	117		
22					157	157
23	133	160	134	176		
30	155	209	195	257	198	324
45	267	317/356	359	476		

*Basic element only, of male lifetime employees at Hitachi Co. (minimum for 18-year-old middle school graduate = 100).
Source: Dore, *British Factory—Japanese Factory*, p. 101.

27

Another crucial factor which contributes to Japanese employees' diligence is their strong loyalty to and identification with their enterprise. Since they stay in the same enterprise for their entire working lives, their fate and well-being depend almost entirely on the prosperity of the enterprise. Furthermore, most Japanese enterprises still function like traditional social groups in which members share a strong sense of belonging and exclusiveness. Thus the relationship between an employer and his employees cannot be reduced to the terms of a contract. Both parties to the relationship "are bound as one by fate in conditions which produce a tie between man and man often as firm and close as that between husband and wife."[13] Westerners are well aware of the fact that a Japanese company often refers to itself as an "enterprise-family" and to employer and employees as "family members." This enterprise-family consciousness produces a total commitment by the employees toward the enterprise. However, this sentimental or emotional commitment is nurtured and reinforced by the welfare policy of the enterprise. In the following section it will be shown how Japanese enterprises take care of the total personal lives of employees and their families.

3. THE LIFETIME "WELFARE" SYSTEM

The employer-employee relationship in Japan goes beyond a mere exchange of labor and wages. First, the newly hired workers need to be trained. As mentioned earlier, most of the employees are recruited when they are fresh out of high school or college; the Japanese educational system as a whole is oriented more toward general education than toward vocational training. Therefore, an enterprise must train its labor force, either in its own training facilities or on the job. During their long career at the same enterprise, workers are likely to be transferred from one job to another. They are trained and retrained, especially after each move. Frequent transfer is one of the characteristics of the Japanese employer–employee relationship. It gives the enterprise greater flexibility to cope with technological changes, the introduction of new products, the expansion of the scope of business, and the opening of new plants ("scrap-and-build") because of innovations and changing business conditions. Dore points out the high degree of job interchangeability in the Japanese factory: "Workers can be 'posted' within the firm from one factory to another for months or years at a time, much as soldiers are posted to a new station."[14] The educational functions of Japanese enterprises are not limited to job training. A variety of courses are provided for the employees in traditional arts like tea ceremony, flower arrangement, or Zen meditation, in addition to general education courses. Some companies run their own adult education programs at a level equivalent to senior high school or college. Graduates of such programs are treated as high school or university graduates in terms of wage and working conditions.

The enterprise also takes care of the education of the employees' children. In contemporary Japan the compeitition to enter the better schools is very keen. The enterprise tries to utilize personal connections with schoolteachers in order to facilitate the admission of employees' children. In case of a transfer to another locality which makes a change of school necessary, one of the most important functions of the personnel division of the company is to secure admission of the employee's children to a good school.

Enterprises also provide recreation facilities such as sports fields and equipment, vacation facilities and recreational courses. In every enterprise, the yearly or twice-yearly company trip is a big event. The company makes arrangements for transportation and hotel reservations and provides substantial financial help, supplementing the amount contributed by the individual employees. During such trips, employers and employees eat together. Heavy drinking is customary during the evening dinner parties. Everybody, including the president of the company, is supposed to become completely frank to release tensions and develop mutual trust between all the enterprise family members. Athletic contests held by companies are also special occasions. Unions join manage-

29

ment in organizing several kinds of such matches and facilitating the pursuit of other hobbies. Exhibitions of paintings, calligraphy, flower arrangements and so on are also very popular. Company newspapers often publish employees' essays, poems and, sometimes, complete novels.

The companies also get involved in more personal matters such as weddings and funerals of employees and their family members. In Japan, even now most marriages are arranged marriages. Arrangements usually are made by relatives or friends, but not infrequently by the employee's superior at the workplace. At the wedding party, in both "arranged" and "love" marriages, the superiors are always invited. An executive, sometimes even the president of the company (depending on the status of the groom or bride), plays the role of go-between in the ceremony. Rohlen describes most vividly how such arrangements were worked out in a Japanese bank.[15] Companies always send flowers to the funerals of an employee or his family members. Fellow employees are also given leave to enable them to help the bereaved. If the death is that of an employee with a record of distinguished service to the enterprise, a company official customarily presides over the ceremony and the company pays all the expenses.

The most important function of Japanese companies is one which, in most industrialized societies, is the responsibility of social security or social welfare. In addition to basic wages, Japanese companies usually provide family allowances based on the number of dependents, cost allowances for housing, commuting and so on. Often they provide company housing facilities and dormitories. Larger plants and offices have their own clinics to supply medical care for the employees. The lump-sum retirement benefits are intended to make it possible for a retired employee to buy a small house or start a small business on which he can depend for the rest of his life without much worry. Because of inflation and the increase in the price of real estate since the end of World War II, these retirement sums are no longer sufficient. In recent years, therefore, some of the public companies have begun to pay pensions in order to supplement the pensions that are paid to retired workers by the national social security system.

Japanese enterprises also are playing an important role in coping with unemployment by refraining as far as possible from dismissing regular employees. Inefficient or lazy workers, rather than being dismissed, are assigned to unimportant jobs and not promoted. Dismissal of regular employees in overstaffed positions is also exceptional and avoided as far as possible. First, surplus labor in a certain division, plant or job category does not necessarily cause problems, because the employees are not attached to a certain job. Employees who are no longer needed in a certain section of the enterprise are likely to be transferred to another unit. Second, the enterprises try to find, or sometimes create, work for surplus labor. The most remarkable case of this sort is that of a large steel company which started to plant trees on the spacious grounds surrounding its steel mill. It thus supplied some work for those who lost their jobs as a result of production cuts during the recession which followed the 1973 oil crisis. Another company began planting orange groves for the same reason.

Using Talcott Parson's terminology,[16] Japanese enterprises are good examples of "functional diffusiveness." They should thus be classified as "traditional" rather than "industrial." However, the fact is that the "traditional" features of Japanese enterprises have contributed to business efficiency, technological development and an astonishing expansion of business operations.

4. RECENT CHANGES IN LIFETIME EMPLOYMENT

It is commonly believed that the lifetime employment system is "traditional" in the sense that it grew out of a practice prevalent over a long period. In fact, it was established by some of the big enterprises during and after World War I,[17] and was institutionalized in its present form after World War II.[18] Certain features of the system have been modified as a result of changes in the Japanese industrial structure and in the labor market. After 1955, the Japanese economy continued to expand, with an annual G.N.P. growth rate of around 17% or 18%. At the same time, the relative output of various industrial sectors changed significantly: primary industries declined whereas manufacturing and construction expanded markedly. Between 1955 and 1967, the number of firms in manufacturing industries increased by 138%, the number of employees by 175%, and the value-added by 677%.[19] Chemical and heavy industries developed greatly during the same period. The machinery industry, which accounted for 18.5% of the manufacturing sector in 1955, increased to 31.4% in 1968.[20]

Changes in the labor market after 1955 directly reflected the rapid expansion of the Japanese economy and its structural changes. The number of employees in manufacturing industries increased by 30% between 1955 and 1959. In 1961 and 1963, the increases amounted to 50% and 70% respectively. By 1966, the number of workers in enterprises with more than 30 employees had increased by 60% over the level of 1955.[21]

It is worth noting that a continuous labor surplus has been a major feature of the Japanese economy throughout the period of modernization. This labor surplus was characterized by high unemployment, disguised unemployment, and very poor living conditions for most of the people living on farms. By the 1960s, this labor surplus had disappeared and, for the first time in Japanese history, a labor shortage emerged. It is particularly remarkable, in this context, that the labor shortage affected young workers the most, especially new graduates from junior and senior high schools. In April 1970, seven job vacancies were reported for each junior high school graduate. The demand for new graduates was especially high in manufacturing industries. After 1962, about 80 percent of the junior high school graduates and 45 percent of the senior high school graduates joined manufacturing industries.

Another noticeable trend in the labor market after 1955 has been the increasing mobility of labor. The total number of employees changing jobs nearly doubled between 1959 and 1962 (from 425,000 to 802,000).[22] Other conspicuous phenomena caused by the labor shortage are the rising participation of women in the labor force and the growing tendency of female employees to stay longer at their jobs. In Japan, as in many other industrial societies, women workers traditionally have been regarded as temporary workers. The labor shortage and other factors such as the changing character of labor caused by technological change, changes in living styles and housing conditions, and the availability of household appliances have contributed to modifying this traditional pattern. The number of female employees nearly doubled between 1955 and 1969. Female employees now constitute one-third of the total employed labor force. The proportion of married women among the total number of women employees exceeded 50 percent in 1969. Part-time female employees account for a significant portion of these increases, especially in the married female employee sector. They have become a last resort for much-needed additional labor.

The labor shortage has caused some changes in the established pattern of the lifetime employment system. First, the shortage of young people in the labor force, especially new graduates, contributed to a decrease in wage differences by age and by size of enterprise. Starting wages have increased more rapidly in the smaller rather than in the larger enterprises (Table 2). The belief that younger workers are more adaptable to rapid technological change has also contributed to narrowing the wage difference between younger and older workers.

Second, as was shown earlier, the labor shortage has led to a growing labor mobility. The urge to move, to seek better working

Table 2
Starting Wage Indexes by Enterprise Size

Enterprise Size Employees	1958	1968
500 and more	100.0	100.0
100–499	69.7	74.5
30–99	54.7	61.7
5–29	43.6	49.3

Source: Ministry of Labor, *Monthly Labor Survey*, 1958 and 1968.

conditions and brighter career prospects is certainly new. Under the lifetime employment system, the better employees stay in a particular enterprise, get promoted and enjoy the privileges of seniority. But, due to an acute labor shortage, especially for competent and adaptable workers with technical knowledge and skills, a number of enterprises have started to recruit employees from other companies. They offer terms equivalent to, or sometimes better than, those of their own regular employees. This trend is in sharp contrast with the traditional pattern, under which most of the employees recruited from other enterprises are regarded as temporary workers or at least are offered less attractive salaries and working conditions than those given to workers recruited immediately after graduation.

However, in spite of the impact of this new practice of "pulling out" workers from other companies, its effect on the employment system should not be overstated. Labor mobility is growing, but this process still does not reflect a general practice. Pulling out has become popular in the case of salesmen, technical engineers and other highly skilled workers, but ordinary workers continue to be recruited from among new school graduates. Enterprises are naturally reluctant to let their own capable employees be recruited by competing companies and, after enticing employees from other companies, they want very much to keep these employees. In this sense, the pulling out practice, while it seems to weaken the lifetime employment system, tends to strengthen it in a modified form. In fact, protection from employee-raiding by other companies was the major motivation for evolving the lifetime employment system in the prewar period.[23]

In this connection, we should also consider Galbraith's contention that the impact of technological innovation and high industrialization may serve to strengthen the identification of employees with their own respective enterprises.[24] In some ways, this observation is true of Japan. However, it is also possible that technocrats, because their knowledge and skills can be used by any company, may be more mobile than are regular employees. This observation may be particularly applicable to technocrats at the lower level of the organization who are still out of the inner circle and are impatient to be admitted to that circle.

Another factor likely to sustain the lifetime employment system is the fact that, because of the labor shortage, temporary employees are staying longer in one enterprise. Female employees especially are encouraged to remain with one organization. The longer they stay, the more they want to be promoted and treated like regular employees. Some of the enterprises have started to promote temporary employees, even part-time employees, to the status of regular employees. This development does not point to a decline but rather to a modification of the lifetime employment system.

Having examined the changing pattern of the lifetime (or permanent) employment system in the 1960s, Cole perceives "a possible weakening of the permanent employment practice." However, he admits that, compared with the American system, the Japanese labor market is tighter, puts greater emphasis on the recruitment of new school graduates and is characterized by a high rate of retention of workers.[25] Looking at the situation in the 1970s, Abegglen pointed out in 1972 that Japan's employment system had not changed in any basic or extensive way: "Any reasonable view of the past two decades, however, must conclude that continuity is the predominant fact, and that substantial change, while often heralded, is yet to occur."[26]

Since most of the significant changes described above originated from a labor shortage during a period of rapid economic growth, the recession caused by the energy crisis is likely to stop or reverse the trend toward the stimulation of turnover. During a recession, employees naturally tend to stick to their present jobs and Japanese companies adhere more closely to the practices of the lifetime employment system as far as their surplus labor is concerned. Perhaps it is still too early to evaluate the impact of the recession. At present it would not be justified to predict the decline of the lifetime employment system in the near future, unless one envisions that a much more serious crisis, indeed a catastrophe, will affect the Japanese economy.

5. PATERNALISM TO WELFARE CORPORATISM

The previous sections dealt with the nature of the Japanese employment system and we concluded with the suggestion that it would remain largely unchanged in the foreseeable future. In order to predict the future trends of Japanese industrial relations in their broader aspects and, especially, the future pattern of labor disputes, we should take into consideration the nature of Japanese industrial society and the union movement. According to Clark Kerr's classic analysis, industrial societies are divided into four types: authoritarian, paternalistic, competitive and class-conscious.[27] The type of industrial relations and the pattern of labor disputes will vary not only according to the type of industrial society prevalent in the particular country, but also according to the characteristics of the union movement. The latter to some extent would be correlated to the type of society. For our present purpose, it appears sufficient to distinguish between the two main types of unionism: business unionism and political unionism.

The development of business unionism in a competitive industrial society is likely to give rise to disputes and, in turn, economic conflicts. Such disputes can lead to "rationalized" settlements, that is, settlements expressed in dollars and cents. According to the orthodox viewpoint, the nature of Japanese industrial society is paternalistic. Within a paternalistic industrial society, disputes are not expected to occur. If and when they do occur, they are usually solved when both parties make an effort to understand each other's point of view and reach accommodation. Such disputes do not result in clear-cut, rationalized decisions. Japanese call such method of dispute settlement *arasoi o mizu ni nagasu* or "let the dispute flow to the water." This idiom is similar to the American adage "It's water under the bridge." In effect, it means simply to forget the cause of conflict and be friendly again.

When two parties are unable to resolve a conflict amicably, a third party attempts to mediate the dispute by appealing to the goodwill and the friendly sentiments of the protagonists. He tries to persuade both parties to make concessions to one another in order to maintain amicable relations.[28] The disadvantage of this procedure is that the conflict is not really resolved, but only set aside. As a result, it is likely to fester and grow. Any emergency then can cause it to burst into the open. Thus if more or less paternalistic industrial societies do not acquire competitive characteristics, industrial relations are likely to become characterized by class consciousness.

In this sense, the Japanese union movement in the prewar period was bent strongly toward political unionism. This trend continued during the postwar period. From its birth until today, the history of the Japanese labor movement has been characterized by a political confrontation of the two main labor federations: in its present form, the *Sōhyō* (General Council of Labor Unions) and the *Dōmei* (Japanese Confederation of Labor). However, in recent years, partly because of economic growth and higher living standards, Japanese unions have gradually started to move in the direction of business unionism. Examples of this trend can be seen in the decline of the influence of the Sōhyō in the private sector; the emphasis on economic goals as well as the criticism by some of the important unions affiliated with the Sōhyō in the private sector against the political objectives of the Sōhyō leadership; and these unions' attempts to form a united front with unions outside Sōhyō. However, considering the fact that the deep-rooted paternalistic undertone of Japanese industrial relations derived from the lifetime employment system is likely to persist, the recent trends just described do not allow one to predict any full-scale development of business unionism in the near future. On the one hand, the obedient character of enterprise unions and the enterprise-family consciousness of union members lead to the development of mild economic unionism. On the other hand, continued dissatisfaction and the accumulation of unsolved conflict provide a basis for the development of radical unionism. Thus it often happens that a moderate faction within a union comes to disagree with the radicalism of the main union body and splits off to form another union. Not infrequently, the new organization made up of moderate groups becomes radical as well after its status has been established. In this manner, the history of the union movement in general and the history of individual unions in particular in the postwar period are characterized by repeated changes of orientation from radical political unionism to mild business unionism and back again to radical political unionism.

This process is well exemplified by an idiom commonly used in Japanese industrial relations: "A chicken grows into a duck." This expression is attributed to one of the American officers who helped the democratization movement of a splinter group reacting against the communist-dominated *Sanbetsu* (Congress of Industrial Unions, 1946–59), at that time the most powerful trade union center in Japan. The outcome of the split was the creation of the Sōhyō in 1955. The Sōhyō is the result of a merger of the *Sōdōmei* (General Federation of Labor, 1946–64), the forerunner of today's Dōmei, which was established in 1964, and those groups which seceded from the Sanbetsu. The members of the Allied Occupation Forces who helped organize the Sōhyō hoped that it would develop into a moderate, pro-American movement. When the Sōhyō started to become involved in political struggles and to display a strong anti-American bias, they were naturally disappointed. The original statement by the officer probably was not accurately translated because his Japanese interpreter was not fluent in English. Nevertheless, he understood that the American was disappointed with the Sōhyō's change of attitude. The expression was so apt that it has been used to describe the process by which Japanese unions split repeatedly into moderate factions which, in turn, become radical again.

In summary, if we adopt Clark Kerr's teminology, Japanese industrial relations are fundamentally paternalistic, yet they also present both competitive and class-conscious features. The modernization of Japanese industrial relations might be achieved only when unions acquire the characteristics of a competitive type of industrial relations. However the issue of modernization in Japan is not simple or clear-cut. Even in those modernized and rationalized companies, which can hardly be described as paternalistic

38

or patriarchal, the Japanese characteristics of industrial relations remain dominant. Ronald P. Dore has called the "collective" paternalism of large Japanese enterprises "welfare corporatism," as distinguished from ordinary paternalism. According to him, "welfare corporatism" is paternalism without a "pater" in which "the same diffuseness characterizes the ties of the workers to his firm. But the responsibilities of the employee's welfare are institutionalized and contractual (so many weeks sick pay guaranteed, so much per child in the family allowance, etc.) and not subject to individual discretion."[29]

Certainly, as Dore pointed out, in larger Japanese enterprises, there exist objective norms such as work rules or collective agreements, and the working conditions of employees are determined in accordance with these written norms. The situation differs from traditional paternalism where the employer exercises responsibility at his personal discretion for the employee's welfare. However, this objectification of norms exists only in principle. In concrete application to individual workers, a certain degree of employer discretion (sometimes arbitrary) is admitted. That, of course, is true in Western industrial relations as well. But there are two differences between the Japanese and the Western situations. First, in Japan, the norms are rather vague and abstract, and therefore likely to cause conflict in their application. Second, when conflict occurs, the method of settlement in Japan is quite different from the Western way of settling disputes in accordance with universal and specific norms.

For example, in recent years, many enterprises have been introducing the Western performance appraisal system, under which a certain portion of the worker's wage and bonuses is determined according to the evaluation of his supervisors. A worker's ability and experience, the job description and the responsibility of individual workers are so vague and flexible that evaluations are difficult. Other criteria of performance appraisal, such as "devotion to the enterprise" or "willingness to work," are also listed in the work rules. These elements inevitably lead to subjective judgments. Quite often workers who are deeply involved in union activities tend to be evaluated lower in their devotion to the company. These workers have charged that such lower evaluations are unfair labor practices. In such cases the subjective criteria of evaluation make it difficult for the Labor Relations Commission to pass judgment on the correctness of the evaluation. In conclusion, it is doubtful whether the development of "welfare corporatism" can overcome the specifically Japanese characteristics of industrial relations, although it will certainly drive out traditional paternalism to some extent.

NOTES

1. Mitsutoshi Azuma, "Futō Rōdō-kōi ni Okeru Niritsu-haihan" [Antinomy in Unfair Labor Practices], *Nihon Rōdō-hō Gakukai Shi* [Journal of Japanese Labor Law Association] 28 (1966): 14.

2. A detailed analysis of labor disputes as "cultural" and "group" conflicts will be found in Part II, chapter 5.

3. For further details, see Part III, chapter 11.

4. John Kenneth Galbraith, *The New Industrial State*, 2nd rev. ed. (Boston: Houghton Mifflin Co., 1971), pp. 261–82.

5. See Part I, chapter 4.

6. Masao Maruyama, "Rekishi Ishiki no 'Kōsō' " [The "Old Stratum" Historical Concept], in *Rekishi Shisō Shū, Nihon no Shisō*:6 [An Anthology of Historical Thought; Japanese Thought], (Tokyo: Chikuma Shobō, 1972), p. 41.

7. Clark Kerr, J. T. Dunlop, F. Harbison and C.A. Meyers, *Industrialism and Industrial Man* (New York: Oxford University Press, 1964).

8. James Abegglen, *The Japanese Factory* (Glencoe, Ill.: The Free Press, 1958).

9. Robert E. Cole, "Permanent Employment in Japan: Facts and Fantasies," *Industrial and Labor Relations Review* 26, no. 1 (1972): 616.

10. Robert E. Cole, *Japanese Blue Collar—The Changing Tradition* (Berkeley and Los Angeles: University of California Press, 1973) gives an analysis of the employment system as it affects blue-collar workers; for white-collar workers, see Thomas P. Rohlen, *For Harmony and Strength—Japanese White-Collar Organization in Anthropological Perspective* (Berkeley and Los Angeles: University of California Press, 1974); Ronald Dore, in *British Factory—Japanese Factory*, provides a detailed comparative study of the two factory systems; James Abegglen, *Management and Worker: The Japanese Solution* (Tokyo: Kodansha International, 1973) is an expanded edition of his original publication *Japanese Factory* and provides an analysis of the changes in Japanese management after 1950. Also see Tadashi Hanami, "The Lifetime Employment System in Japan," *Atlanta Economic Review* 26, no. 3 (May-June 1976): 35–39.

11. *Rōdō Tōkei Yōran* [Summary of Labor Statistics] (Tokyo: Japan Ministry of Labor, 1977), p. 67.

12. Rohlen, *For Harmony and Strength*, p. 136.

13. Chie Nakane, *Japanese Society* (Berkeley and Los Angeles: University of California Press, 1972), p. 14.

14. Dore, *British Factory—Japanese Factory*, p. 40.

15. Rohlen, *For Harmony and Strength*, p. 235.

16. Talcott Parsons, *The Social System* (London: Tavistock Institute Publications, 1952), pp. 51–67, 182–91.

17. Cole, *Japanese Blue Collar*, p. 131.

18. Tadashi Hanami, "Future Industrial Relations—Japan," *Bulletin of the International Institute for Labor Studies* 10 (Geneva, 1972), p. 85.

19. Ibid., p. 100.

20. Ibid., pp. 100–01.

21. Ibid., p. 101.

22. Ibid., p. 103.

23. Koji Taira, *Economic Development and the Labor Market in Japan* (New York: Columbia University Press, 1970), p. 151; Robert Evans, Jr., *The Labor Economies of Japan and the United States* (New York: Praeger, 1971), p. 40.

24. Galbraith, *The New Industrial State*, pp. 145–58.

25. Cole, "Permanent Employment in Japan," pp. 621–28.

26. Abegglen, *Management and Worker*, p. 48.

27. Clark Kerr, *Labor and Management in Industrial Society* (Garden City, N.Y.: Doubleday, 1964), pp. 274 ff.

28. For more details, see Part III, chapter 10.

29. Dore, "Commitment—To What, By Whom and Why?" in *The Social and Cultural Background of Labor-Management Relations in Asian Countries: Proceedings of the 1971 Asian Regional Conference on Industrial Relations* (Tokyo: Japan Institute of Labor, 1971), p. 119.

2

PERSONAL RELATIONS IN INDUSTRIAL RELATIONS

1. EMOTIONALISM IN INDUSTRIAL RELATIONS

a. Transformation of Character: Several years ago, when campus riots were rife in Japan, university professors would complain: "Gewalt-students (those seeking power through violence)[1] are for the most part reasonable people with whom we get along very well under ordinary circumstances"; or "On the personal level, they are quite normal." When talking about a particular student, they would usually say: "He used to be a very good, serious student until he started all this nonsense; his character suddenly changed after he became involved in the student movement." Parents of students who had been arrested tearfully told reporters similar stories.

During the campus riots students took to wearing helmets and wrapping towels around their faces. This was not always for protection or even to avoid recognition. They would also carry "Gewalt-clubs" though they did not necessarily intend to use them as weapons. The purpose of these bizarre and often shocking disguises and accessories was to indicate that they had undergone a personality change—a transformation of their normal familiar selves into something quite different. It is for the same reason that union members invariably wear red headbands and armbands during their labor disputes. Raising red flags, hanging long, narrow strips of cloth with various slogans outside company buildings and putting up posters all have a common basis; namely, they are the ways in which Japanese unions overcome the normal atmosphere of cooperation with management and create a mood of confrontation in order to carry on whatever labor dispute may be at hand.

Although this strange behavior might seem childish nonsense to seasoned Western trade unionists, in Japan it is taken very seriously and regarded as an essential ingredient of industrial relations. Even in the courts or at sessions of the Labor Relations Commission, union members would not appear without wearing their headbands or armbands. No reasonable union members imagine that such behavior is likely to sway the opinion of judges or commission members in their favor. But whenever workers seek legal recourse against employers, they regard these symbolic manifestations as tactics to be used in their dispute.

When employers complain that workers involved in union demonstrations "change their character" and become "impossible to understand," they are actually saying that their workers are basically reasonable and that, under normal circumstances, there exists a mutual understanding between employer and employee. As we have seen in the previous chapter, most Japanese workers stay with a particular enterprise for the duration of their working lives. Consequently, they have a strong enterprise consciousness and loyalty toward their firm. Unions too are organized on the basis of individual enterprises, and their members therefore tend to be markedly enterprise oriented. Each worker is employed as a "total man." The Japanese expression *marugakae* (completely enveloped) fully expresses the nature of Japanese employer-employee relations. Employees are given powerful incentives to identify with their firm, which has all the characteristics of a closed social group analogous with a household, in which members are destined to have an "individual's total emotional participation in the group."[2]

The type of social relationship within a Japanese business is very comparable to those which prevail in a small rural village. Relationships based on emotion and customs are also to be found in large modern companies of present-day Japan. Mammoth international companies observe the traditional practice of sending gifts to their competitors at the end of the year and in early summer. Company executives invite their customers not only to dinners but also on sightseeing trips, golf or mah-jongg parties in an attempt to establish closer ties. This kind of approach is a prerequisite to the formation of a new business connection. Very often business negotiations succeed only after both sides have met at a dinner party and have built up a personal relationship of mutual trust and understanding. It is regarded as "insensitive" and "in bad taste" if, afterwards, one of the parties to the business deal were to insist upon his legal rights and obligations.

Stuart Macaulay's findings indicate that contract law is often ignored in business transactions in the United States as well. He writes that disputes are frequently settled without reference to the contract or potential or actual legal sanctions. This "relatively noncontractual practice" is explained partly by the personal relationship between partners. "Salesmen often know purchasing agents well. The same two individuals occupying these roles may have dealt with each other from five to twenty-five years. . . . Salesmen take purchasing agents to dinner, and they give purchasing agents Christmas gifts hoping to improve the chances of making a sale. . . . The top executives of the two firms may know each other . . . socially and may even belong to the same country club." However, he also suggests that "although a contract is not needed and actually may have negative consequences, businessmen do make some carefully planned contracts, negotiate settlements influenced by their legal rights and commence and defend some breach of contract lawsuits or arbitration proceedings."[3]

Reliance on business contracts is not unknown in Japanese business practice. The motives affecting the use or non-use of contracts in both Western countries and Japan might be the same in the sense that businessmen always resort to planned transactions and legal sanctions when the gains from using a contract are thought to outweigh the costs. The difference does not lie in the actual practices but in the ethics underlying them. In Japan, non-use of contract is consciously applied as a rule of social behavior,

44

while in Western society it is not recognized as a norm but is considered illegitimate and an exception.

Thus, in Japan, a person who stands upon his legal rights is often castigated or at least disapproved of in these terms: "He is the type of person who states shamelessly what can hardly be expressed without hesitation." This widespread expression shows very clearly that in Japan to assert one's legal rights is regarded as unethical behavior. One should not wonder, therefore, that the emotional relationship that prevails within an enterprise makes demands for wage increases or better working conditions appear tactless and indelicate. Under these circumstances, the only recourse for employees who insist upon better conditions of work is to disrupt the day-to-day routine and to undergo a radical change of character. The employees' attitude toward their employer then will vary between two extremes—from polite and respectful intimacy to vile rudeness. What appears on the surface to be an abnormal and extreme attitude on the part of Japanese unions is, therefore, the natural outcome of the emotional nature of human relationships in Japanese enterprises.

The transformation of cooperative enterprise-conscious unionism into militant radical unionism is the same phenomenon at the organizational level as the change of behavior in the individual student engaged in campus activism. R. P. Dore explains the student's attitude as follows: "Rioting students at Japanese universities usually proved to have only two alternative modes of address to teachers—either terse abusiveness or quiet deference signaled by the traditional respectful term of address, *sensei* [Professor]. The egalitarian stand-off was more than they could manage."[4]

b. The Vagueness of Japanese Contracts: As pointed out, all Japanese business relations contain certain emotional elements. Takeyoshi Kawashima remarks that, according to Talcott Parson's terminology, most human relations in Japan are functionally diffuse, while in Western society they are generally functionally specific.[5] In the latter case, when labor and management interact with each other exclusively on a business level, the rights and obligations of both parties can be viewed objectively and most likely can be very clearly defined. In this atmosphere, pay demands by workers can be dealt with calmly and rationally, and negotiations can be conducted with a view to clearly defined rights and obligations. In Japan such discussion of mutual rights and obligations is extremely difficult.

Kawashima has described the Japanese sense of property rights as follows: "I have several times borrowed books from foreign friends. When I was tardy in returning them, they would ask me in a businesslike manner, 'Please return the book to me if you are through with it.' We Japanese always feel awkward about such things, and hesitate to make requests in such a frank and candid way. We can make such requests only after making some excuse (for instance, 'one of my friends asked me to lend him that book, so please . . . ') and even then we do so with a guilty conscience."[6]

In Japanese interpersonal relations one feels "awkward" and hesitates to ask for things even when one is fully entitled to them. This is true especially among friends, for it is believed that relationships can be destroyed simply by standing on one's rights in terms of a borrowed book, contract, or things of that order. In the last section it has been shown that most contractual relationships in Japan are concluded and remain binding solely on the basis of this kind of amicable, personal sense of friendship. If friends hesitate before pressing for their rights, labor unions, who are not in that privileged position, are put in an even more difficult psychological situation when they seek redress of grievances.

Kawashima also believes that the reason for the inability to express discontent directly without hesitation or awkwardness lies in the fact that contractual relationships in Japan usually involve people of unequal social and economic standing. The basis for Japanese business negotiations is not equality but rather patronage and dependence. The bosses are supposed to be aware of their employees' discontent without any direct manner of expression. The workers, on the other hand, assume that their bosses are making an effort to understand them and, consequently, do not take corrective action. According to this concept, whenever conflict occurs, it should be settled by mutual understanding. Direct expression of grievance should be avoided as far as possible, since it is believed that it would destroy the harmony necessary for this kind of relationship.[7] What is more, should one partner express his displeasure directly, the other partner will view it as a challenge to what was thought to be a friendly and amicable relationship. This type of reaction is typical of management. One must remember that the employer-employee relationship in Japanese businesses is something more than a mere trade of labor and wages. It is accompanied by the feeling that the employees' families are subordinated to, and dependent upon, the employer for protection. The establishment of unions within such businesses and workers' demands for salary increases are interpreted by management as a challenge to established and expected human relationships. Those Japanese workers who began organizing themselves in unions are regarded as having undergone a "change of personality" and therefore are "impossible to understand." The workers themselves feel awkward about their own wage demands unless they undergo this "transformation" into different personalities, and consequently feel the need to "disguise" themselves with headbands and armbands. This also explains why employers cannot expect calm, reasonable and rational negotiations in collective bargaining in Japan. Since any request for bargaining on the part of the unions is regarded as a challenge to the employers, the latter will refuse to come to the bargaining table. In most cases, especially in small businesses, this refusal is nothing but the result of genuine surprise at the demands, and an inability to deal with what appears to employers to be an alien procedure in business relations.

Thus bargaining and disputes inevitably turn to confrontation. Japanese society, which attaches great importance to harmony as a social value, does not expect conflict to exist and, where it does exist, ignores it. If we accept that "Only where there is conflict, is behavior conscious and self-conscious; only here are the conditions for rational conduct,"[8] "rational" conduct in the Western sense is ruled out in Japanese industrial relations.

c. Assimilation of Self to Others: There is another type of situation in which labor disputes soon lead to a showdown. It is to be found not only in small, "underdeveloped" enterprises run by "feudalistic" owners, in which oppressive industrial relations still prevail but also in larger, modernized businesses. In this case, either employer or employees behave "mischievously," harassing each other and taking advantage of one another as a matter of routine. We shall now attempt to describe the psychological reasons for this behavior. In this connection, Mitsuo Suzuki's views on the role of conflict in the Japanese society are worth mentioning. He states that there is a tendency in Japanese society to settle conflicts in an amicable manner because, mainly, the Japanese believe in "universal goodness" which precludes the possibility of conflict or antagonism among men. According to this belief, "conflicts exist only in the mind of the individual, and should never be expressed openly. . . . We have neglected the question of conflict as a social problem because we attempted to avoid admitting the fact that the social existence of human beings consists of interaction between independent individuals."[9] The fundamental basis for such personal relationships is *miuchi* (kinship) consciousness. Owing to the development of *miuchi* consciousness, conflict between "us" is impossible since "You and I are both human beings and we both have the same blood," or "We ate rice from the same pot." Thus, accepting this kinship consciousness and living by it means regarding all conflicts as problems between relatives and trying to settle matters through an emotional understanding based on blood kinship. Kinship consciousness has its origin in *amae*.

In a penetrating analysis of the concept of *amae*, Takeo Doi has pointed out the uniqueness of this term in the Japanese psychological vocabulary.[10] Basically *amae* refers to the feeling all normal infants have at their mother's breast: dependence, a desire to be loved, and an unwillingness to emerge from the warm mother-child circle and be cast into a world of objective "reality." It is Doi's basic premise that in a Japanese person these feelings are somehow prolonged and diffused throughout adult life. In this way, to a far greater extent than in the West, they come to shape the whole

48

attitude to other people and to "reality." On the personal level, this means that within our intimate circle, and to a diminishing extent outside that circle, we seek *amae* relationships. In exchange for the assurance of another person's goodwill, we will defer to some extent to this person's claims. Such a relationship implies a considerable blurring of the distinction between subject and object; as such, it is not necessarily governed by strictly rational or moral standards. To outsiders some manifestations of the *amae* attitude may often appear to be selfish; for example, an individual may act deliberately in a childish way as a signal that he wishes to be dependent, and that he seeks "indulgence."

Amae is essentially a matter of dependence on the object—a desire for the identification of subject and object. Thus *wagamama*[11] (a headstrong, self-willed, selfish attitude) with its naked *amae* is an attempt not merely to depend upon another person but also to dominate him,[12] to obtain his indulgence forcibly. According to Doi, almost all childish and headstrong actions and reactions indulged in by adults are the result of their inability to establish an *amae* relationship. This behavior is referred to in everyday Japanese phrases, which also belong to the vocabulary of personnel management, such as *higamu* (to be suspicious or jaundiced in one's attitude), *hinekureru* (to behave in a distorted, perverse way), *uramu* (to show resentment toward or hatred of), and *suneru* (to be sulky); *futekusareru* and *yakekuso ni naru* respectively indicate attitudes of defiance and irresponsibility in speech or behavior associated with a "fit of the sulks."[13] A typical example of such behavior was when union members stood at the entrance of a supermarket and shouted to the customers: "The food is rotten today." On another occasion a company president suddenly started dancing during a wage bargaining session and tried to set fire to his own warehouse which had been occupied by union members. The spiteful and mischievous behavior of labor and management will be discussed in greater detail later on in this book.

A remark made by Kaoru Ōta, former president of Sōhyō, is significant in this context: "Japanese workers react very differently in static or dynamic situations. . . . Under normal circumstances

49

workers are strongly attached to the companies they work for, since labor market conditions are usually not overly favorable. However, should a labor situation become fluid, for example, when a strike is declared, workers forget or disregard the conditions which had been regulating their customary attitude toward, and feelings for, their company and their employers. Under abnormal dynamic circumstances such as these, management also tends to become excited and to react strongly against striking or disruptive workers. When such a confrontation occurs, the situation is serious indeed."[14]

Professional observers of the Japanese human relations scene have attempted to discover the reasons for the striking contrast between the normal amicable and harmonious relationship on the one hand, and the emotionally charged and even violent disruptions on the other. According to Bin Kimura, a distinguished psychiatrist, Japanese drunkards and mental patients are more aggressive and violent than their Western counterparts. From clinical observations in West Germany and in Japan, he concludes: "I could not help but be convinced that the Japanese are somehow especially fragile and tenderhearted by nature. I believe that the constitution and temper of Japanese people are irrational and inconsistent, if our criteria for 'rational' is that one does not lose control even while being drunk or insane."[15] Kimura believes that the rigor and inconsistency of the Japanese climate is partly responsible for the element of irrationality in the Japanese mentality. The climate conditions a society's outlook on life which can be characterized as "stability with possible sudden upheavals and patience with internal turmoil. This is what renders interpersonal relations among Japanese unique."[16] The phrases "patience with internal turmoil" expresses perfectly the psychological atmosphere of labor relations in Japanese businesses and explains the "transformation of character" of Japanese workers. Violent incidents in Japanese industrial relations are clearly related to the concept of "stability with the possibility of sudden upheavals." Kimura further contends that, in Japanese personal relations, rational analysis on the part of the individual becomes impossible in extreme situations and that the individual's absorption by the mass mentality is inevitable. On the other hand, Westerners are basically as systematic and rational as their climate, and the most appropriate attitude in order to maintain good relations with others is to behave consistently and rationally. While in Western society one's actions are likely to provoke individual reactions, in Japan the unpredictability of personal relations commits one wholly to collective action in the same manner as the Japanese submit to their physical environment. It follows, therefore, that "out of empathy for the ever-fluctuating emotion (ki)[17] of others, it is fitting that one should behave in accordance with these constantly changing emotions." Thus the most effective behavior is to "leave oneself in the hands of others," and to modify one's attitude in accordance with them. In this way, the distance between individuals becomes "extremely narrow" and, strictly speaking, the difference between self and others ceases to exist.[18]

In the West, where the phrase *homo homini lupus* characterizes personal relations, to surrender oneself to others is tantamount to suicide. Japanese people, on the other hand, can rely on kinship consciousness and feel they belong equally to the same family or brotherhood, where everyone can understand and trust one another. In other words, "One should not put oneself at the mercy of outsiders whom one cannot understand or trust."[19] These psychological characteristics of Japanese personal relations explain the frequent refusal on the part of Japanese employers to bargain with union leaders who are not their own employees. Company executives often say: "I will gladly negotiate with the union of *uchi* (my family) but not with outsiders." Thus, in many cases collective bargaining in Japan is totally different from bargaining in the West: it is nothing but bargaining "based on kinship consciousness and the assimilation of self with others." Whether in small or large enterprises, the distance between labor and management is "extremely narrow." A number of questions, therefore, arise: How is it possible for respectable unions to exist in Japan? How can they function adequately? How can they ever arrive at collective agreements?

2. THE CHARACTER OF MODERN ENTERPRISES

a. Flexible Collective Agreements: Collective agreements signed by unions and management embody the norms which govern their relationship. One can analyze the nature of the relationship by examining these documents. In Japan, such agreements tend to be more general and abstract than their Western counterparts. In some cases they merely duplicate certain provisions of the national legislation. In others, the details of the contract are so abstract, vague and ambiguous that their intent is all but incomprehensible. The following passage, quoted from a court decision, is a case in point: "Since the provision in question is so obscure, it is almost impossible for the court to ascertain what kind of practices existed in fact and which working conditions were agreed upon by the parties and were to be included in the contract when it was concluded. Consequently, the court can hardly admit the union's claim that an assurance of additional wages was a part of the contract."[20]

This kind of vagueness with respect to contract provisions is yet another consequence of the peculiar nature of Japanese personal relations. As discussed earlier, when business relationships are of a purely economic nature, with the rights and obligations of the parties precisely defined, negotiations can be carried out on a rational basis. Generally speaking, in Western societies, where economic deals are supposed to be functionally specific, it is possible to write into the agreement an exact and detailed description of these rights and obligations and include provisions for every possible disagreement that may occur during the period of implementation of the contract.[21] Thus, when disagreements do arise they can be settled calmly and rationally, with reference to clearly defined and detailed norms embodied in the contract. Japanese looking for long-term accommodations in Europe are often confronted with a typical example of this way of doing things. To their surprise, they are told that a lengthy contract, sometimes comprising more than thirty clauses, must be signed before a residence may be rented.

In Japan, on the other hand, economic deals are often concluded without a written contract. Even in cases where a written contract is drawn up, its contents are usually short, general and abstract. Another characteristic of Japanese contracts is that most of them contain a clause called the "consultation in good faith" or "amicable consideration" clause, usually written as follows: "Should a disagreement arise, both parties will consult each other in good faith," or "Should a disagreement arise, the parties will settle it amicably by consultation." What this means is that Japanese contracts do not provide criteria which can be applied to all possible disagreements. Instead, they express a general policy of settling disputes by mutual understanding.

According to Kawashima, Westerners consider it important to describe in as precise and detailed a manner as possible the standards which are to be applied in every possible disagreement. They feel that there is no way to settle conflicts without reference to a complete description of the rights and obligations of both parties. Japanese think it is both impossible and unnecessary to provide such an extensive written description and make provisions for every possible eventuality. They believe that no matter how detailed the clauses of a contract may be, some unanticipated developments are bound to occur, and that it is more important to establish mutual understanding and trust. Only on the basis of such understanding, Japanese believe, can disagreements successfully be resolved. Since economic deals in Japan are affected by emotional and sentimental factors, the parties to a contract always expect some flexibility in implementation. The detailed enumeration of specific contract provisions would be fatal to this flexibility.[22]

The reluctance to have one's rights and obligations clearly defined is to be found not only in the individual relationship between an employee and his employer but also in the relations between unions and employers. The situation in industrial relations does not differ markedly from the description of personal or business contracts described by Kawashima. Thus collective agreements are short, abstract and often obscure. The fact that the parties to a collective agreement or a labor contract are satisfied with such vague or ambiguous provisions only means that they depend on consultation in good faith should there be a disagreement during the implementation of the contract. There have been cases, however, of unions going on strike when such consultations failed and labor and management could not agree on the interpretation of clauses which, nevertheless, had been accepted by both parties when the contract was drawn up. Such cases resulted in the dismissal of union leaders because they were considered responsible for breaking the contract. Subsequently, the courts have tended to reject employers' claims on the grounds that the ambiguity of the clauses' wording made it technically impossible to break the contract.[23]

In most Western countries, when a collective agreement is signed, an implicit or explicit "no strike" clause guarantees that both parties will respect the content of the agreement and will not go on strike or stage lockouts during the term of the contract.[24] The signing of a collective agreement in Japan does not necessarily result in peaceful relations. Even in those industries where strong unions have matured enough to conclude collective agreements with management, the rights and obligations of both parties to the contract remain so vague and uncertain as to make "consultation in good faith" and "settling things amicably" an implicit provision of the contract. It is only when such consultations fail that unions go on strike and mutual trust and understanding dissolve. When that happens, negotiations become impossible and employers often dismiss union leaders. The dispute then results in a deadlock and the only recourse is to take the case to court. This sketch of the typical progression of a labor dispute in Japan shows that industrial relations are exactly as unpredictable as are Japanese personal relations in general.

b. Collusion (Nareai) in Industrial Relations: In those enterprises where unions are recognized and agreements are concluded between union and employers, labor-management relations are fairly smooth. In these firms there exists a climate of collusion (*nareai*) between the employers and the union representing the majority of employees. *Nareai* is another aspect of *amae* and has almost the same meaning, but *nareai* is a feeling of emotional intimacy between persons outside the kinship group, while *amae* is usually restricted to the kinship group or very close friends. Basically the relationship is one of patronage and dependence, though the unions frequently put on an outward show of radical militancy in their utterances and behavior.

Because the unions are enterprise based and they represent the employees of a particular firm, their activities are carried out for the most part within the confines of that enterprise. The unions are, therefore, dependent on the privileges granted them by management, in the form of office space in company buildings, meeting rooms, telephones, furniture, stationery and sometimes even photocopy services. These facilities, provided free of charge by the companies, symbolize the intimacy of their relationship with the unions. It is also by no means unusual to find full-time union officials being paid, at least in part, by company management, not to mention the common practice of granting employees leave of absence for union activities and providing a free payroll deduction system for union dues. Such extensive privileges are more frequently to be found in the larger enterprises, where it may be said without exaggeration that the unions function at the company's expense.

This can lead to amusing situations, such as in a case over which I presided as a commissioner of the Tokyo Labor Relations Commission arbitrating a case where a firm was forced to rent rooms to hold a high-level company meeting because their conference room was being used by the union. In adjudicating unfair labor practice cases, it has been my experience that unions sometimes take it for granted that the company will grant paid leave to employees attending the hearings either as witnesses or observers for the union. The unions perceive their dependence on the company either financially or in other ways as a routine matter and one by no means inconsistent with fighting a legal battle with the same company. All this will undoubtedly sound strange to anyone familiar with trade unionism in the West where the unions are anx-

55

ious to preserve their independence from management.

In companies where the principle of collusion prevails, the expense in terms of both time and money is discounted, since management knows very well that union activities will benefit them in the long run, no matter how militantly the union boasts of its strength. Actually companies consider the extensive privileges granted to the unions as necessary expenditures for securing good labor relations in the firm. For the perceptive Western observer, the role of Japanese unions as a tool of management is not hard to discern. Cole puts it this way: "The union leaders were not viewed as representatives of workers but as men of superior position, age, experience and status who must be respected. . . . Workers participated in the staged performance [of the union] because, with the union being so closely entwined with the company, it was viewed as part of their job just as punching the time card or pushing the button to start their machines. . . . By participating in the staged performance, workers were buying a harmonious relationship with the company."[25] Rohlen refers to the role of a union leader as follows: "By expressing the needs and problems of the relatively inarticulate lower-ranking majority, he serves management's need to know as well as the union membership's desire to be heard."[26] To be sure, even these "ideal" labor relations, nurtured by "considerate" management, do not eliminate collective bargaining and disputes. But the companies know fully well that the superficially "militant" unions are merely adhering to the game's ground rules. Such is the nature of the "wonderful" labor relations between "modern" management and "strong" unions in Japan.

Travelling abroad some time ago with a number of Japanese union leaders, I was suprised to find delegations from their companies meeting them at each airport with chauffeured cars and invitations to dinner and parties or sightseeing tours. I had the impression, at times, that I was traveling with business executives. In fact, there is nothing surprising about this kind of treatment if one understands that the president of an enterprise union is in effect the company's senior executive in charge of labor relations.

Robert J. Ballon, Professor of Economics at Sophia University, Tokyo, and an authority on Japanese business, once told me: "Trade unions do not exist in Japan." What he meant was that trade unions in the "Western" sense do not exist in Japan. In much the same way, collective bargaining in labor negotiations in Japan is closer to the traditional "consultation in good faith" than to the rational bargaining based exclusively on economic interest, which is characteristic in the West. Such "Japanization" of the Western concepts of industrial relations results from the establishment of a kinship type of relationship within the enterprise-family, which is also at the origin of the particular pattern of dispute settlement in Japan.

The Japanese kinship consciousness has produced a tendency to settle conflicts by mutual understanding based on blood relationships and to regard all disputes as problems to be worked out within a restricted circle. Disagreements and grievances are supposed to be solved "amicably" in a manner known as *nashi-kuzushi*, which sometimes means "step by step," but, in this context, should be understood as settling the matter in a natural way without active efforts. Actually solving problems by *nashi-kuzushi* is little more than softening their impact and postponing any substantive solution. Subordinates are not supposed to express disagreement or to state their grievances openly; they are expected to endure hardships in anticipation of the benevolent consideration by a superior.

Should disagreement and grievances eventually be made public, or disputes come into the open, the parties involved defer to each other and settle matters through "emotional understanding" or by "letting the dispute flow to the water." This uniquely Japanese attitude allows disputes to be settled in a natural way with the passage of time, without introducing positive artificial action by a human agency. An important drawback to this amicable method of settling disputes is that no rules exist to regulate the conduct of both parties except the concept of "amicable mutual understanding." Thus, when the mutual trust inherent in this emotional relationship is lost, disputes erupt and sometimes even become violent. In traditional Japanese society, there is another method of resolving disputes—through conciliation or arbitration by a third party. The third party is usually someone who is respected by or can be said to "have face" (*kao ga kiku*) with both parties. In most cases, this person will be someone who is influential in the small circle to which both parties belong.

Conciliation or arbitration usually takes the form of an attempt to "save the face" (*kao o tateru*) of this influential person and to "entrust" (*azukeru*) the dispute with him. He is not expected to settle the matter in accordance with reason or any universal standard. He does not necessarily make any clear-cut decisions about who is right or wrong, nor does he inquire into the respective rights of the parties. The objective of this procedure of conciliation and arbitration is to settle the dispute in such a way as to restore and to maintain the friendly personal relations within the small society involved. The Japanese phrase for this procedure, *maruku osameru* (to settle in a circle), means to settle things in a way that satisfies both parties equally.[27]

In this content, it is worth noting that this way of solving disputes is not unique to Japanese society. It is frequently found in other non-Western societies which attach great value to kinship and community relations and where harmony, or the absence of conflict, is highly prized. Readers will find several striking similarities between the Japanese style of settling disputes and that of the Ndendeuli tribe in Tanzania or the Mexican Zapotec described by P. H. Gulliver and Laura Nader respectively.

Gulliver summarizes the characteristics of Ndendeuli dispute settlement as follows:

> Ndendeuli have few well-defined rules and norms of social behavior against which men's conduct can be easily assessed.... This marked indeterminacy of norms operates in a situation where adjudicators do not exist and where negotiations and bargaining is vital to the process of settling disputes. . . . There is also no third party, no technique to determine specifically the acceptable, operative, reasonable expectations in

the event of a particular dispute. And while men seek their own advantages and attempt to avoid what is disadvantageous, the process of settlement must depend also on other considerations not directly related to the merits of the matter in dispute. . . . No Ndendeuli whom I asked could say whether the claim for more bride-wealth was or was not "reasonable," "justifiable," or "right." In these circumstances not only the bride-wealth question had to be taken into account, but also the current state of and future effects on the surrounding relationships of kin and neighbors.[28]

Thus the settlement of the intracommunity dispute among the Ndendeuli tends to be

. . . dependent not only on ideas or norms, rights and expectations and on the respective bargaining strengths of both principals and their supporters, but also on other men's interests and the continuance of neighborly cooperation and concord. . . . It is, and must be, an agreed settlement accepted by both principals. . . . A settlement that is acted upon straight away may be no settlement at all, for the whole dispute may have to be renegotiated at a later date, when the claim is actively exerted again. . . . The settlement is really an avoidance of settlement, or agreement to differ. . . . Further, by the immediate completion of a settlement it is hoped to remove the dispute altogether, and thus allow the re-establishment of continued working neighborly relations.[29]

Nader describes a Mexican Zatopec court settling a dispute as follows:

The Zatopec ideal is not "an eye for an eye," but rather what restores personal relations to equilibrium. . . . It is no wonder that zero-sum game (win or lose) as we know it in some American courts would be a frightening prospect to a plaintiff, even though all "right" might be on his side. The plaintiff need not worry, however, for, as we shall see, the *presidente* is equally reluctant to make a clear-cut zero-sum-game decision for a variety of reasons. . . . The judgment that the *presidente* gives on a matter is . . . that the decision is the "result or embodiment of concession or adjustment. Furthermore, there is always a mutual promise, usually signed, to abide by a decision. . . ."[30]

Such a way of dispute settlements is, or used to be, common in most primitive tribes.

The tendency of modern lawyers, particularly in England and America, has been to neglect the "dynamics of early conciliation" in favor of a highly developed system of adjudication.[31] Only recently have some lawyers, reflecting on the work of social anthropologists, come to realize the importance of conciliation and consider conciliation as a middle stage in the evolution of the methods of settling disputes, halfway between the primitive methods of settlement by force and modern settlement by adjudication. Furthermore, even those who accept the validity of conciliation as a method for settling disputes still look at labor relations and international relations as being exceptions. According to them, disputes in these two areas can neither be solved by legal arguments nor by formal adjudication as fully accepted substitutes for force, strikes or war.[32]

The "primitive" method of conciliation is effective in the field of industrial relations when there are no determined norms of settlement and when legal dispute settlement procedures and bodies have not been allowed to develop on a large scale. The guidelines on which the conciliation procedure is based, that is, the reestablishment of a normal relationship rather than the reasonableness of respective claims, preservation of cooperation and harmony, and the avoidance of an immediate settlement, could usefully be introduced into dispute settlement procedures in Western societies. Before going into this point, however, we should examine why the traditional methods of dispute settlement are not always effective in Japan.

c. From Collusion to Upheaval: Settling disputes by the adjudication method which we have just described is only possible on two conditions. First, the parties involved are expected to respond to the appeal of the mediator and to save his "face" because of the emotional relationship within the particular social group. Second, the settlement is reached without recourse to universal standards outside the scope of the group. Consequently, these methods will not work when the dispute extends beyond the limits of a small society, especially in the case of a dispute between persons belonging to different small societies. For example, a dispute between members of a single traditional group, such as a farming community, can be solved through the mediation of a man in a position of power, such as a *jinushi* (landlord) or *nanushi* (headman). But disputes between villages concerning, for instance, the shared rights for gathering firewood or drawing water, can hardly be expected to be solved amicably. The parties to such disputes are likely to become involved in protracted feuds.

Such disputes arise outside the harmonious social group "in a social vacuum."[33] Very often, open antagonism will prevail until one of the parties is able to impose a settlement by force, or a go-between with enough prestige and power to command respect in both communities can be found to settle the matter. In the latter case, the mediator establishes a new order which applies equally to both social groups. In order to secure harmony in this newly extended society, he presides over a rite of reconciliation between the two parties. Disputes between *yakuza* (gangster) groups are often settled in this way by a "superboss" who wields power over both groups.

Labor disputes evolve in much the same way. In so far as the function of enterprise unions is to maintain and improve the working conditions of employees in a particular enterprise, the unions try not to break down the emotional interpersonal relations within the enterprise but, instead, use them to foster industrial relations based on "collusion." However, should the confrontation between labor and management develop to the point where an amicable settlement based on mutual trust is no longer possible, the dispute will continue for a long period, and will often deteriorate to the point of violence. Most protracted labor disputes in Japan, such as those at Mitsui Mining in 1959 and 1960 and at Nihon Steel's Muroran Plant in 1953, began when the company tried to dismiss large numbers of employees. According to Kaoru Ōta, the one-time president of the Sōhyō: "A dispute over dismissals inevitably develops into a large-scale conflict, since dismissal threatens the union members' very livelihood. It would not be an exaggeration to say that the only serious labor troubles in Japan have occurred in cases involving fights against dismissals."[34]

At the time of his writing, Ōta attributed this tendency to the high rate of unemployment in Japan. However, if one leaves aside such factors as the condition of the labor market, the fact remains that large-scale dismissals not only shatter the mutual trust that exists between labor and management but also threaten the very foundation of the enterprise union's existence. This threat is due to the fact that these unions recruit their members exclusively from among the employees of a particular enterprise and, as a rule, employees who are laid off lose their membership. The unions, therefore, have no other way of fighting mass dismissals than by "total opposition." They often resort to desperate means, which they label "honorable defeat," that are reminiscent of the kamikaze tactics used by the Japanese army during World War II. Regardless of the high degree of organization in a union and the success of its bargaining, a sudden brutal fight, similar to that of farmers armed with bamboo spears in premodern Japan, is liable to occur in Japanese industrial relations.

The "permanence with possible sudden upheavals" and "patience with internal turmoil," which, according to the psychiatrist Bin Kimura, characterize Japanese personal relations, also explain why labor disputes develop into full-blown upheavals when the limits of endurance are reached. There is a famous kabuki story, called *Chūshingura*, which serves as a vivid illustration of the nature of labor disputes in Japan. Known in the West as "The Revenge of the Forty-Seven Rōnin," it is the story of a vendetta. In 1701, Kira Kōzukenosuke, a high protocol official, insulted Asano Takuminokami, the feudal Lord of Akō. The latter, meeting his enemy in the shogun's palace, struck and injured him with his sword. Kira's injury was not fatal, but drawing a sword in the palace was against the laws of the time and the Lord of Akō was compelled to commit harakiri. His property was confiscated and all his vassals became *rōnin*, or masterless samurai. Forty-seven of the *rōnin*, with Ōishi Kuranosuke as their leader, vowed revenge. They separated and hid their purpose under the mask of profligate and dissolute lives. Finally, despite tremendous odds, they took their revenge on Kira on behalf of their master. In the industrial relations scenario, the company is cast in the role of Kira, the villain of the story, who tortures the union with contempt until the latter is compelled to commit an improper act after patience and endurance are exhausted. The union identifies with Asano the feudal lord who is ordered to commit harakiri as a punishment for his imprudent behavior. When a union indulges in violent activities in order to protest the company's unjustified measures, they regard their actions as "legitimate" violence, just as Asano drawing his sword within the castle walls. The dismissal of union members on the grounds of practicing what they consider to be "legitimate" violence is for them an "order to commit harakiri." Consequently the union's fight against such dismissals is "the revenge of the forty-seven *rōnin*."

I found this poem in a union report on the dispute at the Kishima Coal Mining Company in 1957:

> Having a common enemy to hate,
> I found it easy
> To talk of money.[35]

This poem clearly illustrates the uniqueness of Japanese labor relations in which, under normal circumstances, union members find it awkward and difficult to talk of money. Only when employees look upon the company as an enemy can they talk freely about economic demands. Japanese labor relations being what they are, one needs to hate the company in order actually to confront it in a dispute. Without hate, employees can muster only half-hearted opposition and are soon ready to compromise. Thus,

Ōta warns that "in the labor movement, sentimental and pathetic moods do not work. . . . To regard a strike as anything like 'fighting spirit' or 'honorable defeat' [kamikaze tactics] . . . of the Japanese army, is a fatal error that is akin to a crime."[36] It still seems true that a fighting spirit and honorable defeat are necessary and sometimes inevitable before Japanese unions can produce a real confrontation.

d. Understanding without Words: As pointed out by psychiatrists Doi and Kimura, one of the characteristics of Japanese personal relations is the lack of "advance through confrontation" of the subject and object, of self and others.[37] In other words, in a society governed by *amae*, personal relationships do not exist between self and other, you and I. Instead, each person being an independent subject, the self exists only in relation to the existence of others. Self, in other words, is nothing but the reflection of concerned others. "Advance through confrontation," on the other hand, implies cooperation between people based on the recognition of the differences in people's interests. Such cooperation through confrontation, however, is almost impossible to achieve in Japanese personal relations.

Mitsuo Suzuki believes that the possibility of "rationalizing" dispute settlement in contemporary Japan depends on acquiring a mastery of this technique. In his view, one can find a model of this technique in a significant episode of the Meiji Restoration, namely, the agreement reached by Katsu Kaishū and Saigō Takamori concerning the surrender of the shogunate to the emperor. Katsu, who represented the shogunate, believed that: "Everyone should be considered an enemy. I do not like friends." This attitude enabled Katsu to establish a truly cooperative relationship with Saigō, who acted on behalf of the emperor, a relationship based on the consciousness of "being *tanin* (an outsider) to everybody." *Tanin* literally means "other person" with the connotation "person with no blood relationship to oneself."[39] Thus it is farthest removed from the parent-child relationship, productive of *amae*. Saigō's and Katsu's very antagonism is what made cooperation possible.

As a result, they avoided a final showdown and the shogunate surrendered Edo Castle to the emperor's army without battle.

In recent years, historians have paid a great deal of attention to the character of Katsu, a major protagonist in the history of Japanese modernization, and have looked upon him as one of the forerunners of the modern individualist. Suzuki considers the agreement between Katsu and Saigō as one of the rare cases of rational bargaining in Japanese history. However, Isaiah Ben-Dasan, who published a comparative study of the respective qualities of the Japanese and Jews, claims that this negotiation was "definitely different from negotiations in the European sense."[40] He points out that after Saigō said, "There might be a lot of serious arguments on your side, but I will take the responsibility at the risk of my own life," Katsu accepted Saigō's proposals without further discussion and left the entire affair up to him.[40] Thus, even negotiations conducted by a person who had completely internalized the *tanin* concept could still not be completely free from the tacit mutual understanding implied in traditional Japanese personal relations. Numerous examples of such tacit understanding are found in contemporary labor disputes.

The Mitsui Coal Mining Company dispute of 1953 was one of the most serious disputes in postwar Japanese labor history. It was called "The Heroless One-Hundred-and-Thirty-Day Fight." The transcripts of the collective bargaining sessions which took place during this dispute document the efforts made by management and the union to "understand" each other, even in the course of a very serious dispute. The trouble began when the company announced its intention of dismissing 5,738 employees for "rationalization." The union decided to fight the dismissal. In an attempt to undercut the union, the company tried to persuade the about-to-be-dismissed employees to accept *osusume* (advice to retire) before October 10, 1953. The following is taken from the transcript of the bargaining session held on October 11.

Company: Perhaps we can go over yesterday's discussion once more.

Union: I am sorry, we can't.

Company: Do you mean that you understand what we have been saying?

Union: No, we mean that we don't understand. What are you trying to do with *osusume*?

Company: We intend to ask each individual personally for his answer. What we meant yesterday by *osusume* was to advise in good faith. That means we will not take any unreasonable steps.

Union: The company probably thinks that the rationalization is the right thing to do. Well, even if it were reasonable from the company's point of view, considering the economic and political situation in Japan today, the company should ask the union members to cooperate and you should talk to us on that basis. Therefore, you should not resort to *osusume*.

Company: We are embarrassed to see that you take *osusume* as something unscrupulous. We will not take any unreasonable action.

Union: I am afraid *osusume* implies enforcing unreasonable criteria for dismissal immediately.

Company: We mean to do *osusume* without referring to individual names for dismissal.

Union: Then this means that you are maintaining your right to rationalize even though you are postponing the posting of the names of dismissed employees. You said that you would respect the employees' individual wishes during the process of *osusume* and that, if none of them volunteered to retire, you could do nothing about it. Do you mean now that you will talk to individuals who refused to retire but whom the company has already listed among the 1,815 inevitable [retirement] nominees?

Company: That's right. And we want to discuss that point.

Union: It is completely out of the question. Your *osusume* is simple *susume* without the honorific "*o*,"[41] that is the truth of the situation. Why are you doing *osusume*?

Company: In order to save the situation.

Union: If so, why don't you give us a concrete proposal? Merely asking us to submit to *osusume* does not make sense.

Company: That is exactly the point we want to discuss with you.

Union: You understand very well what we mean. Nevertheless, you insist that we stop influencing our members' response. That is out of the question. Don't insist on *osusume*! From yesterday's discussion, we understood that you were not going to stick to the criteria you devised for selecting the workers to be dismissed.

Company: We insist upon these criteria.

Union: What? Then there is nothing further to discuss.

Company: We can certainly understand the union's demand for criteria at the conclusion of our talks. But there might be a certain point in collective bargaining where it is not necessary for you to force us to tell everything explicitly.

Union: It is the usual tactic of the company to keep coming back to the same starting point at the conclusion of a long discussion. We will suspend bargaining until the company makes real efforts to save the situation in good faith. The company is really arrogant. Let's stop the bargaining. Besides, we will not accept the company's proposal of holding a small committee meeting in an attempt to come to an understanding.[42]

The company was trying very hard to restore mutual understand by asking the union not to force them to make their intentions clear. The company persisted in asking the union to talk, while it never intended to tell everything explicitly. This is quite common in Japanese industrial relations, just as communication from one person to another is often understood without words.[43] On the other hand, the union was trying very hard to resist this appeal from the company. The union required enormous strength throughout the "heroless" heroic fight just to extricate itself from the network of amicable, sentimental and personal attachments of their everyday place of work. This dispute turned out to be one of the rare cases where the union won out by refusing to accept a settlement based on mutual understanding. But it is interesting to observe that even in the final stages of this serious dispute, the company was still hoping for the traditional settlement and asked the union not to force them to state everything explicitly in collective bargaining. This case illustrates graphically the fact that most Japanese bargaining is actually conducted on the basis of "understanding without words." In order to overcome such "industrial relations—Japanese style," the union had to develop strong organizational power. According to the union's account of the strike, their organizational strength resulted from rank and file solidarity. "During this struggle, rank and file solidarity progressed tremendously. We were only able to resist for such a long time because mass solidarity was organized so resolutely, consistently and systematically. . . . In spite of serious interference and devious plots devised by the company to break our organizing efforts, we did not give them the opportunity to organize a breakaway union."[44]

Despite this historic victory, the same union lost another dispute seven years later. The union defeat in 1960 is attributable mainly to the fact that a breakaway union was well organized and severely damaged the main union's power. The economic and political climate, too, was somewhat different when the later dispute occurred. The final stages of the 1960 struggle became violent. At one point, 10,000 police officers faced 20,000 union members and their supporters, with both groups poised for an open confrontation. At the eleventh hour, the union was forced to surrender when the company announced that it intended resuming production with members of the breakaway union after the police expelled the workers occupying the pits.

The above sequence of events follows a pattern which is fairly typical of a number of recent disputes where the unions lost the struggle. First the union goes on strike and resorts to picketing or occupying the plant to halt production. The company then summons police to disperse the strikers. This move usually fails because in recent years police have been reluctant to get involved in labor disputes. Next the company seeks a court injunction against the workers. The injunction is often denied because the courts also are reluctant to intervene when the unions are not engaged in violent or destructive action, but merely occupying a plant peacefully. Finally, a breakaway union is organized. When enough workers secede to join the breakaway organization, the dispute ends with the defeat of the union which started the strike. The weakening of union power by the organization of a breakaway group will be discussed in greater detail in a later chapter.[45]

In spite of the high degree of union organization (the organization rate in Japan is over 30 percent, well above the level of most industrial countries), unions are concentrated in larger enterprises, and smaller enterprises are often completely unorganized.[46] The above-described Japanese mentality and personal relationships are prevalent in smaller enterprises. Even in larger enterprises, where the labor force is organized and unions appear to be strong, split union organization is not unusual.[47] Even if it is not the case, there is always the possibility of another union emerging because of the very nature of personal relationships within the Japanese enterprise. Employee dissatisfaction which has no free open outlet keeps increasing until it passes the limits of endurance. As long as the unions can provide a channel to express this dissatisfaction, the employer-employee relationship can be one of cooperation. Should the union fail in this function and indulge in an *amae* relationship with the employer, the possibility of upheaval becomes very real.

NOTES

1. In Japan's student movement, violence is called "Gewalt," a German word meaning violence or power. The long club student radicals use for fighting is called a "Gewalt-club." Such frequent use of German words among students reflects the traditional admiration of Japanese students and intellectuals in general (especially in the prewar period) for German culture.

2. Chie Nakane, *Japanese Society*, p. 19.

3. Stewart Macaulay, "Non-Contractual Relations in Business: A Preliminary Study," *American Sociological Review* 28, no. 1 (February 1963): 63–65.

4. Dore, *British Factory—Japanese Factory*, p. 185.

5. Takeyoshi Kawashima, *Nihonjin no Hō Ishiki* [Legal Rights Consciousness of the Japanese] (Tokyo: Iwanami Shoten, 1967), p. 119.

6. Ibid., p. 79.

7. Ibid., pp. 89 ff.

8. Robert E. Park and Ernest W. Burgess, *Introduction to the Science for Society* (Chicago: University of Chicago Press, 1921), p. 578.

9. Mitsuo Suzuki, *Funsō no Ronri to Nihonjin* [Logic of Conflict and the Japanese], *Chūōkōron* 8 [Public Opinion] (1971), p. 298.

10. Takeo Doi, *The Anatomy of Dependence*, trans. John Bester (Tokyo: Kodansha International, 1973).

11. Ibid., p. 99.

12. Ibid., p. 99.

13. Ibid., p. 29.

14. Kaoru Ōta, *Watashi no Keiei-ron to Keieisha-ron* [My View on Management and Managers] (Tokyo: Yūki Shobō, 1966), p. 105.

15. Bin Kimura, *Hito to Hito to no Aida* [Between Persons] (Tokyo: Kōbundō 1972), p. 122.

16. Ibid., p. 123.

17. The word *ki* in Japanese is one of the most important expressions for an understanding of the Japanese mentality. According to Dr. Doi, "*ki* is perhaps most accurately defined as the movement of the spirit from moment to moment. In other words, where *atama* (head), *kokoro* (heart), and *hara* (belly) all indicate the site where the various workings of the spirit take place, and the things that lie in the background of the phenomenon, *ki* indicates the working of the phenomenon as such," Doi, *The Anatomy of Dependence,* p. 97.

18. Kimura, *Hito to Hito*, p. 124.

19. Ibid., p. 125.

20. Kure Kōtsū [Kure Transportation Union] v. Kure City, Hiroshima High Court, December 21, 1965, 16 RKMS 1141.

21. Kawashima, *Nihonjin no Hō*, pp. 113–14.

22. Ibid., pp. 115–17.

23. Nenoki et al. v. Sanseki Taika Renga Co., Ltd., Ōita District Court, Usuki Branch, October 20, 1954, 5 RKMS 628; Mieno et al. v. Iwataya Department Co., Fukuoka District Court, May 19, 1961, 12 RKMS 247; Koyori v. Japan Air Lines, Tokyo District Court, February 26, 1966, 17 RKMS 102;

Sakakibara et al. v. Marui Jidōsha Co., Tokyo District Court, December 22, 1966, 17 RKMS 1423.

24. Gino Giugni, "The Peace Obligation," in *Industrial Conflict—A Comparative Legal Study*, eds. Benjamin Aaron and K. W. Wedderburn (New York: Crane, Russak & Co., 1972), pp. 128 ff.

25. Cole, *Japanese Blue Collar*, p. 250.

26. Rohlen, *For Harmony and Strength*, p. 185.

27. Kawashima, *Nihonjin no Hō*, pp. 154 ff.

28. P. H. Gulliver, "Dispute Settlement without Courts: The Ndendeuli of Southern Tanzania," in *Law in Culture and Society*, pp. 65–67.

29. Ibid., pp. 67–68.

30. Laura Nader, "Styles of Court Procedure: To Make the Balance," in *Law in Culture and Society*, pp. 73–74, 84.

31. Dan F. Henderson, *Conciliation and Japanese Law—Tokugawa and Modern*, 2 vols. (Tokyo: University of Tokyo Press, 1965), 1:3.

32. Ibid., 1:6–7.

33. Takeyoshi Kawashima, "Dispute Resolution in Contemporary Japan," in *Law in Japan*, ed. A. T. von Mehren (Cambridge, Mass: Harvard University Press; Rutland, Vt. and Tokyo: Charles E. Tuttle Company, 1964), p. 45.

34. Ōta, *Watashi no Keiei-ron to Keieisha-ron*, p. 105.

35. Kishima Tankō Rōdō Kumiai [Kishima Coal Mining Employees Union], *Teki yori-mo Ichinichi Nagaku* [One Day Longer Than the Enemy], (Tokyo: Kishima Tankō Rōdō Kumiai, 1958), p. 120.

36. Kaoru Ōta, *Rōdō Kumiai-ron* [On Trade Unions] (Tokyo: Rōdō Keizaisha, 1961), p. 74.

37. Kimura, *Hito to Hito*, p. 166. Doi urges the necessity for Japanese to "transcend *amae* (indulgence) by discovering the subject and object: to discover, in other words, the other person," in *The Anatomy of Dependence*, p. 84.

38. Doi, *Anatomy of Dependence*, p. 36.

39. Suzuki, *Funsō no Ronri*, p. 306.

40. Isaiah Ben-Dasan, *The Japanese and the Jews*, trans. Richard L. Gage (Tokyo: John Weatherhill, Inc., 1972), pp. 123–25.

41. In Japanese, putting "o" at the head of a word always makes the word or utterance polite.

42. Mitsui Tankō Rōdō Kumiai [Mitsui Coal Mining Company Employees Union], *Eiyū Naki 113 Nichi no Tatakai* [Fight for 113 Days Without a Hero], (Tokyo: Rōdō Hōritsu Junpō, 1954), pp. 198 ff.

43. William Caudill contends: "In general, it is my impression that emotion is not so much verbally expressed in Japan as it is lived out." He cites the following words from one of his Japanese interviewees, "Japanese won't express their feelings such as 'I love you' or 'I like you' or 'I dislike you,' or that sort of thing in words. Rather than using words, they often show their feelings in their behavior," in "Patterns of Emotion in Modern Japan," *Japanese Culture—Its Development and Characteristics*, eds. Robert J. Smith and Richard K. Beardsley (Chicago: Aldine Publishing Co., 1962), pp. 119–20.

44. Mitsui Tankō Rōdō Kumiai, *Eiyū Naki 113 Nichi*, p. 12.

45. See Part II, chapter 6.

46. The estimated rate of organization in the private sector by size of establishment in 1975 was 64.5% in the firms with 500 or more employees, 32.1% in the ones with 100–499 employees, 9.5% in those with 30–99 employees and only 3.5% in those with 29 or less employees, see Ministry of Labor, *Rōdō Kumiai Kihon Chōsa* [Basic Survey of Trade Unions], 1975.

47. Enterprises affected by split union organizations include such well-known companies as Japan Air Lines, Mitsubishi Heavy Industry Co., Nissan Automobile Co., and such public and national enterprises as the National Railways and Post Office.

3

LEGAL SETTING

1. UNIONS' RIGHT TO ORGANIZE

a. An "Eternal and Inviolable" Right: Article 28 of the Japanese Constitution guarantees workers' "right to organize, to bargain and to act collectively" as a fundamental human right. Article 12 declares that the rights and freedoms guaranteed by the constitution are "eternal and inviolable." Japanese labor lawyers are proud of such constitutional provisions, since few other countries recognize that the workers' right to organize includes the right to bargain and to act collectively. Not a single Anglo-Saxon country guarantees the right to organize as distinct from the freedom of association in its constitution or bill of rights. Only a few Western European countries, namely West Germany, France and Italy, have constitutional guarantees with regard to the workers' right to organize. The right to strike is acknowledged in France and Italy, but not the right to bargain.

In spite of the fact that in Japan the rights of workers are stated more explicitly than in any other country, Japanese lawyers seem unable to agree on how to interpret these constitutional guarantees. A majority of them believe that unions may ask the courts to force the employers to bargain. Others maintain that the voluntary character of collective bargaining cannot be preserved if it has to be enforced by legal procedure. At the request of unions, a number of courts have indeed issued provisional rulings ordering employers to come to the bargaining table, which is surely an unusual legal procedure. One is, of course, aware that the U.S. National Labor Relations Board also orders employers to bargain with the unions. The difference lies in the fact that in Japan not only such administrative agencies as the labor relations commissions, which correspond to the American National Labor Relations Board, issue orders to bargain, but the courts do so as well.

The constitutional guarantee of the right to act collectively also leads to peculiar interpretations. According to most legal experts, the right to act collectively goes beyond the right to strike. As a result, other union activities beside strikes tend to be regarded as legal. Reflecting the majority opinion, the courts hold that this right permits unions to engage in "positive" actions, something more than the "negative" refusal to work. The attitude of the courts toward violence is the best illustration of this interpretation. For instance, Japanese courts often declare that unions may go beyond peaceful picketing since, in Japan, something more than freedom of speech is guaranteed by the right to act collectively. The result is that it is very difficult to make a clear-cut distinction between legal collective acts and illegal violence. The Supreme Court ruled as follows in a case involving violence, threats and intimidation:

> It goes without saying that the union (and consequently, the union officials and union members who comply with the will of the union) may, by peaceful means of persuasion, request, orally or in writing, that persons starting work cease to do so; but causing such persons to suspend starting work by means of violence, intimidation, or force must be construed generally as illegal. *Naturally, though, whether an act bringing about the suspension of starting work is to be recognized as illegal or not must be carefully determined by particularly taking into account the various circumstances* at the time the appropriate strike or other acts of dispute are being carried out.[1]

The Court concluded its decision on the case in question with the following opinion:

> The union started to go on strike demanding better working conditions. A former president of the union and some others who had close connections with the management started to work. The defendants thought that this group betrayed the cause of the union which started the strike and that the strike would fail if they succeeded in working. Thus, the defendants got extremely angry with the dissident group and joined several others who were sitting in front of a truck in order to obstruct its path. They stayed there, shouted excitedly at the group in the truck, "Kill us by running over us if you want to pass." Judging from these developments, the conduct of the defendants was, so to speak, a matter of the union's internal affairs. Moreover, they only joined others who had already been trying to disturb the moving of the truck. Thus their conduct does not constitute a forcible obstruction of the business of another under the Criminal Code Article 234 and therefore the verdict of the High Court which declared the defendants not guilty is sustained.[2]

The Supreme Court upheld a decision of the High Court in another case as follows:

> The conduct of the defendants occurred in connection with internal union affairs during the dispute. Moreover, the victim, being in a responsible executive position in the union, participated in fractional activities and was accused and summoned to be heard and examined on charges of betrayal by the central committee of the union. . . . [The defendants] seized both his arms, held his shoulders and, when he tried to escape, restrained him for several minutes, finally persuading him to go to the nearby Hotel Botansō. Having committed no other violence or threats, the conduct of the defendants under the circumstances does not constitute the unlawful arrest of another.[3]

75

When I was teaching Japanese industrial relations abroad, I found it almost impossible to make foreign students understand the reasoning of the Japanese courts. First of all, the argument that the defendants' conduct was "a matter of internal union affairs" is not completely persuasive. The students pointed out that, in these cases of conflict among union members, the Supreme Court emphasized that the defendants were incensed by the betrayal of their former associates. They added that, intentionally or not, the court in its judgment gave greater weight to the subjective condition of the defendants than to the objective evidence of violent acts. The students inquired whether criminal conduct was excusable in Japan if a defendant was angry—a very good question indeed. The court ruled in the last case as if the victim, who previously had been trying to escape, suddenly became willing to go along with the defendants, which sounds very unlikely. The Japanese courts often "take into account various circumstances," but in most cases non-Japanese find it very difficult to perceive what these "circumstances" are.

Foreigners ask, for instance, what would Japanese courts say if several *yakuza* (gangsters) apprehended a citizen and, as he was trying to escape, caught him by the arms and brought him, "with his consent," to a hotel. Upon being told that the courts certainly would find this a crime of unlawful arrest and confinement, they would then point out that Japanese courts give extraordinary privileges to unions when they perform similar acts. In answer to this, most Japanese labor lawyers present their favorite trump card, i.e., that the workers' right to act, as guaranteed by the Japanese Constitution, is distinct and goes beyond the mere freedom of association. Furthermore, because the Constitution has proclaimed this right to be "eternal and inviolable," it has acquired a sacred character. In fact, Japanese academics tend to think that the right to organize and to act collectively makes the workers all-powerful. With this right the workers hold a position which is unassailable and often use the guarantee of the right to strike to say that political strikes are legal. The right to organize justifies their demands that companies provide office space and make meeting rooms available for unions, and so on. It is a stand against which no one can argue.

Foreigners, however, do not understand such logic. The only explanation that can be given is that it is a result of "Nihonism," in other words, it is the Japanese way of doing things. One of the best examples of "Nihonism" will be described in the next section.

b. "Nihonism": Between Violence and Power: The two cases mentioned above are not typical of all Supreme Court decisions. In most cases where striking union members prevented others from working by mass picketing or by forcible obstruction, the Supreme Court ruled that the accused were guilty of breaking the law. Labor law scholars are very critical of such Court decisions against labor. They even find fault with the Supreme Court's arguments in the two cases which favored labor. They point out that the Court failed to declare the union members' conduct was an appropriate act of dispute, and only held that their behavior did not constitute criminal conduct given the circumstances of the case. According to most labor law scholars, this opinion constitutes an incorrect interpretation of the law concerning the right to bargain collectively, since obstruction tactics should be recognized as "proper" acts of dispute. Many lower court decisions reflect this opinion.

It should be pointed out that Article 1, Section 2, of the Trade Union Law clearly states that violence is an improper act of dispute. However, labor law scholars say that while violence (*bōryoku*) is not proper, power (*jitsuryoku*) is admissible, a viewpoint which has been sustained by a number of lower court decisions. This is a distinction which foreigners find particularly hard to grasp. Literally translated, *jitsuryoku* means "real power." In a labor relations context it would describe a situation where, for instance, union members sit down arm-in-arm in front of the entrance to a plant, thus preventing the workers from entering, yet without hitting or kicking them. Power in this context is not just psychological but physical as well. To English-speaking people, however, to say that physical power does not involve violence is a mere play on words.

77

This distinction between violence and "real power" has puzzled Ben-Dasan too. The following is his description of, and comments on, an incident which occurred when the Japanese Association of Christians announced its intention to be a participant in Expo 1970. Ben-Dasan used "physical power" as a translation of *butsuriteki no chikara* which means literally "material power."

> The incident started . . . when the permanent representatives of the Association held a fierce all-night discussion with priests, students and other faithful followers who were against the Association's participation in the exhibition. According to accounts, during this discussion one of the organizers of the project "was subject to physical power." First, I could not understand the meaning of the word "physical power," no matter how hard I tried. . . . If you start from the principle that physical power must be a phenomenon obeying the laws of physics and give as examples a meteorite dropping from the sky or a framed picture shaken off the wall by an earthquake, you will have failed your exam in a course on "Nihonism." In reality, the phrase "was subjected to physical power" meant that Professor Yoshizō Kitamori of the Tokyo University of Theology was hit by one member of the anti-exhibition group. Honestly speaking, even I was not able to decode the Japanese phrase and arrive at that meaning.[4]

Ben-Dasan believes that to regard human violence as a natural phenomenon separate from human volition is a way of thinking which has long existed in Japan. This concept is related to the idea that human violence, just as natural calamities, is an act of God. Two justifications were advanced in defense of the attack on Professor Kitamori, both stating that "physical power" was in fact "heaven's punishment." The first claimed that "since Expo itself is a crime, violence is the proper punishment against those who participate in it." The second argued that "although the violence was excessive, the project organizers are to be held responsible for it, since they did not adequately respond to the serious theological questions raised by the naive youngsters."[5] "Physical power" as

78

exemplified in "The Revenge of the Forty-seven Rōnin" is also regarded as "heaven's punishment"; therefore, it is not only justified but also worthy of praise and evokes emotional sympathy in the audience.

The arguments in favor of the "physical power" of unions rest on these feelings of sympathy and on the Japanese "logic" of "heavenly punishment." Similar assumptions underlie the strictures against employers who discipline their employees and criticism of the courts which penalize the behavior of union members. These arguments run as follows: "Intervention in union organization or strikebreaking is a serious crime; therefore, violence is a proper punishment for those who participate in such crimes," or "Violence is certainly excessive, but the employers should be blamed for refusing to entertain the proper demands of the innocent union members." This way of thinking is the basis for the two Supreme Court decisions mentioned in the previous section.

According to Ben-Dasan, the fundamental idea of "Nihonism" is that homicide or acts of violence committed by politically motivated "innocent persons" should not be penalized by law. In his view, this amounts to granting unions absolute authority to prosecute, judge and carry out their own judgments. Thus whenever a union is in difficulty, all it needs to do is to emphasize the political character of the dispute, i.e., to brand the employer as a cruel despot, and present the union's claim as something other than purely economically motivated. If they succeed in portraying themselves as innocent and just men who had to stand up to fight an unscrupulous tyrant, there is a good chance that their violence will be regarded as a just judgment against the employer. In this sense, the doctrine of "Nihonism" justifies the violence which is still more or less prevalent in industrial relations. Why violence occurs frequently in industrial relations is a question which will be dealt with in a later part of this book.[6]

2. FAIR PLAY IN INDUSTRIAL RELATIONS?

a. Unfair Labor Practices—Japanese Style: Under Japanese law, discriminatory treatment against employees because of their union activities and interference into union affairs by the employers are considered unfair labor practices. The notion of unfair labor practices was originally taken from the American labor law system. But in the United States unions as well as management can be sued for unfair labor practices. In contrast to this, the Japanese system admits only the employer's responsibility.

Early American legislation, specifically the Wagner Act of 1935, also recognized only unfair labor practices by employers, but later the Taft-Hartley Act of 1947 introduced the concept that unions as well could be held responsible for such practices. Japan, however, adopted only part of the U.S. system. Japanese labor law scholars contend that unfair labor practices should be admitted for employers only, while the union's excesses should not be penalized. Their contention stems from the fact that the unfair labor practice system is derived from the constitutional guarantee of the right to organize, which applies to the workers exclusively but not to management. This legal concept seems to encourage the union's natural tendency to criticize the employers' misconduct and fails to apply the same standards in judging their own behavior.

I have observed a rather peculiar phenomenon during hearings of the Tokyo Labor Relations Commission. The employers' attorneys often accuse unions or their members of unfair practices such as threats or other mischievous or violent acts. Yet, the union's attorneys do not appear anxious to question the evidence or to present arguments to defend the unions against such charges; they prefer to attack the employers' unfair practices instead. In this way, both parties compete to point out the errors of the other side and seem satisfied when they can show their opponent to be the greater villain.

Not only is the legislation one-sided, but the wording of the Trade Union Law of 1949 suggests that the concept of "unfairness" has been superseded by the concept of "impropriety." The 1945 Trade Union Law, which introduced the American system into Japanese law, referred to *fukōsei rōdō kōi*, a literal translation of the English words "unfair labor practices." The reason for the change in the present laws is more or less accidental. The person who drafted the text chose *futō rōdō kōi* (improper labor practices) simply because the earlier phrase did not sound natural in Japanese. However, there is no general agreement that it is so. Actually, *fukōsei* (unfair) is perfectly appropriate when the criticism is addressed to the government or to other authorities. When it comes to the attitude or behavior of private persons, *kōhei* and *fukōhei*, equivalents of impartiality and partiality, are more suitable. It seems that the Japanese language lacks an appropriate word to express the concept of fairness or unfairness in personal inter-relations.

Isaiah Ben-Dasan concludes that the concept of fairness simply does not exist in Japan. He illustrates his contention by a historical event, the so-called "May 15 Incident of 1932," in which several naval officers visited the premier's residence, were invited in, and then shot the premier to death at the very moment he was offering them cigarettes. According to Ben-Dasan, this was one of the most unfair incidents in Japanese history, but no one in Japan at the time seemed to feel that the officers' behavior was at all "unfair."[7] By the same token, one could conclude that the notion of "unfairness" is almost irrelevant in Japanese industrial relations. Is it fair to accuse an opponent of unfairness, while never applying the same standard to oneself? Japanese labor law scholars refuse to acknowledge the union's unfairness, even when union members invade the residences of company presidents and threaten their mothers, wives and children, or when they follow a company president's wife down the street. What is more, they contend that such behavior should be regarded as permissible acts of dispute for trade unions when the employers refuse to bargain or try to destroy union organizations.

b. Strikes and Lockouts: The right to act collectively, like the right to organize, is guaranteed for the workers only. Furthermore, the concept of conspiracy as a tort is unknown in Japanese civil law. This results in the unions being allowed to go on strike and to engage in other acts of dispute without any risk of being judged liable for the damage caused by such acts. The unions are in fact given legal immunity from acts which amount to breach of contract. For instance, legally speaking, unions could go on strike without being required to give previous notice.

On the other hand, since the right to act collectively is not guaranteed to the employers, lockouts have only limited legal justification. A few court decisions have even denied to employers the right to lockout altogether. Most labor lawyers, however, recognize this right, but the courts have severely limited its application. Lockout is permitted only as far as it is "defensive." It means that employers may lock out workers only when they are on strike or engaging in some other acts of dispute. This attitude of the courts is often a cause of puzzlement to foreign enterprises working in Japan. Such a case, a dispute between the union and Northwest Air Lines, is described below.

The union gave notice that it would go on strike for forty-one hours. A short time later the strike started and lasted the scheduled number of hours. The union members then declared their intention of going back to work. However, the company refused to let them start work on the grounds that they were still wearing armbands, which meant that they intended to continue fighting against the company. The lockout continued for about a month until the dispute was finally settled. The union members sued the company for lost wages. The company claimed that the lockout was legal and that it was not required to pay wages since the dispute had not been settled, as the workers' armbands testified, when the union members tried to go back to work. Management also alleged that the union members had committed illegal activities during the strike which were greatly annoying to their passengers.

All the company's arguments were rejected by the court, and it was ordered to pay the wages which the workers would have received during the period of the lockout. According to the court's decision, "Lockout is permitted only when the damage (including lost earnings) caused to the company by the union's actions exceeds certain limits, or if there is concrete danger or an emergency situation which makes lockout inevitable."[8] In this case, the court estimated that there was no likelihood that the union would resume striking after they went back to work, and that the workers were actually willing to work in spite of wearing armbands. Finally the court felt that the illegal acts which occurred during the strike would probably not be repeated after the strike was over.

Western managers are unlikely to find the reasoning of the court either appropriate or persuasive. First of all, according to the court's findings, the union had declared twenty days before the strike started that they would resort to various kinds of acts of dispute at all working sites of the company until the dispute was settled. Another fact, mentioned in the court record but which attracted little consideration, militates for management's position. After the strike was over, three officers of the union continued to refuse to work, declaring a "designated strike." Japanese unions often engage in "designated strikes," which means that only certain members, designated by the unions, refuse to work. Whether a designated strike is a strike in the usual sense of the term is questionable. While the purpose of an ordinary strike is to put pressure on the employer by causing economic damage, "designated strikes" have no economic objectives. Some, as in the Northwest case, are declared in order for the particular members to carry on union activities.[9] The court said that this partial strike was not related to the original dispute and therefore it could not serve as a justification for the lockout. In spite of all this, the court felt that there was no possibility that the union would engage in any new manifestation of conflict. It concluded, therefore, that the lockout was not "defensive," but "offensive."

Whatever the validity of the legal arguments, most foreign managers will surely feel uneasy when Japanese courts hand down such decisions. This foreboding is all the more true when the same courts declare that wearing armbands, headbands or ribbons do not make union members liable for breach of contract because such acts are permissible acts of dispute. We also have to take into consideration the fact that unions rarely go on strike for an indefinite period, but rather for a specified number of hours or days. They go back to work without waiting for the dispute to be settled, but are likely to resume striking repeatedly. Thus when management is denied the right to lock out, it is left without any effective weapon to cope with the threat of such repeated strikes. Whenever the union decides to start working again, management is expected to accept its offer to work, even if the workers' performance is not up to standards or the work is disrupted by breach of discipline. We can conclude that, as far as the legal setting is concerned, the employers are forced to play a game in which they are seriously handicapped. Whether or not handicapping the employer's conduct in industrial relations is justified is another question.

c. The Courts and Amae Relations: Foreigners coming to Japan, not only managers but also trade unionists, are often surprised to find that union offices are usually located within the company premises. However, for most of the union organizations as enterprise unions, the location of their offices on company premises is not as unreasonable as it appears at first glance. This arrangement is not only convenient but to some extent necessary and inevitable. In contrast with the industrial or craft unions whose functions reach far beyond the company to the local region and even up to the national scene, the Japanese enterprise unions are concerned almost exclusively with the working conditions of the employees of a single enterprise and the daily occurrences at the workplace. In this sense, the functions of the Japanese unions are closer to the activities of work councils or shop stewards in European countries than to those of Western trade unions. Even in Western countries, such bodies often have their offices within the plants where their main functions are concentrated.

Article 7, Section 2, of the Japanese Trade Union Law prohibits employers' control of and interference in union administration, including giving financial assistance to unions. Excluded from this list of unfair labor practices are supplying minimum office space to the unions and providing financial support to their welfare funds. However, in practice, the employers go beyond the allowable minimum and often provide office furniture, telephone service, stationery, etc. Usually unions are also permitted to use company meeting rooms or dining rooms for their meetings and are provided with bulletin boards. The check-off system, in which the company withholds the amount of union dues and fees from the employees' paychecks and passes the amount on to the union, is also practiced widely. Union officers are allowed to take special leave of absence for union activities, sometimes even with pay. Employees elected to full-time union offices are often given leave of absence for their term of office. Such leaves may last as long as ten years or more, especially when the union leaders are elected to national offices in the union federations or central bodies such as the Sōhyō or Dōmei. One well-known example is Kaoru Ōta who maintained his status as an employee of Ube Kōsan Company for several years while he was serving as the president of the Sōhyō.

Some of these arrangements could legally be considered unfair labor practices because they benefit the unions financially. However, the unions rarely bring them to the attention of the labor relations commissions.[10] On the contrary, unions sometimes appeal to a labor relations commission when employers abolish these arrangements. In a case where a company stopped collecting union fees after the union went on strike repeatedly, the commission ordered the firm to resume the check-off practice, even though the agreement to that effect between the company and the union had lapsed for a long time. The commission reasoned that, although the company had no obligation to check-off, the purpose of abolishing the practice, which had been continued after the agreement had lapsed, was to put pressure on the union. In the hope of putting a stop to a series of serious strikes, the company was trying to weaken the union by making it harder to collect union fees without the company's help.[11]

In another case, a company which had been paying the union's telephone charges suddenly asked the union to reimburse them for all telephone expenses for the last two years. Here also, a commission ruled that the company's behavior was an unfair labor practice. The commission admitted that the union should pay its own telephone charges, but it argued that the company's sole intention had been to decrease the union's influence by an attack on its finances.[12] There are many cases where commissions ordered companies to resume providing benefits to unions, after the practice had been stopped. Companies, therefore, are caught in a trap: once the employers agree to provide some benefits, it is almost impossible for them ever to terminate them. As the unions' demands increase, the employers have to make more concessions.

The unions believe that making demands is proof of militancy and that each victory makes the union stronger. As for the employers, they often welcome such union attitudes because they realize that the more benefits they get, the more dependent the unions grow. Thus both parties tend to indulge in a cozy relationship of dependence and mutual reliance. Once the relationship sours, however, the employers try to put pressure on the unions by abolishing or threatening to abolish benefits. To counter that threat, the unions appeal to a labor relations commission, which usually forces the firm to restore the union's privileges. Though the commissions' intention is to protect the unions, it is doubtful whether such decisions actually help to strengthen the unions or only result in making the unions more subservient to the employers who expect absolute loyalty from the unions in return for giving them special favors. By this process the labor relations commissions really foster the growth of *amae* relationships between companies and enterprise unions.

NOTES

1. Japan v. Hirata, Supreme Court, III Petty Bench, December 11, 1956, 10 SSKH 1605–1609. Emphasis added.
2. Ibid., p. 1609.
3. Kido et al. v. Japan, Fukuoka High Court, April 11, 1962, 466 BRHJ 2, Supreme Court, III Petty Bench, March 10, 1964, 525 BRHJ 26.
4. Isaiah Ben-Dasan, *Nihonkyō ni tsuite* [On Nihonism], (Tokyo: Bungei Shunjūsha, 1972), p. 93.
5. Ibid., p. 97.
6. Part II, chapter 9.

7. Ben-Dasan, *Nihonkyō ni tsuite,* p. 74.

8. Koizumi v. Northwest Airlines, Inc., Tokyo District Court, November 11, 1969, 20 RKMS 1451.

9. Unions also resort to designated strikes when union members are dissatisfied with being transferred by the company and refuse to work in their new location. According to the union's way of reasoning, such members are not liable for breach of contract because they are on a legitimate act of dispute.

10. Local labor relations commissions are set up in each prefecture, while the Central Labor Relations Commission is located in Tokyo. The jurisdiction of local commissions applies where one of the parties lives in the prefecture, or their headquarters are located in it, or if the labor dispute occurred there. The Central Labor Relations Commission reviews the orders and decisions taken by the local commissions in the field of unfair labor practices and adjudicates those cases which cover more than one prefecture or which are clearly of national importance. Equal numbers of representatives on the courts are drawn from workers, company management and the general public to make up the membership of the commissions.

11. Kokusaku Pulp Co. Case, August 12, 1958, 18–19 FRKM 184; also see Shōun Kōsakusho Co. Case, November 21, 1962, 26–27 FRKM 152, and Nihon Shintaku Bank Case, April 2, 1963, 28–29 FRKM 206.

12. Fuji Yusōki Kōgyō Co. Case, July 26, 1968, 39 FRKM 157.

$$\boxed{4}$$

ENTERPRISE UNIONISM AND THE NATIONAL SETTING

1. UNION ORGANIZATION IN JAPAN

a. Enterprise Unions and Workers' Organizations: In 1976, there were over 12 million unionized workers in Japan, approximately 35.5 percent of the labor force. The Ministry of Labor Statistics showed that there were 33,771 unions ("Unit Unions"). These ranged from single unit unions in small firms which operate only one plant to headquarters of much larger unions having several local branches. Because such branches are capable of independent activities, their number is sometimes added to that of union proper, for a grand total of 70,039 "Basic Unit Unions."[1]

Among different types of organizations, enterprise unions account for more than 90 percent of all the unions and organized workers. There are few craft and industrial unions in Japan and their membership is quite limited. The figures for the number of unions and organized workers according to the type of organization are available only for 1975 and are given in Table 3.

Among the factors which contribute to the prominence of enterprise unions, two are relevant to the question of union organization. The first factor is that only the employees of a particular enterprise are qualified to be members of the union in that particular enterprise. This organizing principle is the exact opposite of closed shop agreements in Western countries, in which only union

Table 3
Number of Unions and Union Members
According to the Type of Union Organization

Type of Union Organization	No. of Unions (Basic Unit Unions)	%	No. of Union Members	%
Enterprise Unions	65,337	94.2	11,361,378	91.1
Craft Unions	720	1.0	169,569	1.4
Industrial Unions	1,775	2.6	682,728	5.5
Others	1,501	2.2	259,299	2.0
Total	69,333	100.0	12,472,974	100.0

Source: Ministry of Labor, *Basic Survey of Trade Unions*, 1975.

members whose union has entered into an agreement with an enterprise are qualified to be employed by the enterprise. In Japan, because a worker is required to be an employee before he can become a union member, his status as an employee is always the most important thing in his working life, and the union movement stands second in importance. In other words, the union's very existence and functions are tied to the enterprise. The second factor is the lifetime employment system. Since most of the employees stay in a particular enterprise during their entire working lives, it is only natural that their interests are focused on the working conditions of that particular enterprise. Thus enterprise unionism and enterprise bargaining are more suitable to protect the workers' interests.

The only significant craft union in Japan is the All Japan Seamen's Union (*Zen Nihon Kaiin Kumiai*), which organizes seamen regardless of their employment status in each company. The Seamen's Union owes its continued existence as a craft union to its unique history and to the fact that it was able to survive during World War II. Employees of small and medium-size enterprises, whether stores or factories, are often organized in various general unions called *gōdōrōso* (amalgamated unions). In such types of enterprises as well, the lifetime employment system is not generally practiced, and employees often move from one enterprise to another. Although they could be classified as industrial unions, most of the unions in the public sector are in fact extremely large enterprise unions. Public sector employees work under the lifetime employment system and all the members of a particular union have a single employer, either the national government or a public corporation like the National Railways.

b. Industrial Federations and Confederations: The dominance of enterprise unions over other types of union organizations does not exclude the existence of industrial federations in the Japanese labor movement. But, with a few exceptions, including the Seamen's Union, these organizations are exclusively federations of enterprise unions within a particular industry. There were 5,394 such federations in 1976. About 80 percent of them are now advisory bodies. Their functions are restricted to exchanging information and mutual assistance and their decisions are not binding on the affiliated unions.[2] The other 20 percent are genuine federations whose policy decisions are binding on their affiliated member unions. However, even the latter group is characterized by a rather loose organization. Such lack of authority of the main body over the member unions is caused by the strong independence of the affiliated enterprise unions.

Table 4
Number of Unions and Members According to the Size of
Enterprise in the Private Sector (1977)

Size of Enterprises	No. of Unions	No. of Members	%
1,000 employees and over	14,145	4,986,914	57.2
300–999	6,908	1,366,384	15.7
100–299	10,345	1,033,899	11.9
30–99	12,186	466,206	5.4
29 and less	5,743	70,907	0.8
Others*	2,616	789,667	9.0
Total	51,943	8,713,977	100.0

*Others means unions organizing employees of more than one enterprise and those in which coverage is unknown.
Source: Ministry of Labor, *Basic Survey of Trade Unions*, 1977.

Most of the public sector unions have a very large membership. For example, *Dentsūkyōtō* (Joint Council of Telecommunication Industry Trade Unions) has organized more than 320,000 members and the membership of *Kokurō* (National Railways Workers' Union) reaches 250,000. Other important unions in the public sector are *Zentei* (Japan Postal Workers' Union), *Zensenbai* (All Monopoly Corporation Workers' Union), *Dōryokusha* (National Railway Locomotive Engineers' Union), and *Kokkōrōren* (Japan Federation of National Service Employees). The first three of these rank sixth, tenth and fourteenth among the twenty largest unions in Japan (see Table 6).

The following two tables illustrate the strength of some of the private sector enterprise unions. As is shown in Table 4, most unionized workers are concentrated in larger enterprises. Nearly 60 percent of organized workers are employed in enterprises with more than 1,000 employees. Table 5 shows the distribution of unions and organized workers according to the size of the unions. The figures indicate that 70 percent of the workers belong to unions which have more than 1,000 members.

The enterprise unions of large firms are bound to exert a great deal of influence on the industrial federations as a result not only of the number of votes they command but also because of their relatively better financial position. The large enterprise unions have at their disposal comparatively larger amounts of money than smaller unions because big firms pay better wages than smaller firms and union

Table 5
Number of Unions and Members According to the Size of Unions (1977)

Size of Unions	No. of Unions	No. of Members	%
1,000 members and over	1,711	8,489,040	68.3
300–999	3,460	1,797,100	14.4
100–299	7,749	1,302,379	10.5
30–99	12,243	707,725	5.7
29 and less	8,824	140,759	1.1
Total	33,987	12,437,003	100.0

Source: Ministry of Labor, *Basic Survey of Trade Unions*, 1977.

fees are fixed in proportion to each member's income. The larger unions are not always willing to carry out the same policy concerning wages and working conditions as their smaller colleagues in the federations. The overwhelming majority of the industrial federations do not have the authority to bargain collectively, or conclude agreements with the employers, much less call a strike. Since the enterprise unions carry on such important functions on their own, little scope is left for the activities of industrial federations. Their main task is the collection and distribution of information and political activity. The federations publish and distribute a great deal of material to their affiliates. The tone of federation publications is rather abstract and their substance mostly ideological. They are full of high-minded slogans and propaganda for advanced ideas but are not particularly effective or practically oriented. Federations also coordinate the bargaining policies of each enterprise union within the federation at the time of the *Shuntō* (Spring Offensive), the period when negotiations are traditionally opened in Japan.

The political orientation of industrial federations follows closely that of the national confederations with which they are affiliated. The existence of two national confederations, confronting each other along ideological lines, has been a constant feature of the history of the Japanese labor movement. In 1976 the left-oriented Sōhyō had 4,578,911 members, or 36.6 percent of organized workers, while the right-oriented Dōmei had 2,208,864 members, or 17.7 percent of organized workers. The third confederation is the *Chūritsurōren* (Federation of Independent Unions), which was established in 1956 in order to facilitate liaison among several industrial federations not affiliated either with Sōhyō or with Dōmei. This body had 1,354,183 members, or 10.8 percent of organized workers in 1976. The *Denkirōren* (All Japan Federation of Electric Machine Workers' Unions), a very important federation, is one of Churitsurōren's affiliates. Table 6 lists the twenty largest union organizations in Japan and indicates the size of their membership and affiliation to national confederations.

The rivalry between the two national centers is the result of ideo-

Table 6
The Twenty Largest Federations (1976)

Rank	Trade Union (Affiliation)	Occupation or Industry	Membership
1	Jichirō (Sōhyō)	Local government employees	1,196,795
2	Nikkyōso (Sōhyō)	Teachers	642,511
3	Denkirōren (Churitsurōren)	Electrical machinery workers	531,297
4	Jidōshasōren (Ind.)	Automobile workers	530,581
5	Zensen (Dōmei)	Textile workers	470,474
6	Dentsūkyōtō (Sōhyō)	Telecommunications workers	332,602
7	Seihorōren (Churitsurōren)	Life insurance workers	313,952
8	Zenkindōmei (Dōmei)	Metal workers	306,654
9	Tekkōrōren (Sōhyō)	Iron and steel workers	252,793
10	Kokurō (Sōhyō)	National railway workers	247,171
11	Zenkensōren (Churitsurōren)	Construction workers	244,001
12	Zōsenjūkirōren (Dōmei)	Shipbuilding and heavy machinery workers	229,334
13	Shitetsusōren (Sōhyō)	Private railway workers	209,690
14	Zentei (Sōhyō)	Postal workers	202,307
15	Zenkokukinzoku (Sōhyō)	Metal workers	201,528
16	Jidōsharōren (Dōmei)	Automobile workers	192,975
17	Shiginren (Ind.)	City bank employees	184,276
18	Kaiin (Dōmei)	Seamen	156,406
19	Unyurōren (Ind.)	Transport workers	139,666
20	Ippandōmei (Ind.)	General workers	133,882

Source: Ministry of Labor, *Basic Survey of Trade Unions*, 1976.

logical differences which are reflected in their activities. In general, the Sōhyō-affiliated unions are ideologically radical and adopt militant policies. When there exists more than one union in an enterprise, the milder union is often a breakaway union organized in reaction to the militant policy of the Sōhyō-affiliated union. After it gains recognition, the breakaway union usually seeks affiliation with the Dōmei. How such splits in union organization, especially the creation of breakaway unions during serious disputes, weaken the Japanese trade union movement has already been discussed. The causes of this deep-rooted ideological rivalry among Japanese unions will be discussed later in this book.[3]

2. *SHUNTŌ*—INDUSTRIAL BARGAINING IN JAPAN

a. Advantages and Disadvantages of Shuntō: For a number of reasons, the bargaining power of enterprise unions tends to be considerably less than that of industrial unions. The enterprise unions' continued existence and development are tied to the prosperity of the enterprises. Therefore, they are not able to make demands which might jeopardize the company prosperity. If a company is struggling against severe competition from other firms, excessive wage demands by the union would very likely endanger the company's business position.

In order to remedy the shortcomings of enterprise unionism, the Sōhyō invented a unique industrial bargaining system called *Shuntō* (Spring Offensive). The Shuntō scheme is based on the idea that several enterprise unions within one industry, all more or less of similar size and importance, should coordinate their bargaining strategies. Under the leadership of the industrial federation, they harmonize their wage demands and schedule their negotiations and strikes around the same period each year. Through such coordination, the Sōhyō hoped that the unions could overcome the disadvantages of enterprise bargaining, under which only the unions of the prosperous companies obtained higher wages while those of the less prosperous companies were forced to accept lower wages.

When the spring offensive was first introduced, employers showed great reluctance to bargain with the industrial federations. As we have already noted, Japanese employers are loath to negotiate with "outsiders." When, in 1960, the *Gōkarōren* (Industrial Federation of Chemical Workers' Unions) and two of its affiliated unions in the ammonium sulphate industry attempted to bargain jointly, the individual companies refused, on the grounds that "the past practice of bargaining with individual unions is quite sufficient. . . . We would prefer to bargain with each union separately."[4] If the employers accepted industry-wide bargaining, they would be forced to deal with the leaders of the federations who could very well be employees of other companies. This, they felt, would certainly destroy the relationship of mutual trust which they enjoyed with the leaders of their own enterprise unions.

However, over a period of several years, the Sōhyō succeeded in setting up industry-wide negotiations by resorting to several compromises. At first the leaders of the federation attended as observers. In later stages, they attended as representatives of individual unions which had managed to win the right to bargain jointly. Thus a modified form of industrial bargaining, the so-called joint bargaining, was accepted by the employers and today the Spring Offensive is an expected annual occurrence. Nevertheless, serious obstacles must be overcome before industrial bargaining, even in modified form, can totally change the pattern of Japanese industrial relations. In spite of repeated attempts to introduce industry-wide negotiations and strengthen industrial unions at the expense of enterprise unions, the main thrust of Japanese industrial relations today is still to be found at the enterprise level.

The emergence of enterprise unions after World War II and the continuing importance of their role in the industrial relations system, in which enterprise bargaining is a crucial element, has its economic basis in the lifetime employment system. Although the labor shortages of the 1960s increased labor mobility, the majority of the workers are mainly concerned with the working conditions in their own companies. Western workers continue to "grow" throughout their working lives because of their ability to change jobs and to acquire a variety of skills which, in turn, enhance their independence. But in Japan a worker's entire future, whether in the form of wage increases, promotions or retirement allowances, depends upon his length of service in the particular company where he happens to take a job after finishing secondary school or college. Thus, protecting the interests of the workers means first of all improving the prevailing working conditions in a particular enterprise; the enterprise union is the organization best suited for this. Changing companies is still unusual for ordinary workers. They regard working conditions at other enterprises as none of their business, except when their own working conditions are affected.

The survival of enterprise unionism limits the role of industrial bargaining through a Spring Offensive in two important ways. First, it makes the Spring Offensive inevitable in a rather ironic way. For union and management to increase wages and improve working conditions in an enterprise regardless of what the competitors do would be akin to suicide. Any significant change might put their company at a serious disadvantage *vis-à-vis* rival firms. It is here that the economic foundation of the Spring Offensive is to be found because, in fact, joint bargaining takes place only among certain oligopolistic enterprises and within a limited industrial sector only, for instance in the synthetic fiber industry in textiles. Medium and smaller business enterprises participate in such negotiations only as junior partners, or else carry out separate negotiations parallel to those undertaken by the large enterprises.[5] Second, if both union and management occasionally support industrial bargaining in the belief that it is advantageous for their enterprise, the enterprise union naturally tends to forego the united front whenever joint negotiations run counter to the interests of the enterprise. Japanese industrial federations, it must be remembered, are only federations of enterprise unions and their activities and administration are often controlled by the larger unions among their affiliates.

One measure of the dependence of the federations on individual unions can be inferred from the manner in which the federations are financed. We have already indicated that the larger unions receive proportionally much more money in dues than smaller ones because big firms pay higher salaries than small ones. On the other hand, the level of contribution from individual unions to the federation is usually based on what the smaller unions are able to afford. Thus the federation's financial situation tends to be poor while the larger enterprise unions get richer, since they are left with fairly large sums in reserve even after making their donations to the federation. In one instance, "the assets of the *Denkirōren* (All Japan Federation of Electric Machine Workers' Union) hardly reach the level of those of the larger enterprise unions in that sector, which operate at such firms as Hitachi, Toshiba or the Mitsubishi Electrical Manufacturing Company . . . and it is almost impossible to change the situation which is characterized by strong independent enterprise unions and a lack of control by the federations over the individual union."[6] Thus overcoming enterprise unionism by reinforcing industrial unionism remains a goal which can never become a reality: it is, in fact, a union slogan empty of meaning.

The list of obstacles to real industrial bargaining in Japan is almost endless. In spite of numerous demands announced by the unions in the annual Spring Offensive, the main subject of industrial bargaining is in fact limited to wages. Actually, joint negotiations focus solely on the rate of wage increases, while the wage system and wage structure remain the exclusive domain of enterprise bargaining. As a result, even if the same rate of increase is agreed upon by a number of companies, the significant differences in basic wages among these companies remain unchanged. Even such a limited agreement cannot always be reached since, as we have already explained, the bargaining is carried out in separate groups according to the size of the enterprises. Working conditions, with the possible exception of working hours, are rarely negotiated on an industry-wide basis. Since various kinds of fringe benefits figure much more prominently in company personnel practices in Japan than in most Western countries,[7] industrial bargaining hardly contributes to the standardization of working conditions.[8] Conditions vary according to the size of the firm, the industry and the region. Consequently, we can hardly expect that industrial unionism will bring significant changes to the present Japanese industrial relations system.

b. The Concept of the Right to Strike: Matsuta Hosoya, a former *Sanbetsu* (Congress of Industrial Unions) leader, is very critical of Shuntō. His comments, based on his many years experience as a professional unionist are as follows:

> After the Sōhyō was established, the system of the Spring Offensive, that is, a series of confrontations rotating mechani-

cally from one union to another, was practiced regularly. . . .
The Sōhyō decided the timing of the spring confrontation each
year at its annual convention. At the same time, complete
tactical plans and a precise timetable were prepared, ready
to be implemented. Thus serious effort went into the planning
of this schedule. . . .

In short the seasonal confrontation, being nothing but a pre-
ordained event, tends inevitably to reflect standardized ways
of thinking and methodology. . . . Since the whole process of
the labor struggle is planned by the higher echelons of the
union organization, without giving the rank and file any
chance to express their will, its pattern is bound to be characterized by bureaucratic stubbornness. . . .

This trend toward standardization is not only found in the
annual confrontation of the Sōhyō and its affiliated unions
but also can be observed to a greater or lesser extent in every
organization in the Japanese labor movement . . . . We can
find similar trends, too, in most of the unions at the plant
level.[9]

Standardized demands and prearranged strikes planned by the
higher echelons and implemented by means of similar tactics are,
as Hosoya suggests, the product of a standardization of the way of
thinking and the bureaucratization of the Japanese labor movement. At the same time, the practice of Shuntō stimulates and
expands these trends. Since the timetable of the strike is planned
at the highest level of union organization, any criticism of it is
regarded as a betrayal of "class unity." Because the bureaucrats
need time for planning a negotiation strategy and strike timetable,
the unions are required to decide on these matters long before
the date of their implementation. This means that strikes could be
scheduled without taking into account the organizational situation
of each union. Under this system, too, unions are forced to go on
strike according to the schedule regardless of any changes that may
have occurred in the situation.

Generally speaking, it is felt in Japan that the purpose of a strike vote is to legalize strike action, as is shown in the frequent use of the phrase "the establishment of the right to strike." However, the original purpose of any strike vote was to test the individual members' determination to persist in their demands, even if it meant resorting to a strike.

A vote must be taken before strike action is initiated. It is an excercise in discipline, a concerted action controlled by competent agents of the union organization. Thus, for instance, the constitution of each and every union in West Germany requires the support of three-quarters of the membership, expressed by secret ballot, in order to start or continue a strike. The constitutions of some unions require that a strike vote be taken whenever a fresh proposal is made by the employers, or when any other change occurs in the situation. In Japan, the Trade Union Law of 1949 stipulates that unions should have a provision in their constitutions requiring majority support by the members before starting a strike. Most Japanese union constitutions do indeed include such a provision. However, as indicated above, the strike vote often takes place long before the actual strike date, partly as a result of the prearranged strike. Once the "right to strike" has been established, and the collective will of the union determined, individual members are rarely consulted again, even if changes, such as a new phase of bargaining or a new proposal by the employers, alter the situation. In protracted disputes, once the right to strike has been established, unions tend to continue the strike even if the number of members who oppose the strike is increasing. As a result, those dissatisfied members often break with the union and set up a "second union."

In order to obviate the splitting of unions during the course of strikes, Kaoru Ōta advocates a more frequent use of the vote to ascertain whether members still support the strike:

Quite often attempts are made to alienate members from their leaders by propagating rumors that the union is being taken advantage of by power-hungry persons, or that it is being taken over by outsiders. In such cases the leaders should always boldly ask for the support of their members by means of a general secret ballot. If the majority does not support them, or if only a slight majority does so, they should stop the strike . . . . In the case of the dispute at the Muroran Plant of the Nihon Steel Company, the split in the union probably was caused by the decision of the union's central committee to reject the company's proposal without seeking rank and file approval in a general vote. This provided a good excuse for a breakaway. Even when the central committee of a union decides to continue a strike, it is often necessary to take a general vote.[10]

It is quite significant that this procedure, so common in West Germany, requires boldness in Japan and needs to be particularly emphasized by such an experienced union leader as Ōta. The trend toward standardization and bureaucracy in the Japanese labor movement, described above, is certainly related to this attitude of the unions. Unions consider that continuing to strike enhances their strong, militant stance. In their view, once the "right to strike" is established and the strike is "legalized," changes in the situation or in the mood of members are not reasons enough to stop it.

Such attitudes seem to prevail not only in the Japanese union movement but also in "progressive" movements in general. According to Takeshi Ishida, the concept of fundamental human rights has never been firmly accepted by the general public in Japan because, first of all, human rights have been understood exclusively as something to be "extended" in a power struggle with the government (the concept of "power relationship"). Secondly, while much attention has been paid to the "people's rights," the individual's rights have received less emphasis than the "rights of people," e.g., the total group. For instance, the individual's rights in the decision-making process within this total group have been totally absorbed by "group realism" or "group power." In other words, Japanese tend to believe that human rights can be gained only by the application of countervailing power against oppressive authorities. Thus, they rarely look upon human rights as a fundamental "principle" which should not be ignored under any circumstances. At the same time, the human rights of individuals have not been given much consideration because the process of decision making within the total group is not considered important.[11]

Our discussion of the circumstances surrounding a strike vote would indicate that Ishida's remarks are also applicable to the union movement in Japan. Since the right to strike is understood only in relation to the oppressive authorities, attention is paid mainly to "establishing the right to strike," and legalizing the strike. Because the significance of the decision-making process within union organization is considered to be of no great importance, unions often forget that the will of a group never exists apart from that of its individual members. They tend to consider the will of the union as an established and permanent entity once majority support has been gained. Minority opinions within a union are likely to be easily dismissed or suppressed as a betrayal of the union. The majority looks upon itself as the authentic defender of the right to organize; any criticism of union actions is regarded as treachery. Evidently, the concept of "group power" prevails within the Japanese union movement. The trends discernible in the Spring Offensive suggest that its continued practice may further stimulate and extend this tendency.

3. STRIKES IN THE PUBLIC SECTOR

a. Political Strikes: Industrial relations in the public sector are not regulated by the same laws as those which apply in the private sector. The private falls within the scope of the Trade Union Law and the Labor Relations Adjustment Law. The public sector is divided into two categories: one is the national and local civil service, respectively regulated by the National Civil Service Law and the Local Civil Service Law, the second category regroups national government-run enterprises, such as the post office, the telegram service, the mints which print banknotes and postage stamps, the state-owned forests, and the services run by local governments and communities, such as water, gas supply, transportation, and so forth. Public corporations such as the National Railways, Telecommunications and the Tobacco and Salt Corporation also belong to the second category.

Employees in the public sector are prohibited from engaging in strikes and other acts of dispute which hamper the normal course of public services. However, all of them, except policemen, firemen and prison guards, have the right to organize themselves in unions. Civil Service employees, at both the national and local levels, do not have the right to bargain collectively. Changes in their wages and working conditions are made upon recommendation of the National Civil Service Authority (*Jinjiin*). Local Civil Service Commissions (*Jinjiiinkai*) or Fair Treatment Commissions (*Kōheiiinkai*) perform the same function at the local level (see Tables 7 and 8).

The wages and working conditions of employees of public enterprises and corporations are negotiated by their respective unions. Disputes which are not settled through such negotiations are submitted to conciliation or mediation, and finally to arbitration.

Table 7
Percentage Distribution of the Major National Confederations According to the Fields of Application of the Different Laws in 1977

National Confederations	Sōhyō	Dōmei	Shinsanbetsu	Chūritsurōren	Others
Total	36.6	17.8	0.5	10.7	37.5
Trade Union Law (private sector)	17.4	22.7	0.7	14.8	48.7
Public Corporations and National Enterprises Labor Relations Law	86.8	12.3	—	—	0.9
Local Public Enterprises Labor Relations Law	70.0	1.1	—	0.4	29.4
National Civil Service Law	77.8	10.2	—	—	11.9
Local Civil Service Law	90.3	0.6	—	—	9.2

Source: Ministry of Labor, *Basic Survey of Trade Unions*, 1977.

Table 8

**Number of Union Members According to the Application
of the Different Laws in 1977**

Laws	Number of Union Members	%
Total	12,437,012	100.0
Trade Union Law	8,990,627	72.3
Public Corporations and National Enterprises Labor Relations Law	1,019,516	8.2
Local Public Enterprises Labor Relations Law	229,531	1.8
National Civil Service Law	288,495	2.4
Local Civil Service Law	1,908,843	15.3

Source: Ministry of Labor, *Basic Survey of Trade Unions*, 1977.

The Public Corporations and National Enterprises Labor Relations Commission (*Kōrōi*) is an independent body which deals with such disputes on the national level. The disputes at the local government level are handled by the local labor relations commissions, whose main task is to settle disputes in the private sector.

The rationale for this legal setting is as follows: civil service employees work for an employer, the government, which is endowed with sovereignty or supreme authority, and therefore are denied the right to strike or bargain collectively. Decisions on their working conditions belong to the Diet, which represents the supreme authority of the people and controls the national budget. Moreover, they have no need to bargain collectively since the Civil Service Authority issues annual recommendations regarding the improvement of their working conditions. In the government-run enterprises and public corporations, employees are entitled to negotiate through their unions because, budgetwise, these enterprises are more or less independent from the government. On the other hand, because the government still exerts indirect control on the budget of these enterprises and because they perform essential services, their employees cannot be allowed to strike or to engage in other acts of dispute. Their employees' interests in any case are protected by the National Enterprises Labor Relations Commission which is empowered to carry out compulsory arbitration—a privilege which employees of the private sector do not

103

enjoy since it would threaten the autonomy of industrial relations.

In spite of such legal niceties, strikes and other acts of dispute are a matter of daily occurrence in the public sector. Table 9 indicates how frequent these instances of industrial action are in the public sector in comparison with other sectors. The public sector ranks first in the number of acts of dispute and second in the number of participants. The percentage of man-days lost is smaller because acts of dispute in the public sector are carried out only for short periods. If the public sector unions in transportation, communications, electricity, gas and water had been counted with other public service unions, the percentages would have been much higher.

Public sector unions claim that they are unduly deprived of their rights and that they do no wrong when they ignore unreasonable laws. They believe that the Constitution guarantees full union rights to all workers and that legislation restricting their activities, including the right to strike, is unconstitutional. Deeply felt grievances are at the root of the gratuitous militancy of the public sector

Table 9
Number of Disputes Accompanied by Acts of Disputes,
Participants and Man-days Lost in 1975

Industries	No. of Disputes Accompanied by Acts of Dispute		No. of Participants (in thousands)		No. of Man-days lost (in thousands)	
All industries	7,574	100.0%	4,615	100.0%	7,781	100.0%
Mining	53	0.7	29	0.6	14	1.8
Construction	106	1.4	58	1.3	92	1.1
Manufacturing	2,634	34.8	1,688	36.6	4,482	57.2
Wholesaling, retailing	140	1.8	43	0.9	55	0.7
Finance, insurance and real estate	60	0.8	11	0.2	10	0.1
Transportation, communication	896	11.8	1,038	22.5	2,441	30.5
Electricity, gas and water	275	3.6	47	1.0	24	0.3
Private service	746	9.8	475	10.3	375	4.7
Public services	2,645	34.9	1,140	24.7	96	1.2
Others	19	0.4	86	1.9	192	2.4

Source: Ministry of Labor, Annual Report on Statistics and Survey on Labor Disputes, 1975.

104

unions. They resent not only being handicapped in their role as trade unions but also being punished by their employers for their so-called illegal activities. In the latter case, the resentment in public sector unions is not unlike that which prevails in small and medium-size enterprises where the unions are weak and the employers are hostile toward union organization. Actually tactics of industrial actions in the public sector and in small and medium-size enterprises are very similar. The common features are the frequency of work-to-rule, go-slow, recurrent short strikes, wearing headbands and armbands, hanging posters and other manifestations of hostility and disobedience.

However, as mentioned earlier, public sector unions are far from weak in terms of membership, organization and financial resources. In this respect, most of them are equal to or sometimes even stronger than the industrial federations in the private sector. For nearly two decades public sector unions have devoted a great deal of energy to the struggle for "the recovery of the right to strike."[12] As a result of the long-drawn-out controversy and after various political vicissitudes, the government has promised to amend the legislation affecting the public sector and to present concrete proposals concerning the right to strike early in 1978.

b. Avec Strikes: The common features of disputes in both the public sector and the small and medium-size enterprises show that even unions with a large membership and a comparatively good financial situation are not always in a strong bargaining position. Not only are unions prohibited from striking, but the managers of public enterprises are not totally free to negotiate. Their authority is limited by their dependence on state funds and, in the final analysis, by the state's control over their budget. However, it is worth mentioning that both partners in industrial relations in the public sector are often charged with being less than candid in their negotiations. The public often takes a negative attitude *vis-à-vis* disputes in the public sector, because people suspect that the parties are engaged in *avec* (sham) disputes, to act in collusion to cheat the public interest while resting secure in the knowledge that their enterprises can never go bankrupt since the government will always take steps to make up any deficit. It is often said that union and management in the public sector enterprises lack a sense of responsibility and allow disputes to last so long only because their boss, meaning the government, is "the rising sun."

What this phrase implies is that both parties are indulging their dependence by another manifestation of *amae*. Since Japanese industrial relations are characterized by a strong *amae* mentality, it is no wonder that the public sector also shares the same characteristic. The vicious circle of mass punishment and guerrilla tactics in the National Railways is nothing but the fretful behavior of spoiled children. Ironically enough, the National Railways management is frequently accused of being "old-fashioned." Yet it is one of the top-ranking large enterprises in Japan and the world and well-known for its superior technical efficiency, as exemplified by the Super-Express Tōkaidō Line. Naturally it is staffed with first-rate personnel. It is difficult to understand why management of such a high caliber should be "old-fashioned" in its industrial relations.

Elucidating this contradiction will make it easier to understand why labor relations may come to an impasse even in enterprises where management is modern, enlightened and perhaps progressive. These cases of unfair labor practices are the result of the "inward love" type of labor-management relations. Managers are convinced that they fully understand the *raison d'être* of labor unions, that they are friendly toward union leaders, accept their suggestions willingly and are actively promoting progressive labor-management relations. Yet, one day, the whole relationship suddenly becomes deadlocked. The owners complain: "We have been so friendly with the union. We have made many concessions and have been as conciliatory as possible! Now, look how badly they behave! We are betrayed!" This is where all the trouble begins. When you trust someone and feel that there is complete mutual understanding between the two of you and unexptecedly the person starts behaving in a hostile manner, you are at a total loss. In such cases you might feel so upset that you cannot handle the situation and react irrationally. Such irrational reactions are often found in cases of infidelity between husband or wife and, to a lesser degree perhaps, in cases of conflict between parents and their beloved but defiant children. To outsiders, such emotional conflicts often appear silly or absurd, but those involved take them very seriously and they are often impossible to settle.

Why, then, does enlightened management in the public sector habitually interfere in union affairs and hinder its activities? It is because these "considerate" and "sensible" employers expect so much from the "nice" employees of "our family," that they are bitterly disappointed when the workers show signs of defiance. Plots to organize "second unions" also result from this disappointment and from management's consequent efforts to discover "nice" employees. In order to foster more rational industrial relations, therefore, an employer would be well-advised to lower his expectations with regard to employees and even to look upon them as adversaries. These emotional characteristics, however, do not provide a sufficient explanation for the rather abnormal antagonism sometimes found in the public sector. There is another element involved as well, as explained below.

c. The Political Ritual Strikes: One of the reasons for the maladjustment in industrial relations in the public sector is that the confrontation between labor and management in Japan goes hand in hand with the political confrontation between labor unions and the government. The postwar Japanese labor movement, whether the lead actors in the drama were from the Sanbetsu or the Sōhyō, has consistently been connected with the anti-government movement. Needless to say, public sector unions have been playing a major role within the Sanbetsu and the Sōhyō. This maladjustment was investigated by an I.L.O. commission, the Dreyer Commission. In its conclusion, the commission pointed out that the mixing of two functions of government, that of sovereign on the one hand and employer on the other, was one of the main reasons for the troubled state of individual relations in the public sector.[13] Moreover, it can hardly be expected that the successive conservative governments in postwar Japan, who were constantly challenged in their role as sovereign by left-wing oriented unions, would refrain from regulating, and if necessary hindering, these same unions when dealing with them in its role as an employer.

Internal rivalry in union organizations and frequent splits along political and ideological lines have characterized the history of the Japanese labor movement ever since the prewar period. The frequent attempts to organize a united labor front since World War II have always failed. The question of internal attacks against union authority and the union's affiliation with political parties is a complex one. First of all, one must remember that, as far as bargaining with employers is concerned, the effectiveness of unions is severely limited by the Japanese industrial system. Therefore, Japanese unions cannot restrict their functions exclusively to the protection of the economic interests of their members, but have to extend them somewhat by engaging in political activities. Secondly, human factors other than economic realities play an important part in Japanese industrial relations. Consequently, side by side with the economic struggle, the union movement is unavoidably drawn into the fight for the emancipation of the workers as human beings.

As a result, the unions feel responsible for the welfare of the working class, the fate of the Japanese nation, and peace in the world. In other words, they assume a certain responsibility for the souls of the workers. This is yet another example of the functional diffusiveness that Japanese enterprises share with the unions. They exist not only for economic gain but also to fulfill other functions such as securing employment, providing social security, social welfare and sometimes even educational and recreational services. In the same way as the breadth of enterprise functions tends to impede the development of the social services of the government, the unions' extensive take-over of the tasks of the political parties has resulted in stunting the growth of these parties, particularly those of the left-wing. Undoubtedly this process was set in motion because of the weakness of the political parties and the low level of national services.

This functional diffusiveness of the unions results in their main weapon, the strike, being utilized for other than its specific purpose. As a result, political strikes are almost a daily phenomenon in Japan. The frequent use of strikes for political purposes can be explained in terms of one peculiar aspect of strikes in Japanese industry—their efforts to manifest certain attitudes.[14] For a union to demand an end to war as the condition for ending a strike would be an absurdity. The unions do raise a number of political claims along with their economic demands in every year's spring offensive, but it is unheard of for a dispute not to be settled because political issues get in the way. In fact, as soon as wage problems are settled, the unions usually call off a strike and forget all about their solemn and noble causes. The political strike, then, is also no more than a ritual.

d. Conservatism of Unions: The political activities of unions in Japan are lively and flamboyant but not very substantive. It is natural that these activities should remain superficial if their main purpose is to sidetrack or deflect the dissatisfaction and frustration of their members resulting from the ineffectiveness of the union's bargaining function. Furthermore, the political activities of Japanese unions aggravate this weakness still further. It has often been pointed out that splits in union organizations and the ideological obstacles put in the way of a united front have impeded the bargaining power of the unions to a considerable extent.

The political commitment of the unions sometimes directly contradicts their economic functions. For instance, theorists at the Sōhyō headquarters may have to resolve the following dilemma: "If we go on strike, it may decrease the number of votes for union candidates in the upcoming local elections."[15] If one is to evaluate the impact of the political activities of the unions from the point of view of the members' interest, this dilemma can be very real. This is specially true of union leaders at the plant level who closely identify with the individual members. However, most leaders seem to be totally unconcerned about these questions. In fact, the political activities of the Japanese unions mesh smoothly with the dynamics of enterprise unionism. Japanese unions usually endorse a certain party by a majority vote at their annual convention, or declare their support for certain candidates for national as well as local elections. This practice often causes trouble because it undoubtedly restricts the freedom of thought and political rights of the individual members. However, surprisingly enough, it is connected with the kinship-consciousness of the enterprise unions:

> The practice of giving union support to a certain political party originally aimed at organizing a united front of progressive powers such as unions and left-wing parties. However, the result has been that the political activities of the labor unions have been increasingly influenced by extremely conservative concepts and methodology. First of all, this practice extended the egotistic interests of large enterprise unions into the field of politics. When larger unions, especially those in the public sector, which are in fact enterprise unions, support certain political parties, they are not supporting their socialistic programs or policies, but rather they endorse them simply because a number of candidates from that party happen to be members of their own union. This is the "kinship-consciousness" of the enterprise union at work. In an enterprise family, "kinship-consciousness" results in management and labor helping each other's candidates. Management gives financial assistance to the candidates of left-wing parties if they belong to the enterprise union, or tries to collect votes for them by making use of management organizations or business connections, and sometimes grants them leave of absence for the duration of the campaign. Candidates of left-wing parties accept such favors without hesitation. The same concept of "kinship-consciousness" applies when someone from the management level of the enterprise happens to be a candidate for a conservative party. Sometimes the unions do not care to interfere, or at least they refrain from doing so, if union members vote for the conservative candidate put up by the management in the election for the Diet. Union members may very

110

well vote for the management candidate in the local elections and for the union candidate in the national election.[16]

This conservatism on the part of "progressive" organizations is found not only in the election behavior of the unions but is also implicit in the concept of the union's support of political parties. As was already mentioned, the practice of supporting a party by a majority vote infringes on the fundamental human and political rights of the members, or at least of the minority members. At the annual Sōhyō conventions, almost every year for the past several years, the anti-executive factions have proposed resolutions in vain with the objective of doing away with official union endorsement of political parties. However, this claim of the minority against the mainstream has nothing to do with any real consideration for the freedom of choice of minorities. It is but a ploy to enable the Communist Party to receive support from the members alongside the Socialist Party which traditionally enjoys Sōhyō endorsement.

The communist factions today suffer from their minority status within the Sōhyō organization and their demands reflect their frustration with the present union situation. The communists ignored, and even at times suppressed, the freedom of those who supported the socialists when they used to control the Sanbetsu. The Sanbetsu, the reader may remember, was the most powerful labor federation in Japan from 1946 to 1959 and the one a number of socialist unions broke away from in order to create the Sōhyō. Thus, in the history of the Japanese labor movement, genuine freedom of thought never really has been practiced. Furthermore, the concept of "group power" is so strong that respect for individual rights is buried under an overwhelming group consciousness. The situation is exactly the same as that within the conservative groups. This is amply demonstrated by the way the Liberal Democrats rule the Diet with little regard for the claims of the opposition. If these tendencies continue to prevail in the union movement, it is unlikely that the "kinship consciousness" of Japanese industrial relations, not to mention enterprise unionism, will ever be overcome.

111

NOTES

1. Ministry of Labor, *Basic Survey of Trade Unions*, 1976.
2. Ibid., p. 16.
3. See Part II, chapter 6.
4. Gōkarōren Case, Central Labor Relations Commission, April 1, 1960, 22–23 FRKM 89.
5. For a detailed analysis, see Kazuo Koike, *Nihon no Chingin Kōshō* [Wage Negotiations in Japan] (Tokyo: Tokyo Daigaku Shuppankai, 1962), pp. 31 ff.
6. Taishirō Shirai, *Rōdō Kumiai no Zaisei* [Finances of Trade Unions] (Tokyo: Nihon Hyōronsha, 1964), p. 46.
7. For instance, according to Dore, Hitachi Company's total expenditure on housing, medical services, canteens, transport subsidies, sports and social facilities, and special welfare grants other than pay during sickness amounted to 8.5 percent of total labor costs. The corresponding figure for the median British firm was 2.5 percent, including sick pay. See Dore, *British Factory— Japanese Factory*, p. 203.
8. The standardization of working conditions is taking place for other reasons, mainly the changing labor market situation.
9. Matsuta Hosoya, *Nihon no Rōdō Kumiai Undō* [Labor Union Movement in Japan] (Tokyo: Shakai Shisō Kenkyūkai, 1958), p. 218.
10. Ōta, *Rōdō Kumiai-ron*, p. 67.
11. Takeshi Ishida, "Nihon ni Okeru Hōteki Shikō no Hatten to Kihonteki Jinken" [Development of Legal Thinking and Fundamental Human Rights in Japan], in *Kihonteki Jinken* [Fundamental Human Rights], 5 vols., (Tokyo: Tokyo Daigaku Shuppankai, 1968): 2:17 ff.
12. The most extensive and profound analysis of how this process operated until the early 1970s is found in Ehud Harari, *The Politics of Labor Legislation in Japan—National-International Interaction* (Berkeley and Los Angeles: University of California Press, 1973).
13. International Labor Organization (I.L.O.), "Report of the Fact-Finding and Conciliation Commission on Freedom of Association Concerning Persons Employed in the Public Sector in Japan" (Dreyer Report), *Official Bulletin*, Special Supplement, vol. 49:1 (Jan. 1966), p. 516.
14. For a detailed analysis of this particular aspect of Japanese strikes, see Part II, chapter 7.
15. Yoshiaki Kamizuma, *Rōdō Undō Nōto* [Notes on the Labor Movement] (Tokyo: Rōdai Shinsho, 1965), p. 73.
16. Taishirō Shirai, *Kigyōbetsu Kumiai* [Enterprise Unions] (Tokyo: Chūō-kōronsha, 1968), pp. 182–83.

Part II

Labor Disputes

5

GENERAL THEORY
OF LABOR DISPUTES

1. THEORIES OF INDUSTRIAL CONFLICT

The commonly held view of conflict is that it is a destructive process which disrupts the order of society. Traditional sociologists look upon conflict as a threat to the *status quo* and as something which should be eliminated or at least avoided. On the other hand, a small number of social scientists consider that it is the *status quo* which is the "problem" and, therefore, are inclined to welcome conflict as a solution to this problem. Lewis Coser, one of the proponents of this new approach, believes that conflict is "functional" and results in "balancing and hence maintaining a society as a going concern."[1]

In the field of industrial relations, too, conflict is often viewed as undesirable or as a "last resort" social process, "a poor substitute for more civilized and less destructive modes of determining social policy."[2] If one applies Coser's viewpoint to industrial relations, it ensues that industrial conflict could become self-regulating. This outcome takes place when industrial conflict observes the "rules of the game" and thus becomes institutionalized. In fact, industrial conflict is frequently characterized as institutionalized conflict.[3] Although no one questions the presence of serious conflicts of interests in industrial relations, most observers are convinced that, at least in the majority of industrialized societies, "the mode of this conflict [has been institutionalized] through collective bargaining."[4]

In Western industrialized countries, trade unionism is acknowledged to be "an essential part of the mechanism of social control."[5] As the unions mature, they become progressively integrated not only into the administrative structure of the enterprise but also into the social and political systems of the given society. This assumption is the basis of Dahrendorf's theory of "mature" industrial relations. He asserts that "industrial conflict has become less violent because its existence has been accepted and its manifestations have been socially regulated."[6] Lipset has taken a further step by asserting that "trade unions should not be viewed primarily in their economic-cleavage function. They also serve to integrate their members in the large body politic and give them a basis for loyalty to the system."[7]

The above theories of industrial conflict call for two comments. First, most Western academics who take a more or less positive view of industrial conflict believe that the present industrial relations system is the outcome of the efforts made to institutionalize conflict in the first place. Second, because they consider these efforts to be the most significant part of the process, these scholars tend to neglect the spontaneous character of industrial conflicts and the difficulties of their regulation.

The most obvious example of this shortcoming of Western theories is the theory of the "withering away of strikes" which was current in the 1950s. Ross and Hartman contended that strikes were going out of fashion: "Man-days of idleness in the late 1950s are fewer than in the late 1940s or the late 1930s, despite the increases in population and union membership. . . . The decline is more dramatic when described in comparative terms."[8] The authors did not see "any substantial evidence of any impending revival of strike activity in Northern European countries."[9] However, this prediction was proven false by the occurrence of strikes, especially wildcat strikes, in some of the Scandinavian countries and West Germany in the late 1960s and early 1970s, not to mention the earlier "strike explosion" in Great Britain.[10]

2. NATURE OF INDUSTRIAL CONFLICT

a. Cultural Elements: When comparing Japanese labor relations to Western (particularly American) labor relations, it is often said that Japanese workers do not enjoy equality with their employers, that the employers are "feudalistic" and the workers servile. Certainly it is true to some extent. American employers and workers are regarded as equal citizens. American workers do not bow politely to their employers when they meet on the street as their Japanese counterparts always do. However, in some Western countries, England for example, the social gap between labor and management is broader than it is in Japan. The different residential areas, schools, pubs, newspapers, magazines, in short the whole English way of life, is so pronounced that a Japanese observer finds it very hard to believe that both groups share the same culture. So we have to admit that social cleavage follows different rules in each country and that it is impossible to make generalizations, at least as regards private life.

As far as the workplace is concerned, however, there is less class distinction between managers and workers in Japan than in Western societies. Dore describes the difference between British and Japanese factories:

> English Electric employees have a conception of the status system of the factory (and, for that matter, of their society) in terms of a few more or less homogeneous layers separated by marked gaps. The extent to which people are conscious of the gaps depends on the variety of differentiating criteria which coincide on the same line of division—income, method of payment, toilets, canteens, holidays, pension rights, dress, accent, union membership, etc.—in addition to functional authority positions. In the Hitachi system, there are far fewer discontinuities—toilets, canteens, etc., do not demarcate status groups. Pay scales are a single continuum.[11]

The distinction between management and labor at the workplace has its origin in the nature of the labor contract. Regardless of differences in culture and social stratification, wherever there exists a system where wages are paid for labor provided by workers, distinctions of this nature can be observed. In general, the characteristics of wage labor might be summarized as follows: 1) the goods provided by the workers' labor are indivisibly connected with their personalities; 2) the specific content of the job and the actual method of performance are decided by management;[12] and 3) unlike ordinary contracts such as sale or purchase, there is no possibility of change in the position of the parties, namely, the seller remains seller and cannot become buyer.[13]

Because of these characteristics of wage labor, especially regarding points one and two, labor disputes are by nature "cultural conflicts." According to Kenneth Boulding, they arise "out of the cultural difference," and must be distinguished from "issue conflicts" which emerge in such exchange as sale and purchase.[14] In the case of issue conflicts, there is a certain point when the parties can perceive both a community of interest and a conflict of interest at the same time. Once the transaction is completed, the parties may be better off than if the game had not been played (the concept of "positive-sum game" in game theory). Because labor disputes differ in nature from issue conflicts, they cannot be settled in the same manner. The above-mentioned characteristics of wage labor, particularly points one and three, preclude the possibility of a community of interest between the parties in a labor dispute.

In general, what causes the dispute is a conflict of interest as "perceived" by the parties, rather than the actual conflict of interest. Kornhauser, Dubin and Ross point out that "the perceived relationship depends not only on the 'economic facts of life' but also on the social interpretation current among the people involved."[15] One can say that labor disputes also result from the fact that both parties have a different conception of the nature of the exchange of wages for labor. For the workers, the labor contract is an exchange of their labor for money, whereas for the employer it refers to a mere exchange of goods. The employer is not able to understand that work has a personal meaning for the

118

workers. It becomes clear, therefore, that labor disputes can be caused by other than economic factors, that they may arise even in the absence of economic conflict, and that they could be prolonged until they actually become harmful to the workers' economic interests.

b. Everyday Labor Disputes: The relationship established by the labor contract is a continuous one, but the nature and specificity of the relationship is determined as it develops. At the time a worker is about to perform his job, the exact content and scope of the duties he has to perform are undecided, no matter how precisely they have been prescribed by contract or work rules beforehand. Collective agreements or work rules usually specify in detail working hours, rest periods, holidays, leaves, wages and other allowances. However, these provisions establish only general guidelines. Problems always arise as to how to apply these guidelines to individual workers in specific situations. The content and scope of specific jobs are also a source of difficulties.

In such cases, commonly accepted legal theory holds that employers have the right to direct and supervise and that their orders should be obeyed by employees. But this rule does not solve the problem at all, since specific problems arise every day that cannot be brought to court one by one whenever individual workers have grievances. In commercial exchanges disputes are exceptional events. In any case, the detailed provisions of a commercial contract provide a basis for the parties to reach a settlement in questionable cases, either by going to court or by submitting to arbitration. In labor relations, as we have seen, disputes are a day-to-day occurrence, normal rather than exceptional events. Thus, most industrialized countries have autonomous institutions such as works councils to process grievances and to settle disputes.

c. Labor Disputes as Group Conflict: In industrial relations, disputes tend to become institutionalized by the emergence of unions and their involvement in dispute settlement, especially through the collective bargaining process. However, group conflicts in labor

119

relations are not necessarily "organized." In fact, labor disputes are often started by unorganized groups, as in the case of wildcat strikes or other unauthorized strikes. This is a frequent phenomenon in small and medium-size enterprises in present-day Japan, not to mention during the early stages of the trade union movement in every industrialized country. Generally, the development of such institutions as collective bargaining, works councils, grievance committees, as well as arbitration, has come after prolonged efforts to replace spontaneous group conflicts at the workshop level with organized conflicts. However, although any worker organiztion is based on a certain group, either at the workshop level or on a wider scale, the fact remains that labor disputes are originally and fundamentally group conflicts.

In Western countries, until recently, the employees' representatives at the shop level were chosen spontaneously and elected in an informal way by the group of employees on the work floor. The strikes organized and led by these representatives were more akin to group conflicts than to organized conflict. Nowadays, these informal representatives have been more or less integrated into formal union organizations, like the shop stewards in Great Britain and the *Betriebsrat* (works councils) in West Germany. Even today, their acts of dispute are sometimes not endorsed by the unions and may be considered illegal by state authorities. Today in the highly industrialized countries, where workers' organizations play a major part in dispute settlement, the disputes which are not resolved by such well developed institutions emerge in the form of wildcat strikes. This process underlines the fact that industrial disputes are fundamentally group conflicts. This is the reason why there is a hard core of conflicts with which existing labor institutions find it very hard to cope, no matter how well organized they are.[16]

d. Labor Disputes as Organizational Conflict: Labor disputes, being group conflicts, are usually associated with the so-called mirror image phenomenon, according to which "reality is not the same for observers belonging to different groups."[17] Needless to say, the economic interests of both parties are perceived by each as diametrically opposed. This phenomenon also affects the way in which each party views itself and its adversary. The workers' group, especially, tends to regard the employer as a miser, or a bad character. This tendency, another example of the "cultural" nature of labor disputes, opens the door to the possibility of violence in the dispute. "Members of competing groups build up and maintain differential images of reality, images so formed that 'our' group is virtuous and free from sin . . . 'their' group is bad, aggressive, treacherous, and not quite human . . . if we can perceive the opponent as less than human, superego controls do not operate and no guilt is felt over a resort to violence."[18] The above quotation makes it clear that industrial violence occurs elsewhere besides in Japan. In fact, the author quoted above distinguishes the hostility between labor and management from ordinary economic conflict and lists industrial conflict alongside civil and international conflict by pointing out the similarities in picket-line violence to the violence of a lynch mob and of the Nazi SS men.[19]

Most scholars in industrial relations imply that violence in labor disputes is a pathological phenomenon. According to their theories, such violence is characteristic of "underdeveloped societies" and is disappearing from the "relatively developed industrial societies."[20] Boulding expresses this view in more general terms: "There is a strong tendency in human society for the unorganized group to develop organization . . . consequently group conflict tends easily to pass over into organizational conflict."[21] This remark is applicable to industrial relations. Following the establishment and recognition of unions, labor disputes tend to be organized and "rationalized," and thus pass over into organizational conflict. Unnecessary disputes are avoided, and the "rationalized" settlement of disputes is likely to be stimulated by the development of union organization. Sayles and Strauss have observed that "the union is sometimes required to discipline its members in order to make a more effective fighting force. Unauthorized strikes are frowned upon as a dissipation of union strength. . . . Union officials who earlier may have spent much of their time agitating the members now find themselves forced to urge patience and restraint."[22]

On the other hand, the development of a union organization is just as likely to have an opposite effect on the frequency and nature of labor disputes. Namely, the presence of a union may lead to disputes which otherwise might not have occurred. It is Boulding's opinion that "the growth of organizations themselves may create conflict where no previous consciousness of conflict existed," and that "[when] organizations frequently organize themselves against something and in the absence of perception of conflict, their reason for existence is weakened or disappears."[23] In this sense, the introduction of organized conflict may have two different consequences. One is to rationalize conflict and the other is to extend conflict. Which of these two tendencies will prevail in a particular society at certain periods is determined by a complex set of factors such as the living standards of workers, the degree of civil and political rights achieved by them, and the character of the union movement and the industrial relations system in the particular society.

A full-scale analysis of this intricate problem would require another book. I shall limit myself to considering political unionism and business unionism, the two extreme types of unionism Clark Kerr describes when discussing four types of industrial societies: authoritarian, paternalistic, competitive and class-conscious.[24]

When the society is inclined to be authoritarian and class-conscious, the unions tend toward political unionism. As a result, labor disputes usually become an aspect of the class struggle. The unions are not satisfied with defending the economic interests of their members; they also try to further their cultural and political interests. This general principle does not apply in societies where labor disputes are suppressed or settled in a completely authoritarian way. In such societies, the substance of labor disputes is fundamentally political even if they take the form of economic disputes. Also they usually extend beyond the framework of industrial relations.

By contrast, in competitive societies, unions tend to be business-

122

minded and concentrate their efforts on the protection of their members' economic interests. The development of business unionism facilitates the dispute settlement process, since the majority of labor disputes are likely to be economic rather than cultural conflicts. Economic conflicts are easier to solve because it is possible for the parties to find a position where both of them benefit, as in the "positive-sum game." In such societies where disputes are "rationalized," the parties avoid power confrontation and institutions for peaceful settlement of disputes are well developed. Paternalistic societies borrow aspects from the two types described above. The degree to which they incline toward one pattern or the other depends on the interplay of the factors listed above.

3. ECONOMIC RATIONALISM OF DISPUTES

Business unionism results in rationalizing all labor disputes except those which are primarily group and cultural conflicts. First of all, horizontal union organizations, such as industry or craft unions, only succeed in establishing standards for working conditions, especially minimum and uniform standards within a craft or industry. Disputes concerning the application of such standards to individual enterprises and individual workers may still arise. Aside from the collective bargaining process, some institutions, such as workers' consultations, grievance committees or arbitration systems, are needed to resolve these disputes. Once more, one of the outcomes of disputes is the growth of the organizing machinery. Disputes also take place when the application of general standards to the shop floor leads to higher production requirements. The numerous efforts to organize and institutionalize this last type of dispute have not been successful in any country so far.[25]

Secondly, the pursuit of business unionism drives unions to organize as many workers as possible and the need for united action impels them to consolidate their members' diverse demands into packages of uniform demands. Thus "organizing" a dispute leads to a massive growth of union organization and to the standardization of their demands. In adopting this pattern, the unions are only following a general trend. In other segments of society, the push toward modernization and industrialization has had the same results. Trade unions have always contributed a great deal to society by solving labor disputes which otherwise could have seriously challenged the social order. However, as union organizations grow into mammoth organizations and become increasingly bureaucratic, they become less capable of coping with the frustrations of their individual members. Of course, such is also the case of most other social organizations in modern industrial societies.

In industrial societies, blue-collar workers, who make up the majority of union members, are gradually being replaced as the main work force by white-collar workers.[26] Technological changes and the growth of information industries cannot but increase this trend.[27] The economic demands of blue-collar workers provided some justification for unified union demands. However, the improvement in their living standards means that eventually they, too, will no longer be satisfied with gains that are solely economic. A uniform union program is not likely to meet the needs of white-collar workers who, like intellectuals, easily fall prey to the anxieties of modern life. Hitherto the class conflict between labor and capital has been regarded as the most serious of all social confrontations. Nowadays, however, conflicts flare up between groups divided along lines other than the traditional ones, i.e., along generation, race or sex lines. Confrontation also occurs along a new line of social cleavage. On one side is "the establishment" which includes not only the "ruling class" but also workers who are integrated into established society. On the other side is the "new class," namely the intellectuals and the students whose potential lies in the future.[28]

Many recent industrial conflicts originated from outside the framework of traditional industrial relations systems, and were characterized by the participation of some of the new groupings described above. Notably this was the case with the wildcat strikes in Great Britain, Germany and Australia, the common front of workers and students in France and West Germany, and the strikes by professionals in Scandinavian countries. These conflicts demonstrated that existing union organizations had a limited capacity to solve the new types of industrial conflict.[29] In other words, the traditional way to settle industrial disputes through a process of economic growth and organization is not as universally effective as was generally thought.

Finally, the process of dispute settlement through rationalization and organization is intrinsically limited. Generally speaking, organizations and institutions have a tendency, inherent in their nature, to lose their dynamism and power of adaptation as soon as they are established. Therefore, it is impossible for these institutions to organize successfully all kinds of disputes which arise out of fluid and constantly changing social relationships. This raises a fundamental question about the institutional method of dispute settlement, and especially about the tendency to ask legal institutions to resolve disputes by the application of legal criteria.

NOTES

1. Lewis Coser, *The Function of Social Conflict* (New York: The Free Press, 1956), p. 137.
2. R. Dubin, "Industrial Conflict and Social Welfare," *The Journal of Conflict Resolution*, Vol. 1 (1957), pp. 179–85.
3. J. B. Atleson, "Work Group Behavior and Wildcat Strikes: The Causes and Functions of Industrial Civil Disobedience," *Ohio State Law Journal* 34 (1973): 753.
4. R. Dubin, "Constructive Aspects of Industrial Conflict," in *Industrial Conflict*, eds. A. Kornhauser, R. Dubin and A. M. Ross (New York: McGraw-Hill Book Co., 1954), p. 47.
5. A. Fox and A. Flanders, "The Reform of Collective Bargaining: From Donovan to Durkheim," *British Journal of Industrial Relations* 7 (1969), p. 156.
6. Ralf Dahrendorf, *Class and Class Conflict in Industrial Society* (Stanford: Stanford University Press, 1959), p. 257.
7. S. M. Lipset, "Political Sociology," in *Sociology Today*, eds. R.K. Merton et. al. (New York: Basic Books, 1959), p. 113.
8. Arthur M. Ross and Paul T. Hartman, *Changing Patterns of Industrial Conflict* (New York: John Wiley and Co., 1960), p. 4.
9. Ibid., p. 176.
10. See R. Hyman, *Strikes* (London: Fontana, 1972), pp. 83 ff. The evaluation of the theories of conflict in this section is developed from Hyman's analysis.

11. Dore, *British Factory—Japanese Factory*, p. 258.

12. John R. Commons, *Legal Foundations of Capitalism* (New York: MacMillan Co., 1957), p. 28.

13. This even applies to a large extent in the United States where the vertical mobility is higher than in other industrial countries. According to Kenneth E. Boulding: "The worker is on one side of the exchange of life, and the employer likewise," see *Conflict and Defense: General Theory* (New York: Harper & Brothers, 1962), p. 212.

14. Boulding, *Conflict and Defense*, p. 213.

15. Kornhauser, Dubin and Ross, *Industrial Conflict*, p. 14.

16. The resurgence of wildcat strikes in most industrialized countries is diverse and depends on the nature of industrial relations in each country: wage drift in England, dissatisfaction of white-collar workers in Scandinavian countries and minority groups in the United States. However, a more fundamental and universal cause is the failure of established industrial relations systems to solve the problems and to remove the dissatisfactions caused by the very nature of the technological setting of today's work processes. In the U.S., for instance, several studies indicate that the main cause of wildcat strikes is the incapability of centralized bargaining and contract administration and the established grievance procedures to resolve the frustration and dissatisfaction of the individual workers, see Leonard R. Sayles, "Wildcat Strikes," *Harvard Business Review* 32, no. 6 (1954), pp. 42–52, and Atleson, "Work Group Behavior," pp. 751–816.

17. Ross Stagner, "The Psychology of Human Conflict," in *The Nature of Human Conflict*, ed. Elton B. McNeil (Englewood Cliffs, N.J.: Prentice-Hall, Inc., 1965), p. 47.

18. Ibid., p. 51.

19. Stagner, "Psychology of Human Conflict," p. 51; also see Boulding, *Conflict and Defense*, pp. 248 ff.

20. Abraham J. Siegel, "Method and Substance in Theorizing about Worker Protest," in *Aspects of Labor Economics—A Conference of the Universities— National Bureau Committee for Economic Research* (Princeton, N.J.: Princeton University Press, 1962), pp. 41–45.

21. Boulding, *Conflict and Defense*, p. 145.

22. Leonard R. Sayles and George Strauss, *The Local Union*, 2d rev. ed. (New York: Harcourt, Brace and World, 1967), p. 9.

23. Boulding, *Conflict and Defense*, p. 145.

24. Clark Kerr, *Labor and Management in Industrial Sociology*, pp. 274 ff.

25. "Deciphering the proper solution to a wildcat strike is difficult because the issue which seemingly causes the wildcat is often not the basic problem, but merely a symbol of more generalized frustration. Even when the actual root cause of the wildcat is found, the parties to the agreement may nevertheless consider the cause trivial. . . . Issues involved in wildcat strikes are usually of little interest to labor unions officers and managers," see Atleson, "Work Group Behavior," p. 758. "The prevalent *legal* conception that workers should use the grievance system and not engage in wildcat strikes may there-

fore need amendment . . . . Here we are referring not to the merits of the grievance, but rather to the futility of presenting it in a system in which union and management may have mutual interest in common," ibid., p. 769.

26. In the United States, in the fifteen years from 1958 to 1973, white-collar workers—professional, managerial, office and sales workers—increased by 13.5 million. In these years blue-collar workers—craftsmen, operatives, and laborers (excluding farmers and miners)—increased by only 5.5 million. By 1974, there were 10.5 million more white-collar than blue-collar workers— 40.3 million as compared with 29.8 million. During these years, the number of professional and technical workers increased about 80 percent—a greater rate of increase than for any other category. During these years the percentage of white-collar workers among total employed increased from 42.6 percent to 47.8 percent while that of blue-collar workers declined from 37.0 percent to 35.4 percent. United States Department of Labor, *Manpower Report, Report of the President: Report on Manpower Requirements, Resources, Utilization and Training* (Washington, D.C.: Government Printing Office, 1974), pp. 267–68.

27. Galbraith states that: "Within the system the blue-collar proletarian is sharply in decline, both in relative numbers and in influence . . . that it will have a large and growing requirement for qualified talent is evident. Technology, planning and the coordination of the resulting organization all require such talent. This requirement, it is perhaps unnecessary to notice, is for educationally qualified, as distinct from skilled, manpower. At the same time, the industrial system reduces relatively, and it seems probable, absolutely, its requirement for blue-collared workers, both skilled and unskilled," *The New Industrial State*, pp. 236–37.

28. In Europe today one expects that "an increasing degree of property ownership might well 'embourgeoisify' the workers, lessening the intensity of class conflict . . . political cleavages will no longer be based on the economic conflicts but will, increasingly, be polarized according to differences in underlying value priorities. This new axis of political cleavage would, initially, oppose one section of the middle class to the remainder of society," see Ronald Inglehart, "The Silent Revolution in Europe: Intergenerational Change in Post-Industrial Societies," *The American Political Science Review* 65 (1971), pp. 991–1017. Inglehart suggests that a new ordering of values will manifest itself first and most fully among those groups with high education connected with parental affluence. According to his research, this group is most likely to choose the post-bourgeois set of value priorities while the lower socioeconomic groups, including the working class, are much more likely to select acquisitive value priorities.

29. Norman F. Dufty, *Changes in Labour Management Relations in the Enterprises* (Paris: Organization for Economic Co-operation and Development [O.E.C.D], 1975), pp. 12 ff.

$\boxed{6}$

LABOR DISPUTE CHARACTERISTICS

1. MISCHIEF IN LABOR RELATIONS

a. Harassment: The *Asahi Shinbun*, one of the leading newspapers
in Japan, reported the following story on February 7, 1972. A union
had pasted about 400 posters on the wall of a company building
protesting the dismissal of several members. The company hired
workers to tear off the posters and to clean the building and then
asked the union to pay the cost of the cleaning work which
amounted to 5,415 yen (about $18.00 at that time). Upon the un-
ion's refusal to pay, the company deducted this amount from union
dues which were collected automatically from the members' wages
under a check-off arrangement. The company gave further notice
to the union that they would deduct another 836 yen (about
$4.40) for the cost of cleaning another plant which had also been
defaced by union posters.

Pasting posters on the walls as well as on the windows of company buildings is a common practice of Japanese unions, whenever
they wish to attack the "reckless" policies of management or ad-
vertise their "modest" demands. The content of the posters often
refers to the personal affairs of the company president or other
management personnel in scurrilous language. These attacks are
scrawled on paper of poor quality. When the company has the
posters torn down, new ones are pasted up immediately. As a re-

sult the buildings become completely defaced by the starch paste. Even though such practices are certainly a nuisance and cause trouble between labor and management, they are so commonplace that they have little news value. Why, therefore, should the newspaper report the incident cited above?

In this instance, the management, angered by the union's mischief, demanded reparation for the damage. Generally, Japanese employers, unlike their Western counterparts, do not require unions to pay for damages caused by its members. Instead, they prefer to dismiss the union leaders (who, in most cases, are employees of the company) who have led unlawful activities. This contrast in the employers' response can be explained by the fact that in Western society union leaders are usually professionals rather than company employees: rendering dismissal as a means of punishment would be impossible. For the most part, Japanese employers seem to be more interested in maintaining relations with cooperative and loyal employees than in recovering economic losses resulting from union activities. They consider it of greater benefit to expel militant union leaders from the enterprise and to encourage obedient union activities than to make an issue of a small amount of money for damages.

In this context, the reaction of management in the above-mentioned case appears businesslike and rational. However, taking into account the small amount of damage, the steps taken by management were, on the contrary, bordering on the malicious: the main intent was to embarrass the union. The aftermath of this incident is striking. The June 6 edition of the *Asahi* related that the union had brought a charge against the director of the company alleging that he had embezzled the union's money. The police reported the case to the prosecutor, but whether or not it was brought to trial was not reported.

It is not at all exceptional in Japanese labor relations for unions to level charges against management, as we can see in this case. Companies also punish union leaders by disciplinary measures or charge them with violence and other crimes. In fact, both parties often indulge in emotional confrontations. In small, medium-size

129

and large companies, the union's red flags can be seen flying on the top of company buildings. In one instance, a company removed a union flag from the top of a building and threw it in a nearby river. The union then took a photograph of the flag drifting in the water and submitted it in court as evidence that management unlawfully interfered with the administration and activities of the union. When management removes posters or flags put up by a union, they are often accused of seizure of property. In innumerable cases, especially in disputes of small and medium-size industries, collective bargaining takes the form of a mass meeting, where both sides harangue each other and often clash violently. Far from being exceptional, such harassment practices are daily occurrences.

b. Japanese Unions—Weak or Strong?: Most foreign visitors come to Japan believing that Japanese industrial relations are ideal and that unions, having a strong enterprise consciousness, are friendly and cooperate with management. According to Robert E. Cole, American employers think that Japan is a paradise as far as industrial relations are concerned. They feel that American union leaders are arrogant and workers are not interested in their jobs and far from loyal to the enterprise, while Japanese workers are as obedient to their employers as children to their parents. Americans are told that Japanese unions identify strongly with the enterprise, never raising economically harmful demands and that, as a result, increases in productivity always exceed increases in wages.[1]

Foreigners who come to Japan with such preconceptions will soon feel puzzled when faced with emotional confrontations between labor and management. They will be perplexed when they come across workers' furious street demonstrations and find that unions in the public sector, such as the National Railways where any kind of act of dispute is prohibited by law, frequently go on strike and resort to work-to-rule and stage slowdowns. They will begin to doubt whether unions in Japan are really obedient to employers and whether the collective bargaining system is functioning.

130

The fact that unions and management frequently indulge in mutual harassment indicates that while unions are not strong enough to confront management openly, at the same time, they are not so weak enough to be completely controlled by management. In order to paint an accurate picture of Japanese industrial relations, we have to examine how discord exists alongside harmony. It is this very coexistence which is one of the decisive factors essential for an understanding of Japanese industrial relations.

2. BREAKAWAY UNIONS

a. Is Betrayal a Japanese Tradition?:   Donald Keene, an authority on Japanese literature, and Ryōtarō Shiba, a well-known novelist, once held the following exchange on the subject of the battles fought during the feudal age of Japan.

> Keene: I have been meaning to ask you. Reading Japanese history, it struck me that there were many battles fought during the Genpei and Sengoku periods,[2] but . . . in most cases a traitor appeared at the most crucial moment and the outcome was usually determined by such a betrayal. Isn't this true of all the significant battles, like Dannoura or Sekigahara?[3]
>
> Shiba: You are right. Traitors always appear at the very climax of the battle. Furthermore, contrary to what one would normally expect, they are not condemned until later. . . . Perhaps this is because Japan is a kinship society and most of the people involved are somehow related to each other. Because of often minor and ill-defined reasons, they become divided into friends and enemies. There is no such clear-cut cause for the outbreak of wars in Japan as religion— Catholics against Protestants, for instance. . . . Generally speaking, in drawn-out family quarrels, a time

comes or an occasion arises which enables one group to make overtures to some members of the other group with a view to breaking their resistance. Then somebody will afterwards reveal that he was told: "Why don't you betray your side?" Both sides are playing the game by the same rules.

The Battle of Sekigahara is considerably larger in scale, even from the perspective of world history, and could be compared, for instance, to the Battle of Waterloo. It could, therefore, have been a more serious confrontation. In fact, however, it was nothing of the kind. In the morning the West Army was leading, in the afternoon it was the turn of the East Army, and meanwhile—betrayals! Thus it may not be very interesting as a battle. But for the Japanese, the interest lies behind the scenes, and the battle itself is just a pageant. Already Kobayakawa Hideaki, the general of the West Army, . . . had been exhorted by Kita no Mandokoro, the mother of Tokugawa Ieyasu, to join the East . . . but he hesitated, since in the morning the West had been leading. Meanwhile a messenger arrived from Tokugawa Ieyasu urging him to betray and reminding him of his earlier promise. At that Kobayakawa made up his mind, declaring, "Then I cannot help it." In short, the battle itself was only a pageant. The story had already been written the day before the battle. Thus drama exists behind the scene but not in the battle itself.

Several important points concerning the characteristics of conflict in Japan are raised here. First, the outcome of the war is often decided by betrayal. Second, betrayal is a normal practice since conflict is not based on any definite "cause." Third, the outcome is determined behind the scenes and the battle in the field is merely a pageant.

Hard as it is to believe, these three points are exactly applicable

132

to labor disputes in Japan. In the first place, the outcome of labor disputes is often determined by a split in the union organization. Second, the confrontation between labor and management is not "defined" because the relationship between labor and management is ambiguous and the personal relations between employers and employees are influenced by the process of "assimilation." Employees soon become frustrated at being told: "The company's interest is your interest." Thirdly, the outcome of a labor dispute is often decided by dealings behind the scenes. It is quite common for union leaders to utter militant slogans at the bargaining table, while they are making back-door deals with the company.

In the 1960 dispute at the Miike Pit of the Mitsui Coal Mining Company, the union was defeated because of a split in union organization. The following account of this dispute by Kaoru Ōta shows how the characteristics of conflict, as described above, are exactly applicable to this case.

If we had been more careful, we could easily have been aware of the weakness of the union as a federation within an enterprise. . . . Before Mr. Hara [then President of the Coal Mining Workers' Union] and Mr. Hatakeyama [then President of the Mitsui Miners' Unions] knew of it, the unions of several other pits had already decided not to follow the Miike Pit Union in their strike action. This forced the union into a situation where they had no alternative but to stop the strike. . . .

The unions of other enterprises, each courted and threatened by their own companies, also concluded that they could no longer continue to fight and withdrew from the common front. At the same time, a plot had already been devised by the employers, who were negotiating with one of the branch leaders of the Miike Pit Union with the objective of starting a breakaway union.

. . . . The Coal Miners' Union tried to change its tactics. Curiously enough, at that moment, the wage increase issue in the coal mining industry was settled within a day through conciliation by the Central Labor Relations Commission, a process that usually takes two or three weeks. This means that, considering the impact of a wage dispute on the Miike problems, the Labor Relations Commission tended to settle the wage issue as early as possible. . . . I suspect some back-door dealings took place between the employers of the coal mining industry and some of the union leaders.

Thus the Miike workers lost the support of other unions and were left alone to carry on their struggle. Around this time, we received information that a former chairman of one of the branches of the Miike Union, then vice-chairman of the Local Assembly of the city of Ōmuta and a socialist, had decided to move to the second union, taking about 5,000 followers with him. At that time, the second union was already organizing about 5,000 members. This additional membership of 5,000 for the breakaway organization would have made the union's struggle extremely difficult. We decided that we would make out somehow though we knew that the rank and file members would be hard to persuade.[5]

The most decisive factor which forced the leaders of the Sōhyō and the Coal Miners' Union to capitulate was behind-the-scenes dealings and betrayal. Furthermore, some weakness of the labor management relationship in the enterprise made the creation of a second union possible:

The Miike Union was known for having a strong union organization. However, the general practice among the unions affiliated with the Coal Miners' Union was for the companies to buy drinks for union leaders at the pits. After the struggle began and union leaders were trying to maintain discipline among their members, the workers pointed out that the union leaders themselves continued to drink with management people. The leaders often felt uneasy about this situation and hesitated to exert pressure on the rank and file. When questioned about it, I usually told them that drinking with management was all right because it had been the practice at the pit, and ought not to be regarded as a betrayal: a reasoning

134

which I knew all too well made little sense. On the other hand, the workers would be disciplined if it were known that they were drinking with company executives in the midst of the present struggle in which the very life of the union hung in the balance, and where it was quite evident that the company was trying to bribe workers. I made this speech which I myself did not fully understand. In short, this kind of weakness was more or less endemic to the union, and the company exploited it.[6]

The weakness of the affiliated enterprise unions and the lack of a clear issue with which to confront the enemy turned the final stages of the struggle into a catastrophe for the Coal Miners' Union, which prided itself on being the most militant of the Sōhyō-affiliated unions. The grass roots of militant unions are teeming with "Nihonists" who are in the habit of drinking with management. Mr. Ōta shows himself to be a first-class "Nihonist" when he advocates discipline in a speech which he "did not quite understand," and urges his audience to forget all previous mistakes and to try harder.

b. Lack of Commitment to Unions: It is worthwhile examining in greater detail the process by which unions split, or what can be termed "betrayal Japanese-style." The splitting of unions has been the issue in numerous legal cases. The most representative of these cases is probably the Shinagawa Shiro Lenga Company case which was decided by the Supreme Court in 1957.[7]

The original union, Union A, had a membership of 611 when a number of members got together to oppose the policy and the type of leadership of union executives. Fewer than 100 members publicly expressed their dissatisfaction with the executives. At this point, the official leaders upbraided them as traitors, put pressure on them, and rejected their call for a general meeting. On April 28, 1950, more than 100 members seceded from Union A and organized two unions called the "Second Plant Union" and "Third Plant Union" respectively. On May 2, these two unions merged to form the "New Labor Union." Around May 8, several score more workers seceded and established the "First Plant Union," but around May 18 they merged with the "New Labor Union," thus increasing its membership by about 100. Then on June 1, some of the members of Union A forced a number of "New Labor Union" members to rejoin Union A. A large number of Union A members felt that this action was going too far and became critical of their leaders. As a result, by the middle of June, some 300 members had defected and, on the June 18, the number of members who had left Union A totalled about 350. At first they organized an informal interim group. Then on July 23, all the workers who had defected from Union A joined together to form a new union, Union B. Eventually with the addition of newly seceded members, the membership of Union B reached 511.

This is a typical case of a trade union split, in the sense that the moderate union members withdrew because of their dissatisfaction with "militant" union executives. Usually these anti-executive groups start out as minorities, but, within a short period, they emerge as majorities, leaving the original union in a minority position.

Breakaways often occur in the course of labor disputes and play a decisive role in their outcome. Being fully aware of this, the companies naturally try to instigate such breakaways. The "second union" is often organized with the support, if not the active initiative, of the company itself. However, a split cannot take place unless there are workers who are ready to respond to the company's efforts. The rapid growth of the second union is certainly due to company inducements and the promise of favorable treatment, but there must always be a number of members who are willing to accept such inducements. We must assume, therefore, that the real cause of the decline of a union already existed within the organization which boasted the support of the overwhelming majority of its members.

It may be said without exaggeration that most unions carry within them the seeds of a split, no matter how strong their organizing capacity. There are several good reasons for this assumption. Most

Japanese unions are enterprise unions and these unions exist in most developed enterprises. As new employees start working in enterprises, they consider joining the union as a matter of course. In extreme cases, which are not altogether rare, newcomers are treated as union members even before they know it and find union fees deducted from their paychecks under the check-off arrangement. Newcomers join a union for no particular reason, except perhaps that everyone else does. They feel that if they refuse to join they might be regarded as being strange and might even be called upon to explain their reluctance to join. Those who do not join are often labelled "reactionaries"; clearly, it takes some courage to withstand this kind of pressure. While it takes courage and independence to stay away from the union, neither of these qualities is needed in order to join. Here we find a reversal of the original spirit of trade unionism, when it took enormous courage for workers to organize and join a union. Indeed, workers often risked their lives resisting the oppression of employers and government, only because they considered union organization an absolute necessity.

Even in the industrialized countries of the West, the voluntarism of traditional trade unionism has long since faded and "apathy" among union members has become a popular subject of investigation by specialists.[8] The peculiar situation of Japanese unions in this context is that workers interact with their own union exclusively at the workplace and that their identification with the enterprise union is often based upon, and does not contradict, their identification with the company. Union leaders often complain of "union organization without spirit." According to Wakao Fujita, Japanese unions are neither "voluntary" nor "sworn" organizations. "Employees join their organizations [unions] only because they are working at a certain plant. They neither join voluntarily not are they sworn in. They find themselves members without their prior knowledge."[9]

However odd this may sound to Westerners, it is not always clear in Japanese society whether one has joined a group or not. According to Chie Nakane, in the case of a group with a horizontal social structure, "It is immediately obvious to an outsider whether he may join the group or not, because of the clarity with which the criteria for membership are laid down. In the case of a group with a vertical structure, there is no such obvious rule governing membership, so that any outsider, provided he can become acquainted with and accepted by one of the members, may join."[10] Thus if a person has been accepted by most of the members of a particular group, he may find himself a member of the group without having actually taken steps to join it of his own free will. In such cases, filling out application forms and the like are just a formality which has no significance.

Thus, since most union members join a union because everybody else does, they do not hesitate to withdraw from it once they encounter any trouble or feel uneasy about staying in the union. They just as easily join the newly established breakaway union when they find that "everybody" is now joining the new group.

c. Vertical Relationships in Unions: Nakane, who submitted the "vertical principle" as a key concept for analyzing the unique characteristics of Japanese society, points out the difficulty of forming and maintaining voluntary associations in Japanese society. According to her, it is almost impossible for the Japanese to form a functional group without either a "frame," or "vertical links."[11] In the case of enterprise unions, enterprises are likely to be interpreted as being the "frame," and the personal relationships within the enterprise provide "vertical links" which enable the formation and the maintenance of the union organization.

It is Nakane's opinion that the vertical structure of groups in Japanese society leads to instability and makes the group particularly susceptible to fission.[12] The vulnerability of such groups to a split is attributed to the fact that the cohesion of the group depends on the vertical links between members. Once the power and authority of the leader is at stake, the group will easily split or be taken over by one of the subleaders since the horizontal links, if and when they exist, are very weak. In groups based on a horizontal structure, on the other hand, each member, regardless of status, shares the same attribute which is the basic requirement for the formation of the group.[13] Thus as long as this attribute is viable, any change in leadership does not weaken the cohesion of the group as a whole.

Unions are not different from other groups in Japanese society in the sense that the personal relationships between members count for so much that if these relationships are strained, the entire organization is disturbed and, in extreme cases, can even be destroyed. Employers are well aware of this possibility, and are able to control the course of union activities by dismissing leaders at a crucial point, or perhaps by engaging in a policy of appeasement toward them, thus creating internal friction among members.

In vertically structured groups, a change of leadership is generally a difficult process because it always drives a wedge between members on the personal level and the lack, or weakness, of horizontal links causes a substantial degree of frustration within the group. The dismissal of a union president, like the death of a *oyabun* (boss) of a traditional social group, leads to an internal struggle, *oiesōdō* (family quarrel). Similarly, when a rival of the president increases his power, which is comparable to the emergence of a powerful *kobun* (subordinate) with a large following, the rival either takes over the organization and expels the former president, or pulls out his "family and retainers" and forms a new union. In the case of an enterprise union, the expulsion of the president can easily be caused by a conspiracy with the employer, since all union leaders, including the full-time union officials, are employees of the company. In theory at least, dismissal from the company means that the employee is no longer eligible for union membership.

Almost all the legal cases concerning a split in union organization are disputes concerning the legitimacy of their own organization (often referred to in Japanese as "disputes for position as head of the family"). In most cases, breakaway unions claim the original union's assets. They assert that the original union, now reduced to a minority, "unreasonably" monopolized these assets in the first place. It may appear unscrupulous for those who began the internecine fight and initiated the breakaway to demand recognition as the authentic union and claim the spoils. Furthermore, one might reasonably ask why they did not remain within the organization and take over the entire organization with the majority they so quickly gained. They should perhaps have stayed and worked to win the majority through persuasion. This procedure, however, presupposes that the unions function on the principle of democracy and majority rule.

d. Lack of Samurai Spirit: An examination of union splits indicates that most of the anti-executive groups tend to break away rather hastily and easily. They do not discuss the matter patiently with other members; when they do separate reluctantly it is only as a last resort. Matsuta Hosoya, a union leader of many years standing, describes the prevailing trend in prewar Japanese unions as follows:

> Democracy, which is so vital to the union movement, did not prosper. The opposing left- and right-wing factions did not fight their battles in a spirit of democracy. Rather they indulged in conspiracies and trickery, resorting to any available means to crush their opponents. Minorities started neglecting resolutions soon after they were adopted in general meetings and mobilizing an anti-leadership movement. On the other hand, the majorities did not attempt to prevail by persuasion, according to the rules. . . .
>
> Unions at the plant level could resist unsatisfactory orders issued by union headquarters, concerning anything from daily activities to strikes, only when they were backed by some other central organization. Thus the relationship between the various branches of union organizations tended to rely on the spheres of influence commanded by each faction, thus intensifying the complicated antagonism of these factions.[14]

The postwar union movement adopted democracy as the ruling principle in union administration, but, according to Hosoya, "Here again the situation merely goes to show what democracy is like without individual independence, that is, it leads to unbridled rivalries and endless series of internal conflicts and splits in union organization."[15] Hosoya attributes the frequent splits in the Japanese union movement to the immaturity of its internal democracy. Needless to say, democracy is a principle for regulating the administration of groups, whereby decisions in the group are made in accordance with majority rule—presuming that there is a difference of opinion among individual members. Majority rule does not exclude the recognition of, and respect for, minority opinions. Compared to these generally held premises, we can easily see that there can be no democracy in a union movement which does not admit the possibility of different opinions within its organization, and in which opposition all too easily develops into a split.

However, in my view, there are more fundamental reasons, connected with the Japanese mentality, for the unstable nature of the union movement. The question to be asked is why democracy has not matured into a working principle. For instance, the following is suggested about trade unions in Hong Kong: "In the Hong Kong case, it is clear that the traditional social values do not provide an atmosphere in which trade unions might flourish and collective bargaining develop. . . . For example, the reluctance of the Chinese people to express direct disagreement . . . leads to the creation of splinter groups when differences occur within a union."[16]

In traditional Chinese and Japanese society, where extreme importance is attached to harmony as a social value, it is extremely difficult, if not impossible, for internal criticism to find expression within the group. In postwar Japanese society the situation is even more complex. People still retain the traditional values but, at the same time, democratic values (especially freedom of speech) are strongly emphasized. Internal criticism is therefore quite common; in the case of labor unions, perhaps this criticism is too common. This rather popular practice of internal criticism does not contradict the above-mentioned traditional negative attitude toward directly confronting fellow group members, since the members who wish to criticize the group's majority have a habit of doing so only when they are in contact with outsiders.

Yukio Mishima, the world-famous writer who killed himself by harakiri, wrote an open letter to the writer and Diet member Shintaro Ishihara reproaching Ishihara for the way he had criticized his own Liberal Democratic Party:

> What I have to say has to do with the attitude toward internal criticism. . . . To belong to a party, no matter how it may have degenerated, means to assume a certain discipline, and unequivocally to renounce a part of your freedom. . . .
>
> I am angry not only with you but also with the general trend of carrying out internal criticism rather lightheartedly, as if it were a distinguished service. There is no tone of sorrow in your words: they are too lightly expressed. The samurai of ancient times killed themselves by way of admonition when they experienced serious dissatisfaction with their feudal clan. Those who chose not to commit harakiri endured their bitterness silently. To belong to something must be this way. Human beings who are free face a serious choice exactly at this point—to be beautiful or not while belonging to something.[17]

Mishima's anger at Ishihara's "lighthearted" criticism of his own party as though it were a distinguished service sprang mainly from the fact that it had appeared in the press, that is, outside the party. In feudal society where internal criticism was forbidden, one criticized only by sacrificing one's own life. In contemporary Japan, criticism, which is ostensible, is completely free because democracy is recognized, at least formally, as an undeniable social right. However, since the custom to avoid any open confrontation is still strongly entrenched within social groups, internal criticism tends to be superficial and lacking in the energy that brings about a true confrontation. Such criticism then, which is devoid of any serious intent, is nothing but an irresponsible utterance, and is easily exploited by hostile outsiders. In order to strengthen "progressive" movements in a real and basic sense, perhaps what is needed is some of the old samurai spirit; a spirit that was dramatically stressed by a writer who, somewhat ironically, killed himself for a conservative cause.

NOTES

1. Robert E. Cole, "America no Nihon Rōshi Kankei-kan to Genjitsu [American Ideas on Japanese Industrial Relations and Reality]," *Nihon Rōdō Kyōkai Zasshi* 161 (1972), pp. 27 ff.

2. The Genpei and Sengoku periods stretch from 1156 to 1600.

3. The Battle of Dannoura in 1185 brought the Heike's final defeat at the hands of the Genji and the Battle of Sekigahara in 1600 resulted in the hegemony of the Tokugawa Shogunate.

4. Ryōtarō Shiba and Donald Keene, *Nihonjin to Nihon Bunka* [The Japanese and Japanese Culture] (Tokyo: Chūōkōron, 1971), pp. 66–68.

5. Kaoru Ōta, *Tatakai no Nakade* [In the Midst of Struggle] (Tokyo: Aoki Shoten, 1971), pp. 149–50.

6. Ibid., p. 148.

7. Tanaka v. Shinagawa Shiro Lenga Company, Okayama Plant Union, Supreme Court, I Petty Bench 1957, 11 SSMH 1943.

8. A major contribution to the literature on trade union apathy is Joseph Goldstein's *Government of British Trade Unions* (London: Allen & Unwin, 1952). Also see G. W. Brooks, *Sources of Vitality in the American Labor Movement*, New York State School of Industrial and Labor Relations, *Bulletin* 41 (Ithaca, N.Y.: Cornell University Press, 1960).

9. Wakao Fujita, *Rōdō Kumiai Undō no Tenkan* [Conversion of Labor Union Movement] (Tokyo: Nihon Hyōronsha, 1967), p. 267.

10. Nakane, *Japanese Society*, p. 41.

11. Ibid., p. 59.

12. Ibid., p. 48.

13. Ibid., pp. 40–48.

14. Matsuta Hosoya, *Nihon no Rōdō Kumiai Undō* [Labor Union Movement in Japan] (Tokyo: Shakai Shisō Kenkyūkai, 1958), p. 267.

15. Ibid.

16. Joseph England, "Equilibrium and Change in an Industrial Relations System: The Hong Kong Case" in *Social and Cultural Background of Labor Management Relations in Asian Countries* (Tokyo: Japan Institute of Labor, 1972), p. 232.

17. Yuko Mishima, *Ranryō Ō* [King Ranryō] (Tokyo: Shinchōsha, 1971), p. 321.

7

STRIKES

1. SWEET MEMORIES

Kaoru Ōta, who led several nationwide strikes during the ten years he was president of the Sōhyō, from 1958 to 1968, contends that strikes in Japan are generally of short duration, being limited to one or two hours or, at the most, one or two days. He writes:

> The Federation of Private Railway Unions carried out a two-day strike in the spring of 1956. But when the companies did not concede an iota, the unions quickly gave up, claiming that the management position was too strong to continue the strike. To begin with, it is completely erroneous to think that a mere one- or two-day strike can bring any wage hike at all.[1]

Later Ōta explains why Japanese unions do not undertake long strikes. In his opinion, right after the end of the Second World War, people were starving and demands for higher wages were almost desperate. Company officials, on the other hand, were paralyzed by the shock of losing the war and unable to resist union demands. In addition, management could increase profits to cover wage increases by selling their goods on an extremely inflated market.

Thus all the union leaders had to do in order to obtain higher wages was simply to shout and pound on the bargaining table while the mass of union members sang militant songs and waved red flags outside. Although the circumstances are completely different today, union leaders still cling to these sweet memories under the assumption that if only they wave red flags, bargain collectively and pretend to go on strike, they will get higher wages.[2]

The above comments were written in 1961. Even if the easygoing attitude of the unions at that time could be explained solely by the "sweet experience" of the postwar period, the accumulated experience of the last thirty years ought to have cured the union leaders of their naiveté. Yet, ten years later, Ōta observed that Japanese unions were still not ready for long strikes and gives the example of a general meeting of the National Railways Union he addressed in 1964. When he began to emphasize the necessity of a three-day strike in order to achieve wage parity with other public corporations, the participants as well as the observers suddenly became uneasy and fell silent.

This is the outstanding difference between the Japanese and the American or Western union movement. It clearly exemplifies the weakness of unions not only in the National Railways but also in all sectors of the economy in postwar Japan. How could the unions win their struggle without careful preparation in regard to the exact amount of economic damage to be inflicted on the company in order to achieve the desired wage hike? . . . Since strikes were limited to half a day in the past, the workers' only experience had been with strikes which were little more than rituals. They were startled when they were told to go out for three days.[3]

While Ōta's observations on the reluctance of Japanese unions to undertake long strikes are correct, the motives for this reluctance go beyond wishful thinking and nostalgia for the "sweet experience" of the postwar period. In fact, the reasons can be found in certain fundamental characteristics of the Japanese union move-

145

ment of which most union leaders, including Ōta, are certainly well aware. In short, on the one hand, the Japanese unions are not capable of carrying out long strikes; on the other hand, they do not need prolonged strikes in order to obtain satisfaction of their demands.

2. STRIKE CHARACTERISTICS

Before going into an analysis of the characteristics of Japanese strikes, we have to examine whether strikes in Japan are really shorter than ones in the West and if so, how short. The following graph (Figure 1), prepared by Kazutoshi Kōshiro[4] and based on

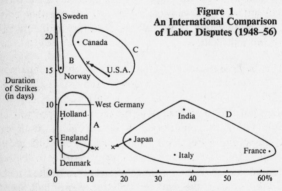

Figure 1
An International Comparison
of Labor Disputes (1948–56)

Note: x indicates a country's position 1960–66.

Rate of Union Member Participation in Strikes
   A   North Europe–I
   B   North Europe–II
   C   North America
   D   Mediterranean–Asia

Source: Kazutoshi Kōshiro, "Dantai Kōshō to Sōgi" [Collective Bargaining and Dispute], in *Nihon no Rōdō Kumiai* [Trade Unions in Japan], ed. Taishirō Shirai (Tokyo: Nihon Hyōronsha, 1967), p. 232.

146

research done by Ross and Hartman,[5] presents a comparison of strike participation rates and strike duration in selected countries.

Figure 1 shows that the strike participation rate is low while strike duration is long in some Scandinavian countries (Sweden and Norway), Canada and the United States; strike duration is short and the participation rate is low in West Germany, Holland, Great Britain and Denmark; and the participation rate is high and strike duration is short in the Mediterranean countries, France, Italy and in some Asian countries (India and Japan). Ross and Hartman published their findings in 1960. After 1960, the strike participation rate increased and the duration became slightly shorter in Great Britain, while the participation rate declined and the duration became slightly shorter in Japan. As a result, the strike patterns of Great Britain and Japan seemed to be moving closer together. The change in Great Britain might have been caused primarily by an increase in wildcat strikes. But a more recent trend in that country shows a gradual lengthening of strike duration —a trend also found in the United States.[6]

Robert Evans pointed out that only 24.5 percent of all work stoppages in the United States lasted more than a month, while disputes lasting four days or less made up 27.7 percent of all disputes in 1966 and 24.3 percent in 1968. At the same time in Japan, such short-term strikes accounted for 75.1 percent and 55.5 percent of all disputes respectively. In 1968 the average number of days lost per strike was 2.4 in Japan and 18.5 in the United States.[7]

A comparison of international statistics on labor in six major countries (Table 10) shows that France is the only country where strike duration has been shorter than in Japan. However, the fact that the countries surveyed do not collect labor statistics by the same methods makes it difficult to draw accurate conclusions. For instance, Japanese, figures do not include strikes shorter than four hours, whereas other countries include only strikes longer than eight hours. Table 11 shows that in Japan the number of strikes shorter than half a day has exceeded that of longer strikes in every year since 1966.

Table 10
Trend of Labor Disputes in Six Major Countries

Year	Japan				U.S.A.				U.K.			
	A	B	C	D	A	B	C	D	A	B	C	D
1965	1,542	5,669	2.0	3.4	3,968	23,300	3.8	15.0	2,354	2,925	1.2	3.3
1966	1,252	2,742	0.9	2.4	4,405	25,400	4.0	13.0	1,937	2,398	1.0	4.4
1967	1,214	1,830	0.6	2.5	4,595	42,100	6.4	14.7	2,116	2,787	1.3	3.8
1968	1,546	2,841	0.9	2.4	5,045	49,018	7.2	18.5	2,378	4,690	2.0	2.1
1969	1,783	3,634	1.1	2.6	5,700	42,869	6.1	18.6	3,116	6,846	3.0	4.1
1970	2,260	3,915	1.2	2.3	5,716	66,414	9.4	20.1	3,906	15,980	4.8	6.1
1971	2,527	6,029	1.8	3.2	5,138	47,589	6.7	14.5	2,228	13,551	6.1	11.5
1972	2,498	5,147	1.5	3.3	5,010	27,066	3.7	15.8	2,497	23,910	11.0	13.8
1973	3,326	4,604	1.3	2.1	5,353	27,950	3.6	12.3	2,873	7,200	3.3	4.7
1974	5,211	9,663	2.7	2.7	5,074	47,991	6.1	17.3	2,922	14,750	6.6	9.0
1975	3,311	8,016	2.2	2.9	5,031	31,240	4.1	17.9	2,282	6,010	2.7	7.4

Year	West Germany				France				Italy			
	A	B	C	D	A	B	C	D	A	B	C	D
1965	20	49	0.0	8.2	1,674	980	0.7	1.4	3,191	6,993	7.9	3.0
1966	205	27	0.0	0.1	1,711	2,523	1.7	2.4	2,387	14,474	16.5	7.7
1967	742	390	0.2	6.5	1,675	4,204	2.8	1.5	2,658	8,568	9.5	3.8
1968	36	25	0.0	1.2	1,103	423	0.3	0.9	3,377	9,240	10.2	1.9
1969	86	249	0.1	2.8	2,480	2,224	1.4	1.5	3,788	37,825	41.2	5.0
1970	129	93	0.0	0.5	3,319	1,742	1.1	1.5	4,162	20,887	22.3	5.6
1971	624	4,484	2.0	7.8	4,358	4,388	2.7	1.4	5,598	14,799	15.7	3.8
1972	53	66	0.0	3.0	3,464	3,760	2.3	1.4	4,765	19,497	20.0	4.4
1973	732	563	0.3	3.0	4,253	3,910	2.4	1.6	3,769	23,402	:	2.4
1974	890	1,051	0.5	4.2	3,831	3,380	:	:	5,174	19,489	:	:
1975	202	70	0.2	1.9	3,876	3,876	:	:	:	:	:	:

Source: Seisansei Honbu (Japan Productivity Center), *Katsuyō Rōdō Tōkei* (Practical Labor Statistics), 1977 (Tokyo: Japan Productivity Center, 1977), p. 159.

A = Number of labor disputes; B = Number of man-days lost; C = Number of man-days lost per 10 employees; D = Duration of dispute (number of days).

Note: Japanese figures exclude going-slow and strikes shorter than 4 hours. Figures for other countries exclude strikes shorter than 8 hours.

148

Table 11
Number of Strikes in Japan

	Strikes longer than half a day	Strikes shorter than half a day
1966	1,239	1,452
1967	1,204	1,403
1968	1,537	2,021
1969	1,776	3,282
1970	2,256	2,356
1971	2,515	4,653
1972	2,489	3,531
1973	3,320	6,667
1974	5,197	6,378
1975	3,385	5,475

Source: Ministry of Labor, *Rōdō Sōgi Tōkei Chōsa Nen Hōkoku* [Annual Report of Statistics and Survey of Labor Disputes], 1975, Ministry of Labor, Tokyo, 1976.

3. THE ULTIMATE WEAPON?

Evans contends that ". . . the fact that only 24.4 percent of all work stoppages lasted more than a month clearly suggests that most American strikes are in the nature of tactics rather than ultimate solutions."[8] Although he admits that this trend is "more evident in Japan," his assertion is tantamount to saying that the difference betweeen industrial disputes in the United States and Japan is only a matter of degree.[9]

In Western countries, especially Britain, West Germany and the United States, the strike has traditionally been regarded as the ultimate weapon to be utilized only when all possibilities of bargaining have been exhausted. Recently, however, there has been a change in viewpoint. For instance K. G. J. C. Knowles writes: "Yesterday they were battles; today few of them are more than protest demonstrations."[10] However, while the strike nowadays may have become essentially a demonstration, it also means that "'sporadic' . . . and spontaneous strikes give way to the new-fashioned strike which has become 'enlightened, orderly, bureaucratic' . . . almost chivalrous in its tactics and cold-blooded in its calculatedness."[11]

149

Because it results from unemotional and cool calculation in contrast to the former desperate and impulsive revolt, a strike tends to be deferred as long as there exists a possibility of peaceful negotiation. For instance, in West Germany a strike vote often fulfills the function of the strike itself. When the vote in favor of a strike approaches 100 percent, German employers become conciliatory. When it does not exceed 80 percent, it is the union that reconsiders its position. Thus in West Germany, even when negotiations are deadlocked and a strike is decided, both parties endeavor to make concessions up to the last moment.[12]

Generally, in Western countries a strike can be considered an ultimate weapon only in the sense that workers do not go on strike or companies declare a lockout until several bargaining sessions have been held and both parties realize that further conciliation is impossible.[13] English-speaking nations commonly refer to a strike as a "walk-out," reflecting the fact that workers usually leave the job site and will not return until the dispute is settled. Therefore, it is quite natural that, while strikes are rare, once they have begun they tend to be prolonged.

4. STRIKE AS THE STARTING POINT

Until recently, Japanese strikes were radically different from the Western pattern described above. Every year during the Spring Offensive[14] it was an almost established procedure for both parties to appeal to the Central Labor Relations Commission (CLRC) for conciliation without having engaged in any serious prior bargaining themselves. The late Professor T. Ishii, then chairman of the CLRC, wrote the following in response to criticism of the Commission's alleged inactivity during the 1971 Spring Offensive:

It is not the function of the Labor Relations Commission to stop strikes. There seems to exist some misunderstanding among the public as well as employers and unions regarding this. . . . It is my strong conviction that the Commission should

150

not be reduced to an institution that stops strikes. . . . The labor law emphasizes the principle that all factions reach a settlement without outside intervention. . . . It is their responsibility to prevent strikes and to that end they should negotiate in good faith. Only after they have failed to settle a dispute by serious bargaining, should they come to the Commission . . . otherwise both parties harboring misunderstanding or hoping that the Commission will settle the strike alone conveniently neglect their responsibilities and thereby cause unnecessary harm to the public.[15]

Ishii's message is that the Commission should work to settle disputes only after both parties have made a serious attempt at settling their disagreements. The Commission should not be held responsible for a strike if the parties have not worked earnestly toward a settlement. However, the parties usually go on strike in order to put pressure on the Commission so that it will submit proposals for settlement while the parties concerned tend not to bargain seriously.

In the Spring Offensive of 1972 a dispute between private railway companies and unions resulted in transportation stoppages which greatly inconvenienced and irritated the public. The dispute lasted until the CLRC made a proposal which set a pattern for the year and actually settled various other current disputes. The public was very critical of railway companies and unions because they did little bargaining and merely waited until public pressure forced the Commission to intervene. The irresponsible attitude of both parties was all the more scandalous because they were well aware that the government would allow a fare increase. They simply needed public support for a wage increase so that the fare increase would seem more reasonable.

In more typical cases where disputes are not brought before a commission, it is not unusual for strikes to start without any bargaining at all. Indeed the employer will begin to bargain in good faith only after a strike has started. We can say that, in most cases, the objective of a strike is to bring the employer to the bargaining table. If management procrastinates about negotiations, unions are unduly hasty about declaring strikes and frequently call a strike as soon as they have put their demands forward. In extreme cases, management might not know what the union's demands are, even after a strike has already begun. When the workers of a small enterprise succeed in getting organized, they celebrate the creation of the union by going on strike immediately, picking any problem at hand. The strike is merely a means to demonstrate their determination and their will to fight. Under such circumstances one can see that a strike is not the final stage of bargaining but its starting point.

5. STRIKES AS DEMONSTRATIONS

If a strike is only a means to show the workers' will to fight or to demonstrate the union's strength, it is unnecessary and even absurd to continue striking during all the time it takes for the negotiations to be completed. Instead a strike should last for one or two hours or, at most, one or two days and stop in order to assess the reaction of management; it may be repeated if needed. Thus even if a dispute lasts for a long time, unions do not continue the strike for the entire period. Such tactics are not unknown in Western countries. Benjamin Aaron describes various forms of sporadic strikes, switch-strikes, rotating strikes, and hit-and-run strikes, also called *grèves tournantes* and *débrayages*. However, such "irregular" industrial actions are uncommon and illegal in most Western countries, except France and Italy.[16]

It has been pointed out that in Western countries strikes have assumed the function of protest demonstrations and are becoming more calculated, rationalized and formalized.[17] Although there is a gradually emerging trend among large enterprises toward taking strikes more seriously, Japanese unions usually go on strike without much thought and regardless of the consequences. To initiate a strike, a union need not have any serious grievance. The workers will go on strike quite readily if it is understood that they will be called out only intermittently. The Japanese labor law system, which safeguards the right to strike to a greater degree than Western counterparts, encourages this easygoing attitude of Japanese unions toward strikes. The strike, which is the system's offspring, has been pampered by excessive legal protection and, as a result, has become a lusty overgrown problem child.[18]

Since strikes in Japan are protest demonstrations, a mere work stoppage is not considered sufficient to achieve the purpose. A strike is not a "walk-out" as in English-speaking countries, but a "walk-in." Typical Japanese strikes are carried out with the workers staying at the work site and resemble the sit-down strikes in the West.[19] A strike where workers do not stay at the workplace is considered an ineffective one. It used to be called a *ne-toraiki* (*ne*-strike), a tongue-in-cheek compound word, *ne* meaning to sleep or to lie down in Japanese. The Japanese terminology reflects the demonstration function of strikes.

In the United States as well as in Great Britain, the strike is the most typical form of labor dispute. Thus the term "act of dispute" is not used frequently in industrial relations. The right to perform acts of dispute is always called "the right to strike." In Germany there are terms like *Kampfmassnahme* (means of dispute) and *Kampfhandlung* (act of dispute), but the right to perform acts of dispute is always called *Streikrecht* (right to strike). In Japan the terms "act of dispute" and "right to perform acts of dispute" are used more frequently. This difference in terminology shows that the strike is neither the most typical nor the most important kind of act of Japanese labor dispute.

Japan might be regarded as one of the most remarkable countries in the world in the sense that the greatest variety of acts of dispute occur there daily. Japanese unions can be proud of their rich imagination. Of course, if we look at the history of the labor movement, we can easily find a variety of acts of dispute in Germany and in English-speaking countries as well. But, at the present time, disputes for the most part are limited to strikes, picketing and perhaps boycotts. Cases of lockouts by employers, slow-downs and work-to-rule are the exception rather than the rule.[20] On the contrary, in Japan, many acts of dispute, beside the strike, are resorted to frequently. Any act which might effectively shock employers and arouse their attention as well as that of the public will accomplish the purpose, without necessarily resorting to the strike. Since the objective is to shock and annoy the employer, it follows that many kinds of malicious acts are performed. In the following chapter we will describe the various kinds of acts of dispute which are frequently carried out in Japanese industrial relations.

NOTES
1. Ōta, *Rōdō Kumiai-ron*, p. 7.
2. Ibid., p. 7.
3. Ōta, *Tatakai no Nakade*, p. 204.
4. Kazutoshi Kōshiro, "Dantai Kōshō to Sōgi" [Collective Bargaining and Dispute], in *Nihon no Rōdō Kumiai* [Trade Unions in Japan], ed. Taishirō Shirai (Tokyo: Nihon Hyōronsha, 1967), p. 232.
5. Arthur M. Ross and Paul T. Hartman, *Changing Patterns of Industrial Conflict*. The purpose of the author is not to evaluate Ross and Hartman's typology of strike patterns. For detailed criticism, see Benjamin Aaron, "Methods of Industrial Action: Courts, Administrative Agencies and Legislatures," in *Industrial Conflict—A Comparative Legal Survey*, eds. Benjamin Aaron and K. Wedderburn (New York: Crane, Russak and Co., 1972), pp. 72–126.
6. Ben C. Roberts, "Die Zunahme in der Entwicklung Industrieller Unruhen seit 1945 und ihre Tendenzen," in *Arbeitskonflikte und Arbeitskampf*, edited by International Stiftung HUMANUM (Cologne: Peter Hanstein Verlag, 1973), p. 24.
7. Robert Evans, *The Labor Economies of Japan and the United States* (New York: Praeger, 1971), p. 29.
8. Ibid., p. 30.
9. Ibid.
10. K. G. J. C. Knowles, *Strikes—A Study in Industrial Conflict* (Oxford: Basil Blackwell, 1952), p. 4.
11. Abraham Siegel, "Method and Substance in Theorizing about Worker Protest," in *Aspects of Labor Economics: A Report of the National Bureau of Economic Research* (Princeton, N.J.: Princeton University Press, 1962), p. 44.
12. Takuji Ishiguro, "Nishi Doitsu ni Okeru Dantai Kōshō [Collective Bargaining in West Germany], *Kikan Rōdō-hō* 39 (1961), p. 145.
13. France may be the most significant exception to this pattern. French strikes are considered as actions taken by individual employees, who then are joined by other workers. However, the situation has been changing in recent years. Today, strikes are being called by unions and have become a part of the

strategy and tactics of collective bargaining. See Folke Schmidt, "Industrial Action: The Role of Trade Unions and Employers' Associations," in Aaron and Wedderburn, *Industrial Conflict*, p. 48.

14. For a description, refer back to Part I, chapter 4.

15. Teruhisa Ishii, "Rōdō Iinkai ni tsuite" [On the Labor Relations Commission], *Chūrōi Jihō* 519 (1973), pp. 6–8.

16. Aaron, "Methods of Industrial Action," pp. 92–94.

17. The notable exception among Western countries is France. The French strike is never the disciplined action of a group, but rather the materialization of agitation and the concordance of different displeasures. See Folke Schmidt, "Industrial Action," p. 48.

18. See Part I, chapters 3 and 4.

19. Sit-down strikes do occur in most Western countries today, but they remain little more than a symbol of the world-wide labor unrest in the 1930s. In almost all countries in Europe as well as in the United States, they are illegal, see Aaron, "Methods of Industrial Action," pp. 95–97. However, Ben Roberts refers to the new trend emerging with the "sit-in" or "gherao tactics" (non-violence as practiced by Ghandi) in Britain, France and Italy in the 1960s. See Roberts, "Die Zunahme," pp. 20 ff.

20. Slow-downs and the practice of working-to-rule are widespread and effectively used in the United States and, to a lesser degree, exist in some other Western countries; however, they often are illegal, see Aaron, "Methods of Industrial Action," pp. 81–83. For a description of other acts of dispute in the West, see Knowles, *Strikes*, pp. 10–19.

8

OTHER ACTS OF DISPUTE

1. PASTING UP POSTERS

The pasting up of posters by unions is a very troublesome aspect of many labor disputes. In some extreme cases several hundred or even several thousand posters are glued on walls and windows with bucketfuls of paste. The covering is so thick that, when the paste has dried, it is almost impossible to clean off. In other instances, unions pour paste on office desks or stick several sheets of paper over windows, one on top of the other, until the room is completely dark. One union put up 1,500, 2,500 and 4,500 posters over a period of three days while management repeatedly took them down. After the dispute, the company had to hire workers specialized in cleaning buildings. The cleaning process took several days. First the wall surface had to be soaked in hot water, the layers of paper had to be sliced off with knives, then brushes were used to scrub the walls. In spite of this cleaning, thousands of tiny pieces of paper and hardened paste remained on the windows and numerous scars were left on the walls after the cleaning was done. In this case the Supreme Court found the union guilty of destruction of property.[1]

Articles 260 and 261 of the Japanese Penal Code dealing with the destruction of buildings and the damage of goods respectively, and Article 1, Section 33, of the Minor Offenses Law concerning the placement of posters, specify under which conditions the pasting of posters is a criminal offense. The criteria applied consist of determining whether a building or property has become unusable for its essential purpose. The pasting up of posters by unions is usually regarded by the courts as a proper act of dispute as long as it is not carried out in an extraordinary way and does not result in permanent damage to goods or buildings. Thus, the courts penalize the unions only when their actions are excessive.

Legal penalties are, however, less to the point than the question of the union's purpose in distributing or pasting up posters. Posters are, one would think, a means of communication intended to convey information on the position, claims and viewpoints of the union to its members, the company's customers and the general public. If this were the case, posters should be easy to read, pleasant to look at and neatly made to appeal to the aesthetic sense of the public. Yet most union posters are printed on cheap paper and sometimes even made from old newspapers; the message or slogans are roughly or clumsily drawn; and the posters themselves are put up anywhere the union deems fit. The messages or slogans are mean, abusive and sometimes even hit below the belt with unfair personal attacks; they only result in alienating viewers.

Communication is not, in fact, the sole objective of these posters. Rather, the union's main intention is to annoy the employer, give customers and the public unpleasant feelings and thereby disturb the normal operations of the business. In this perspective, the more repulsive and unpleasant the posters are and the more shocking impressions they give, the more effective they will emphasize the dispute.

It has already been pointed out that the reckless pasting of posters and their threatening and libelous content constitute criminal offenses in the eyes of the law. The general public as well, aggravated by the maliciousness of pasting posters and their distasteful style and content, feels the union's actions are disgraceful. Because the union movement stands for human rights and dignity, such behavior by unions is without a doubt a betrayal of the underlying ideal of the movement. We should bear in mind that cases

157

in which union leaders are prosecuted for putting up posters occur most frequently in small enterprises and in the public sector where strikes are prohibited and unions so weak that leaders cannot carry out a full-fledged strike and must resort to such tactics. However, poster pasting, even though it may be only a desperate effort by powerless unions, cannot help but erode public support for the organization in the same manner as violent actions often do.

2. RECEIVING WAGES DURING STRIKES

The financial condition of Japanese unions is another important reason why unions avoid strikes and prefer other acts of dispute. During a strike, union members do not receive their regular wages and must rely on union funds. On the management's side, too, normal business cannot be carried out in the midst of a strike. Thus the outcome of a dispute largely depends on which side is able to hold out longer. In this sense, the bargaining power of the union rests largely on its financial position.

Japanese unions, being enterprise based, have on the average a small number of members and, as a result, their financial resources are quite limited. Small unions in small enterprises, with only twenty or thirty members (a common situation in Japanese industry) can barely provide for the living expenses of their striking members, even for a few days. In fact most of the money collected from union dues is expended on day-to-day activities.

In 1952, the *Tanrō* (Nihon Tankō Rōdō Kumiai, or Japanese Coal Mining Workers' Union), then one of the most powerful unions in Japan with 260,000 members, carried out a 63-day strike for a wage increase. This was the longest wage strike until the *Kaiin* (Zen Nihon Kaiin Kumiai, or All Japan Seamen's Union) struck for 90 days in 1972. When the Tanrō started the strike, its funds amounted to less than 2,000 yen (less than $10.00) per member. Total wages lost amounted to an approximate figure of 100 million yen per day, or 6 billion yen for the duration of the strike, a total of 24,000 yen for each worker. Since the finances of large unions like the Tanrō were so meager, even in its most prosperous period,[2] one can easily imagine the situation in smaller organizations. Therefore, in most prolonged strikes, unions have to rely on the voluntary contributions of friendly organizations or on loans from the *Rōkin* (Rōdō Ginkō, Labor Financial Bank). The Rōkin is a banking facility set up by the government in 1953 to promote the workers' welfare. Its fundamental purpose is to give financial help to individual workers. Actually it gives loans to unions under the pretext of aiding workers who are having financial difficulties during a strike.

The Kaiin, which was able to carry out a strike for 90 days, is the only union which could genuinely be considered an industrial union. Its members are affiliated directly with this industrial organization, whereas most so-called industrial unions are only federations of enterprise unions. Its method of raising strike funds is unique. The Kaiin allocates 15 percent of the total fees collected for a strike fund in the same manner as most Western unions; other Japanese unions make a separate collection for strike funds, the proceeds of which are usually deposited in banks or other financial institutions in the name of the individual members.

The reason for this special procedure for raising strike funds is because of the strained financial situation resulting from limited membership: Japanese unions are compelled to levy heavy fees on their members in order to meet routine costs. It has been calculated that, on the average, union dues in Japan amount to 1.30 percent of the worker's salary, while the proportion in the United States is 1.15 percent and only 0.75 percent in Great Britain.[3] Since regular fees alone almost exceed the limits of the worker's ability to pay, unions are allowed to collect an additional amount needed for a strike fund only on the condition that it be deposited in the names of the individual members. Legally speaking, the strike funds of most Japanese unions are the property of the individual members and, in theory, the unions are using money borrowed from their own members when they go on strike. This means that the Japanese unions' finances are totally unsound and that unions always have to "start war with a totally vacant armory."[4] Given these circumstances, it is quite natural that the unions always try to make do with acts of dispute that require little or no expense. Many such free or inexpensive acts are commonly used by Japanese unions. A perfect example is the case when the union members take their annual vacations at the same time.

3. VACATIONING FOR STRIKE PURPOSES

When members of a union take their vacations simultaneously, the effect on the company is the same as if they were going out on strike. This tactic was invented by unions in the public sector.[5] If challenged by management, the unions can claim that they are not engaged in a strike at all, but that their members are merely taking the vacations to which they are entitled by law. Their intentions are clear, however, since when management refuses to pay vacation wages, the union often takes the case to court. Private sector unions also resort to this tactic,[6] not only out of financial need but also because their organizational weakness makes them unable to carry out a successful strike.

The courts usually rule against the union's wage claims in cases concerning vacationing for strike purposes on the basis that the intent of such an action is to hamper the normal course of business, which is not the case with regular annual vacations.[7] According to recent decisions of the Supreme Court, an employer can refuse to provide vacation time with pay only when the normal course of business is disrupted.[8] These judgments refer to cases where a union mobilized small contingents of its members from one or several plants to another target plant within the same enterprise. Such action is a relatively recent trend in union tactics. Its object is to concentrate efforts on a particular plant chosen as a target for holding mass meetings or for picketing. Of course, the ultimate aim of the union is to disrupt work at the target plant. However, according to the Court, the employees from other work sites are not disturbing the operation of their own plant by taking a vacation. Therefore, their claims that they are entitled to receive wages for so-called vacation time should be upheld.

Such reasoning may seem like a bit of legal trickery and fly in the face of common sense. However, the Court's opinion is not as unsound as it first appears, if we take into consideration another aspect of this difficult legal problem— the principle that employees are entitled to complete freedom of choice as to how they spend their vacation time. Consequently, management has nothing to say if the workers use vacation time for union activities. Sometimes it is almost impossible to distinguish whether workers used their vacations for union activities or for striking. In one case, a union whose petition for a bonus was pending in court ordered its members to use their vacation time to attend court in order to watch the proceedings. The employer refused to pay the workers who took time off and the Labor Relations Commission turned down the union's claim that the employer's refusal was unfair, taking the position that the union's order to go on vacation was meant to put pressure on the company for the purpose of getting the bonus. At the heart of the dispute the vacation tactic was considered a strike in fact, and the workers were not entitled to receive vacation pay.[9]

4. PECULIAR WAYS OF SPENDING VACATIONS

Besides the ambiguity of the legal definition of what constitutes a vacation, the workers' peculiar way of spending their vacation time contributes to the union taking advantage of the concept of vacation. Japanese workers, in general, do not take long vacations. Instead, they take time off at intervals to tend to private business, when they are ill or to go on short trips, and then usually for just one or two days. In Western societies, on the other hand, extended vacations are traditional. Recommendation No. 47 (1936) of the International Labor Organization suggests that vacation time be divided into no more than two parts. The I.L.O. Convention No. 52 (1936), a legal code ratified by a number of countries, also prohibits the use of vacation time for illness. A West German federal law regulating vacation time is based on similar principles.

Western people look on their long annual vacation time as an occasion to get away and recuperate from the physical and mental fatigue that builds up during the work year. In Japan, Article 39 of the Labor Standards Law provides for taking vacation time "consecutively or separately." Yet, the majority of Japanese workers spend their vacations a little at a time, which enables them to tend to private matters as they arise. These private matters include visiting home, attending weddings and funerals, and attending family memorial services, all of which are very important in Japanese family life. Also included in such private matters are participating in class reunions, meetings with people involved in a common hobby and political gatherings.[10]

In many companies union officials are allowed a certain amount of time outside their vacations to engage in collective bargaining or joint consultations, and even to attend regular union meetings. They must use their vacation time, however, for other union activities such as attending federation meetings or liaison work with other unions. Since most Japanese unions cannot afford full-time officers, they have to make do with part-time officials. Therefore, it is usually necessary that these officials be given some kind of leave of absence during working hours for union activities. In fact, the Labor Relations Commission once found an employer guilty of unfair labor practices for refusing free time to a union official who intended to use his time for union business.[11]

Unions also take advantage of the fact that the procedures by which one requests leave are often not followed to the letter. In most enterprises, it is required that employees fill out a form and get it stamped by their supervisor several days before they take time off. In actual practice, however, employees usually take their leave without prior permission. Quite often, on the morning of the day the worker plans to take off, he simply calls the supervisor or a co-worker informing him of his intentions. The employee might even take it off without contacting anyone, and go through filling the form and getting the seal of the supervisor only after he has returned to work.[12] Unions make good use of these relaxed procedures by ordering their members to fill in the vacation forms and leave them on the desk of the supervisor just before leaving the workplace. If a union orders its members to take a leave of absence without filling any forms, they can always argue that, since this is a common practice, there are no grounds for prohibiting it during a dispute.

5. PARTIAL STRIKES

A partial strike is often resorted to as a means of achieving the same effect as a full-scale strike without exposing all the union members to losing their wages. In this kind of strike only one part of the plant is shut down. It is not even always necessary to order an entire division or section to stop work since the union can often command the same effect with only a few individuals on strike. Another variation is to have certain employees refuse to perform certain parts of their assigned tasks. Since most of the union members remain on the job, a partial strike is ideally suited to the organizational needs of the union and helps them to keep control of the plant during the strike at very little cost.

In the coal miners' strike of 1952, the Tanrō used full-scale strikes and partial strikes or "nominated" strikes, together with forced entry into the mines by union men who had been fired and mass demonstrations, as the situation required. Even today, partial strikes and the refusal to perform certain tasks are tactics used when the unions deem them necessary. However, as a way of saving union funds while carrying out a strike, these tactics are not always successful. Often a worker out on a partial strike holds a key position in the line and his absence forces the rest of the crew into idleness. As in the case of annual vacations, employers often refuse to pay the wages of union members who participate

163

in the partial strike. In these cases, employers claim that these union members, even though they reported for work, did not in fact work up to the standard outlined in their employment contracts and, therefore, ought not to be paid.

At first glance, a partial strike appears to be a very effective weapon for the unions since it can have a strong impact on the enterprise while requiring a minimum of sacrifice on the part of the union. However, it is not difficult for employers to take advantage of the weaknesses inherent in the partial strike tactics. A partial strike shuts down only a part of a business concern and it is relatively easy for an employer to replace the work force in the striking section by a few strikebreakers. Management can then reduce the effectiveness of a slowdown by putting pressure on union members still on the job, especially since the plant is the area where management is most powerful. Employers also try to influence the workers who are on partial strike or "soldiering" on the job.

In a case involving a trucking company where the union ordered a work stoppage, management directed the supervisors to ask each driver whether or not he would comply with the union's order. The supervisors were to refuse work to those drivers who answered in the affirmative by not letting them sign in. Shortly before work started in the morning, the union cancelled the strike and some of the union members went to work as usual. However, the employer refused to pay all the union workers for that day, whether they had worked or not. In this case it was easy for the firm to put pressure on the union members by asking them where they stood in terms of the dispute as they signed in that morning. The Labor Relations Commission held that the employer's questioning of the drivers constituted interference in union administration because it incited union members to work in spite of the union's strike order. The company's denial of work to union members and refusal to pay their wages was found to be an unfair labor practice.[13]

The Commission's ruling remains open to question since legally employers have the right to refuse admission to workers who have no intention of working to the letter of their contract. They also have a legal right to refuse to pay, or at least to reduce, the wages of those who do not put in a full day's work. Quite likely, the ruling was based on the supervisor's interference in union activities.

In fact only a minority of the trucking company workers belonged to the union. Their weakness in numbers made a partial strike appear to be the most effective tactic. However, when a union is not strong enough to withstand the pressure management will inevitably exert, such tactics quickly fail. Concerning this point, Kaoru Ōta's comments are very much to the point:

> What counts most in the conduct of a dispute is not tactics but more fundamentally the nature of the union's organization. If the union does not have the power to carry out a full-scale strike, it cannot be successful in a partial one.[14]

6. ONE-PERSON OR NOMINATED STRIKES

A one-person strike, also called a "nominated" strike, has the same objective as a partial strike, that is, to disturb work on a large scale at little cost to the union. More often it is a means to ignore a management order that is disagreeable to the union. Usually, the purpose of such a strike is to force an employer to grant certain demands. But in some cases unions can have their demands realized through the strike action itself. An example of this is when workers go on strike on the first of May, Labor Day in Japan, for the purpose of obtaining a leave of absence on that day.

This type of demand is at the origin of most nominated strikes. For instance, let us take the case of a union member who does not wish to comply with a transfer order issued by management. He appeals to his union who takes up the case with management, requesting cancellation of the transfer. If the union's request is denied, the union can then order the worker to go on strike. He refuses to work at the new job, justifying his behavior on the grounds of compliance with a union order. This nominated strike is regarded as a legitimate action as long as it is carried out by order of the union.

A difficult legal problem arises concerning wages in cases of nominated strikes. Since it is a strike, the employer theoretically need not pay the worker's wages. But unions often order the worker to stay at his original job and request that he be paid as usual. Since his attendance at the regular working place is not regarded by the employer as fulfilling his work contract, the company usually refuses to pay him regardless of whether he reports in or not. However, if the transfer order were judged to be improper, the employer would be forced to pay him for the time he was out on strike. The following is one such case:

> In the Kyoto plant of the Sekisui Chemical Company, as a result of a labor surplus created by technological changes, management decided to transfer four employees to another plant. While two of them went willingly, the other two employees asked to negotiate individually. They talked to their superiors but could not reach an agreement. Subsequently, they received a written order for transfer on June 18. They protested and refused to accept the order.
>
> The plant manager urged them to comply with the order, warning them that they would be dismissed if they did not. They received six such warnings between June 18 and June 21. Meanwhile the union and the plant manager negotiated on this matter but without success. The union declared that the two employees would go on a nominated strike on June 26 and thereafter they continued their refusal to be transferred.[15]

The Labor Relations Commission held that the company's intention in transferring the two employees had been to remove from the plant two influential union militants. Thus the employer was ordered to cancel the transfer and to pay back-wages to the workers. The Commission's remarks on this case are noteworthy:

> Given that the transfer of the two employees constitutes unfair labor practices, their rightful place of work is in the Kyoto

166

plant, even though the company refuses to accept their working there. Since, under these circumstances, they were unable to work, the nominated strike carried out was not, in the Commission's estimation, a strike in substance. Therefore, the employer should pay their wages for this period.[16]

It is not very clear for what reason the Commission judged that the nominated strike was not a strike in substance. Perhaps the transfer order was improper and therefore the two employees had the right to work at the Kyoto plant. Since the company refused the employees' legitimate offer to work, they had to pay the wages regardless of whether or not the nominated action was formally called a strike. In this case, it was a strike although it did not affect their wages because the transfer was illegal.

If a transfer is legal, a refusal to be transferred is improper and a worker cannot expect to get wages for the time he has spent away from his work to protest the transfer. Even if his action is designated as a strike, the result is the same since one does not receive wages during a strike. On the other hand, if a company dismisses an employee who has refused to work at the place to which he has been ordered in accordance with a union-ordered strike, the legal repercussions of the dismissal depend on whether or not the action is considered a strike, since it is an unfair labor practice to dismiss an employee because of union activities. In the above case, the union ordered a nominated strike to protect the two employees from dismissal, which would have resulted as the penalty for disobeying the transfer order. In fact, when the company ordered the transfer of another employee some time later, he too went on a nominated strike and was subsequently suspended for three days as a disciplinary measure.

Since a nominated strike is regarded as an act of dispute, it is protected by the constitutional guarantee of the worker's right to act collectively. An employer is not permitted to penalize workers for such acts even if the order of transfer is proper because the legality of an act of dispute is always recognized. It makes no difference whether the union demands pertain to something to which they are legally entitled, as in unfair labor practice cases, or whether the union fights for a raise in wages, which is not guaranteed to them by law. For instance, should an employee be dismissed for carrying out a nominated strike and refusing to work at the place of transfer, it is very doubtful that the court would recognize the legality of such a dismissal. Such actions, even though they are rarely found to be a strike in substance, are nevertheless often performed with the worker and the union claiming that they are indeed on strike. Only under this guise can the worker expect to avoid being penalized. It is a deeply embedded tendency of the Japanese union movement to rely, perhaps unconsciously, on legal arguments as compensation for the organizational weakness of unions.

Many union members come as spectators to Labor Relations Commission and court hearings which are held during working hours. Article 7 of the Labor Standards Law acknowledges the employee's right to exercise his franchise and other civil rights and to perform his public duty during working hours. If many employees attend the hearings, the work schedule of the company is necessarily disrupted. Even if this were not the case, it is not pleasant for management to see the entire courtroom packed with union members. Companies try to prevent their employees from attending the hearings by denying that it is a public duty and refusing to grant them leave of absence. On the other hand, employees are unwilling to have these absences taken from their vacation time or entered into their records as "leaving early without permission or just cause." Therefore, the unions declare that the members who are attending the hearings are out on a nominated strike. In this case the objective of the nominated strike has little to do with attempts to pressure a company into granting specific demands.

In one case I examined as public commissioner of the Tokyo Labor Relations Commission, only two union members participated in all the sessions. One was the president of the union who had been dismissed by the company. The other member had not been dismissed, but did not appear to be working either. Upon being questioned, he answered that he was on strike for an indefinite period. Taking into consideration the fact that the whole procedure took more than one year, it is surprising that he was continuing a nominated strike for such a long time.

7. UNUSUAL FORMS OF STRIKES

Unions declare partial strikes for other reasons than their belief that they are a less costly substitute for full-scale strikes. In the following case, the union was opposed to the introduction of certain new tasks and ordered its members to refuse to perform them.

Early in August 1968 the board of directors of the Nishi Nihon Newspaper Company contracted to do the printing and distribution of a political party newspaper. The company planned to introduce this new business in September and asked the union to cooperate. On August 22, during the course of negotiations, the union declared it was opposed to the project because speeding up the pace of work would have an adverse effect on the health of union members. The union also objected to the main newspaper abandoning its image of political neutrality and feared that this departure would have negative effect on public opinion.

The printing of the political paper was set to start on August 31. Since the union persisted in its opposition, the company hired temporary workers and ordered some of the regular employees to work one hour overtime. On the same day, the union voted 87 to 35, with one abstention, in favor of a strike action to protest the introduction of the new business. The printing of the political paper had no sooner started then union officers went through the plant and ordered the union members assigned to this job to refuse to work. The next morning, the union ordered all its members not to work on the political organ and to work only on their usual tasks for the main newspaper. The partial strike was carried out until October 15.

In September, the company notified the union that some of

its members were engaged in an illegal act of dispute by declining to work on the new task and refusing to work overtime. Management warned that if they continued this illegal activity, appropriate steps would be taken against them. Even after this warning, the union refused to comply. Next, the company suspended four union officials, including the president, for periods of one to three months.

The Labor Relations Commission held that the suspension of the union officers was, in fact, a punishment for union activities "recognized by law," and therefore unfair. The Commission also ruled that the company's actions were "careless and inappropriate," citing the unilateral introduction of the new printing contract over the union protest, the lack of adequate planning for avoiding work speedup, as well as the harsh attitude toward the union. Nevertheless, the Commission acknowledged that the company's behavior was partly due to the union's demand that the new printing contract simply be rescinded and to the stubborn refusal even to negotiate possible changes in working conditions.

In spite of these strictures on the union's attitude, the Commission found that the union's refusal to work was a lawful act of dispute because it had been a concerted action.[17] If, on the other hand, the Commission had found that the union's actions were "careless and inappropriate," it would have upheld the company's disciplinary measures. Courts and commissions usually regard punishment of union activities by companies as an unfair labor practice, if the act of dispute which led to the punishment was lawful and the union demands are not extremely unreasonable. The partial strike described above was not a strike per se since the objective was to put pressure on the company by an action which the union actually forced the realization of its own demand, i.e., putting an end to the printing of the political newspaper. Even such an act is usually deemed proper as long as it is carried out by union order. Another feature of this case is that the dispute concerned an attempt by the company to expand its business. If unions are permitted to wage disputes in cases like these, with no interference whatsoever, they will have the power to stop all changes in business policy and to interfere effectively in company planning. This type of dispute will be examined in the following section.

8. UNION TAKE-OVERS

The so-called *seisan kanri* (union take-over) is an act of dispute in which unions expel management, assume the administration of an enterprise, and control production themselves. This tactic was first used in 1945 in the Yomiuri Newspaper dispute. It spread rapidly to a number of disputes until the fall of 1946 and thereafter declined, gradually disappearing after 1950. During the years which followed World War II, strikes were not effective because most companies were not so anxious to produce in a chaotic economy. Around that time the Sanbetsu (Congress of Industrial Unions), then the most powerful union confederation, made the following statement:

> In times of persistent inflation, capitalists tend to neglect production and to wait until the price of materials and inventory rises rather than to produce goods for sale with the materials on hand. The former is more profitable than the latter. Thus many capitalists bide their time, neglect production or even close their factories.[18]

Under these circumstances, claimed the Sanbetsu, union take-over was "an inevitable act of dispute." At the same time the Sanbetsu was well aware that, in order to carry out this kind of act of dispute, unions would have to obtain materials and funds by themselves as well as sell the products. Only in the confused economy of the postwar period was this type of industrial action possible, and the Sanbetsu anticipated that these conditions would not persist for long.

Although the union take-over tactic fell into disuse after 1950, it is a topic of study which is relevant to contemporary labor relations. This is due to the fact that it has characteristics in com-

171

mon with several other kinds of acts of dispute which remain popular today. First union take-over was resorted to at a time when strikes were ineffective and was considered the most effective and appropriate means of protecting the workers' interests. As described above, one of the reasons why many Japanese strikes are ineffective is that unions do not have the power to carry them out successfully. Thus workers often have to exert their imagination to the limit and invent new types of acts of dispute. Second, take-over could not be undertaken by craft unions, which are usually unable to control an entire production system. Only enterprise unions, which organize blue- and white-collar workers alike, and the workers in a particular enterprise would able to carry out such tactics. In this sense, union take-over fits the Japanese labor situation very well. Third, the act of taking over, by its very nature, is such that it enables workers to achieve their demands, that is, to protect their livelihood by running the business themselves against the employer's will. This also is the case of some of the acts of dispute described above. Fourth, union take-over inevitably results in the occupation of a plant and conflicts with management's authority. Regarding this conflict with management rights, the Supreme Court ruled that "acts of dispute which shake the basis of property rights are not allowed."[19] Nevertheless, many acts of dispute which are commonly carried out in Japan today infringe more or less on management rights.

The refusal to take telephone calls or go out for business, keeping silent, wearing ribbons, headbands or armbands and work-to-rule tactics are kinds of partial union take-overs in the sense that union members do work, but only in the ways prescribed by the union. This is also the case in nominated strikes, partial strikes and the refusal to work overtime. The *nōkin-suto* (see following page), seizure of car keys and vehicle registration papers, removal of tires from cars in the taxi industry and the like also exemplify partial union take-over in the sense that unions control the property and the means of production of the company. While the strike is a passive yet effective action and union take-over is an active, positive and impressive tactic, the types of disputes which stand halfway between the strike proper and total union take-over appear to be timid half-measures. On the other hand, they testify to the creative imagination of the workers.

9. NŌKIN-SUTO

Nōkin-suto is an act of dispute which was invented by the *Densan* (Electrical Workers' Unions of Japan) after cutting the supply of electricity during a strike was prohibited by law in 1953.[20] The word itself means an act of dispute whereby a union orders its members to hold on to the fees they are collecting on behalf of a utility company.[21] Union officials who start a *nōkin-suto* are usually charged with embezzlement. In one of these cases, the Supreme Court ruled that since the union officials had deposited the money in a bank in the name of the union president and since their intention was to keep it only for the duration of the strike, they were not guilty of embezzling the company's money.[22] *Nōkin-suto* has been regarded as a short-lived phenomenon since, in most instances, this tactic was used immediately after the promulgation of the Strike Regulation Law of 1953. However, in 1966, public attention was called to this type of act of dispute when a union in the taxi industry resorted to it. The following is an excerpt from the court's judgment on the case:

> As an act of dispute, *nōkin-suto* is carried out as a pressure tactic to win certain demands made by the union. It is not only a refusal to perform a specific work, i.e., to pass on the money collected by the union members; it also involves the seizure of money resulting in financial damage to the business and is intended to bring economic and psychological pressure on the employer in order to gain an advantage in negotiations.

Thus according to the court:

> Such actions can hardly be considered as being within the scope of the lawful concerted actions of unions which are

protected by law as a means of maintaining the balance of power between labor and management in negotiations. This law restricts the employer's actions to a certain degree so that a balance is maintained between the possible losses or sacrifices of employer's interests and union's gains brought about by acts of disputes.[23]

The court concluded by expressing strong doubts as to the legality of *nōkin-suto* because it keeps money indefinitely until a dispute is settled; its reasoning was based on the fact that this tactic goes beyond a mere refusal to supply labor. While union take-over "shakes the basis of property rights," *nōkin-suto*, at least partially, threatens these rights.

Besides *nōkin-suto*, unions in the taxi industry often turn to such actions as taking away car keys, registration papers and tires during a strike. The purpose of these measures is to keep the employer from running the business during a strike by employing temporary labor to drive the cars. Enterprise unions in the taxi industry are driven to take such actions because only a minority of taxi drivers are union members. Even when this is not the case, it is generally easy for the employers to find part-time drivers. In the following case, the Labor Relations Commission ruled that this type of action as well was illegal.

Although the fundamental legal rights of labor should be respected, property rights as well should not be neglected. Therefore, protection of the rights of labor is sanctioned only to the extent that it does not infringe upon the rights of property. There is no reason why an employer should be defenseless when a union seizes registration papers and keys or takes away tires owned by the company.[24]

The Commission seems to have adopted the view that in Japan an act of dispute consists of an action which disturbs the normal course of business and aims at causing economic damage to the employer. It ensues from this view that acts of dispute include not only the passive refusal to work, such as strikes, but also positive actions. An action taken by a union is illegal if it clearly contradicts the principle of fair play, rather than because it is aggressive. Japanese unions often resort to malicious or mischievous actions which, even though they do not exactly interfere with the property rights of employers, can hardly be regarded as fair. These tactics will be examined in the next section.

10. MALICIOUS OR MISCHIEVOUS ACTS

On August 2, 1958, in a department store called Iwataya located in Fukuoka City, a union went on strike for a summer bonus. The union picketed the store entrances and appealed to the customers not to enter.

Seeing the union members surrounding the store, most of the customers left. Union members and their supporters blocked the way of the few who tried to get in, saying: "We are on strike today! Come back tomorrow!" and "Goods at Iwataya are expensive!" or "Goods are rotten today!" Now and then they challenged customers who tried to enter, asking, "Tell us why you want to enter?" and started arguments with them, which made the customers angry.

When customers still tried to enter, the picketers repeatedly approached them, demanding, "Don't enter because we are on strike," "Please do your shopping at other stores"; or "Do not buy here, buy at other stores." Shouting, the picketers gathered round the entrance, pushing from both sides and blocking the passage.

One union member tapped a woman on the shoulder as she came to the door and said: "What are you fooling around here for?" Another pulled the belt of an elderly man from behind while others grabbed the parasols and clothing of women customers and bodily tried to prevent their entrance.[25]

In the case of the Hichijūhichi Bank dispute which took place in 1961, the struggle was politically motivated. The union wished

175

to keep the government from introducing a bill in the Diet that would regulate the use of violence as a political weapon.

On the October 26, upon the orders of union executives, the members started to wear yellow ribbons pinned on their chests during working hours. The ribbons were 2 cm. wide and 10 cm. long (approximately 1 inch by 4 inches) with the words "Wreck the Bill" written on them. Some employees stopped wearing these ribbons in November, but others continued until some time in December. The union also pasted about 130 posters on utility poles and walls located next to one of the branch offices of the bank. On the posters were the following statements: "The Hichijūhichi Bank makes big enterprises get bigger and small enterprises go bankrupt"; "The Hichijūhichi Bank does not lend money to those who need it"; "Attack Hichijūhichi, enemy of small enterprises and enemy of the workers"; "Frenzied Management! Resign at once!" "Management of Hichijūhichi almost killed a pregnant woman"; "Vice-president of Hichijūhichi is a bloodsucker! The people demand that he be fired"; "The management of Hichijūhichi is stopping at nothing to destroy the union, even almost committing homicide"; "Beasts, mad, inhuman, cruel. . . We protest the dismissal!"; and "Don't deposit money at Hichijūhichi with its wicked management."[26]

The union's activities in these two cases were far from fair. The wearing of ribbons, in particular, can give the customers unpleasant feelings and is especially detrimental in service industries like hotels, restaurants and banks where an employee's attitude and appearance contribute significantly to the customer's impression of the entire business.

Work-to-rule also amounts to mischief making when it is carried to extremes. On September 10, 1972, the press reported that the National Railways Union would start a "fixed number struggle."[27] The union claimed that the railway company violated a provision of a law passed in 1900 which stated that the company was not

176

allowed to run cars carrying more passengers than there were seats. The newspaper reported that the union had decided to start an "intensive work-to-rule struggle," and use various kinds of "guerrilla tactics" from September 14 onwards. The union appealed to all of its members to participate in this action and circulated a booklet entitled "How to work-to-rule."

Among the tactics to be used were the following: (1) "the tactic to issue certificates for lateness": the National Railway issues certificates to passengers when the trains are delayed as an excuse for being late at their offices and the union intended to cause confusion at stations during rush hours by encouraging many passengers to ask for this certificate; (2) "a movement to accept ordinary commuter tickets on express trains"; (3) "a movement to search for lost articles in cars full of passengers during rush hours": in order to search the baggage rack of each car carefully, the conductor would have to ask the standing passengers to get off until the search was over; (4) the ticket takers were to punch tickets only after examining them meticulously for the date, destination and so forth; and (5) union members working at ticket windows were to speak very slowly but in a loud voice when telling the passengers how much they were to pay and how much change they would receive.

Also reported in the article were the railway authority's comments on the proposed tactics, namely, that all of them were of a malicious and mischievous nature. There is no doubt that most work-to-rule tactics are mischievous in character. The reason is that in such a situation both parties in the dispute disregard the gap between the written rules and day-to-day reality. Let us take for example the "fixed number struggle," based on the obsolete but never repealed 1900 Railway Business Law. Article 15, Section 2 of this law states that: "Passengers with tickets may ride the train only when there is a seat for them." Article 26 of the same law states that: "Employees who allow passengers to ride the train beyond its capacity will be punished." In view of the traffic jams that plague the big cities today, nobody expects that all passengers will be able to sit comfortably during rush hours. The law has become a joke in the crowded cities of Japan where every morning "pushers," employees specifically hired for that purpose, with all their strength literally push passengers into cars already jam-packed with people.

Work-to-rule was originally resorted to by public sector unions who claimed that their members were not engaged in an act of dispute since they were merely observing regulations to the letter. However, there is no doubt that work-to-rule is an act of dispute in that it disturbs the usual course of business. In the case of the railways, it is not quite certain whether the usual is normal or abnormal. In any case, the National Railways authorities bears a share of the responsibility for the chaos which resulted from the union's mischievous tactics. At the root of the new strategy was the union's indignation over the "mammoth punishment" of 3,800 union members by the railway company scheduled for September 14. The punishment package included warnings and dismissals of workers who were involved in illegal activities during a dispute the previous year.

The International Labor Office's Dreyer Commission pointed out "excessive legalism" as one of the most important causes for the troubles prevailing in industrial relations in the Japanese public sector.[28] However, when it comes to intensive work-to-rule on the part of the union or mammoth punishment on the part of the employer, these actions are too malicious to be the result of legalism, whether or not it is pushed to the extreme.

NOTES
1. Kito et al. v. Japan, Supreme Court, III Petty Bench, June 10, 1966, 20 SSKH 274. Also see chapter 6.
2. Tanrō suffered greatly in terms of membership as a result of the decline of the coal mining industry and now has only some 18,000 members, see *Directory of Major Trade Unions in Japan*, 1977 (Tokyo: Japan Institute of Labor, 1977).
3. Taishirō Shirai, *Rōdō Kumiai no Zaisei* [Trade Unions' Finances], pp. 26, 63 and 67.
4. Ibid., p. 256.
5. The only similar kind of industrial action found in the West might be the "sick-out," a form of secret or disguised strike, sometimes practiced by em-

ployees who are prohibited by law from taking such industrial action. See Benjamin Aaron, "Methods of Industrial Action," p. 94.

6. For example, see Ichikawa v. Dai Nihon Bōseki Co., Osaka District Court, June 8, 1962, 13 RKMS 707.

7. See Hasegawa et al. v. Japan, Tokyo District Court, April 18, 1962, 304 *Hanrei Jihō* 4 [Case Journal], September 29, 1966, 17 RKMS 1240, and several other decisions concerned with vacationing for strike purposes. The majority of these cases concern disputes in the public sector.

8. Ono et al. v. Japan, March 2, 1973, 27 SSMH 210; Asano et al. v. National Railways Corporation, March 2, 1973, 27 SSMH 191.

9. Nagoya Shōken Torihiki Jo Case, Aichi Labor Relations Commission, June 28, 1965, 32–33 FRKM 271.

10. Concerning the different ways in which British and Japanese employees spend their vacations, see Dore, *British Factory—Japanese Factory*, pp. 187–88.

11. Kashiyama Kōgyō Case, Nagano Labor Relations Commission, March 25, 1965, 32–33 FRKM 198.

12. The reader will find a vivid description of such practices in Dore, *British Factory—Japanese Factory*, p. 25.

13. Kintetsu Daiichi Truck Co. Case, Shizuoka Labor Relations Commission, January 14, 1970, 42 FRKM 89.

14. Kaoru Ōta, *Gendai no Rōdō-undō* [Modern Labor Movement] (Tokyo: Rōdō Hōritsu Junpōsha, 1970), p. 35.

15. Sekisui Kagaku Kōgyō Co. Case, Kyoto Labor Relations Commission, January 12, 1970, 42 FRKM 27.

16. Ibid., pp. 54–55.

17. Nishi Nihon Newspaper Co. Case, Fukuoka Labor Relations Commission, February 13, 1970, 42 FRKM 49.

18. Eizaburō Morinaga, "Seisan-kanri" [Production Control], in *Shin Rōdō-hō Kōza* [New Lectures in Labor Law], ed. Japan Labor Law Association, 8 vols. (Tokyo: Yūhikaku, 1967), 4: 172.

19. Odaka v. Japan, Supreme Court, Grand Bench, November 15, 1950, 4 SSKH 2261.

20. The Strike Regulation Law (Law Concerning the Regulation of the Method of Acts of Dispute in the Electric Business and the Coal Mining Industry) was introduced in 1953 when unions in the electric and coal mining industry repeated a series of strikes which seriously threatened the nation's economic stability.

21. *Nōkin* means the handing over of money and *suto* is an abbreviation of strike.

22. Kamata et al. v. Japan, Supreme Court, Second Petty Bench, September 19, 1958, 12 SSKH 3047.

23. Universal Taxi v. Kurisu et al., Osaka High Court, February 10, 1972, 812 *Rōdō Hōritsu Junpō* 6 (1972).

24. Tomin Kōtsu Co. Case, Tokyo Metropolitan Labor Relations Commission, January 5, 1971, 44 FRKM 461.

25. Mieno et al. v. Iwataya Department Store, Fukuoka District Court, May 19, 1961, 12 RKMS 347.

26. Yoshida et al. v. Hichijūhichi Bank, Sendai District Court, May 29, 1970, 21 RKMS 689.

27. Asahi Shinbun [Asahi Newspaper], 10 September 1972 (morning edition).

28. International Labor Office, *Official Bulletin* (Dreyer Report), p. 496.

9

VIOLENCE
IN INDUSTRIAL RELATIONS

1. SIT-INS AND VIOLENCE

a. Legal Ambiguities: We have seen that the term "act of dispute" is frequently used in Japan. Article 7 of the 1946 Labor Relations Adjustment Law defines it as follows:

> In this law, act of dispute shall mean strikes, slow-downs, lockouts and other acts and counteracts impeding the normal course of work of an enterprise, performed by the parties involved in labor relations with the object of attaining their objective.

The purpose of this definition is to clarify the meaning of the term "act of dispute" in the context of the dispute settlement procedure. This is because the settlement process starts only after actions hampering the normal course of business have already taken place or are about to take place (Articles 6 and 12 and other provisions of the Labor Relations Adjustment Law).

According to the above definition, acts of dispute are not limited to strikes and slow-downs but also include any action taken by the union which upsets the normal operation of business. However, defining an act of dispute for the purpose of dispute settlement is one thing and deciding on its legality is quite another. Theoretically the question of legality and propriety is dealt with in the

Trade Union Law of 1949. Article 8 therein specifies that:

> No employer shall claim indemnity from a trade union or members of the same for damages received through a strike or other acts of dispute which are proper acts.

This provision implies that not only strikes but also other acts of dispute are considered proper. Article 1, Section 2, of this law also declares that "appropriate collective bargaining and other acts of a trade union" are deemed to be covered by Article 35 of the Penal Code which states, in part, that no person shall be penalized for acts done "in accordance with . . . an appropriate business function." However, the law does not provide any standard for judging the appropriateness of "other acts" except for the provision in Article 1, Section 2, that ". . . in no case shall the use of violence be construed as an appropriate act of a labor union."

Decisions handed down by the Supreme Court tend to regard only the collective refusal to work as a proper act of dispute, and to exclude aggressive actions from the scope of "appropriate acts."[1] This tendency of the Court gave rise to much criticism because the interpretation stigmatizes any act besides the strike and slowdown and contradicts the provision quoted above. The opinion of the Supreme Court notwithstanding, the fact that the Trade Union Law acknowledges the propriety of "other acts" has contributed to the erroneous conviction, frequently held by union activists, that any action taken as an act of dispute is legal. The lack of a clear standard for judging the appropriateness of acts of dispute greatly facilitates the spread of a variety of kinds of dispute in Japanese industrial relations.

Some labor lawyers go further and intentionally try to extend the concept of proper acts beyond its usual limits. In one case a union invited the legal advisers of the Sōhyō to give lectures to its members on the legal limitations on picketing and other activities in preparation for a strike. During the strike the lawyers stayed at the union offices along with the top union leaders, directing the strike and giving advice to the union. The employer went to court and the union and its officers were found guilty of illegal activities and had to pay over 1,000,000 yen in compensation to the employers.[2] In this case the on-the-spot legal advice was of little avail since the union was made to pay for the carelessness of its advisers.

In general, Japanese unions and employers are overly concerned with the letter of the law. It is of course advisable for a union to consult with lawyers about the limitations on acts of dispute so as to avoid illegal acts and unnecessary suits. However, there are times when a union is put in a position where it has no recourse but to act illegally. Given that those who suffer imprisonment, dismissal or fines in such cases most likely will be the unions and their members, the decision to take illegal steps must be made very responsibly and the union members must have resolution enough to carry their plans through. In the same manner, lawyers should observe the limits of their function as legal advisers and warn the unions about possible adverse rulings if there is any doubt about the legality of their acts. Lawyers should also explain the countermeasures that might conceivably be taken by an employer or the police so that a union can be aware of the potential repercussions of a given act of dispute.

Even when the leaders are careful, there is always a chance that rank and file union members will behave irresponsibly and that provocation on the employer's side will result in violence. In such instances, Ōta warns:

> When a union gives the police an excuse for intervention and members are arrested or dismissed because of excessive actions, people forget the original cause of the dispute and the dispute itself often takes an unexpected turn. For example, in the case of the Nissan Company strike, union members entered the plant and occupied it. While this might have been exciting for the militant members, it was but a momentary pleasure. It is extremely doubtful that this move was effective in terms of gaining the union's objective. On the contrary, it gave the company an excuse to dismiss the union leaders. In short, the main objective of a strike is to win the dispute by way of leaving the workshop and stopping production. Concentrating mainly on

this goal, unions should carefully avoid illegal actions and should never indulge in superficial militancy.[3]

It is interesting to note that Ōta's concept of industrial action closely resembles that of the Supreme Court. However, in spite of his warnings against momentarily gratifying but superficially militant actions, these types of actions are a daily occurrence in Japanese industrial relations.

b. The Workplace during a Strike: We have seen that the Japanese strike is not simply a walk-out. Union members show up at the workplace in order to picket, sit-down or carry other activities like holding meetings or putting up posters. Particularly in small and medium-size companies, unions often occupy the company facilities for an extended period. One case concerning a prolonged sit-in involved a small publishing company. When the workers organized a shop union, numbering fifteen employees in all, the president of the company announced his intention to shut down the business as a result of the establishment of the union. He asked for the voluntary retirement of the union members and when they refused he fired them.

> Those who did not simply accept their dismissal went to the office and found the main entrance locked and a sign on the door saying, "Closed for the time being." Then they discovered the shop had been completely cleared out the day before. Several non-union employees were staying at the company president's residence next door and the president and his family were nowhere to be found. So the union members sat-in at the office, demanding that their dismissal be rescinded and the business reopened.[4]

In this case the Labor Relations Commission ruled that the dismissal of the union members was unfair and ordered their reinstatement on the condition that the union end the occupation of the office. As can be gathered from the Commission's report, the occupation had continued for more than one year.

In another well-known case, a union occupied the warehouse

184

and retail store of a company for more than five months until the strikers were arrested by the police. Here, too, the day after the union had been established, the members ". . . went to the office and found that all the doors were locked and that there were signs on them saying that the company had closed."[5] At this juncture they decided to stage a sit-in. The incident was reported in the press as an example of "violent bargaining" in which the "anti-Yoyogi Sect," a radical violence-prone group which is strongly against the Japanese Communist Party,[6] was involved. The arrested union leaders were found guilty of trespassing. Although the union acted recklessly, the employer appears to have behaved strangely as well. While engaged in bargaining with the union, the company president suddenly started performing a traditional Japanese dance. Later on, he poured gasoline and paint thinner on his own building, then occupied by union members, in an attempt to set it on fire.

In most of these cases, according to the findings of the commissions involved, the companies closed their businesses and dismissed the union members with the intention of destroying the union organization. Under such provocation the union's occupation of company offices amounted to self-defense. A strike, i.e., a mere stoppage, would have been a completely ineffective act of dispute in such a situation. Given these circumstances, the labor relations commissions have sometimes ordered the reinstatement of employees, even though they had been found guilty of illegal actions in criminal court.

Even in the case of large companies it is not uncommon for striking workers to occupy company facilities. The following case is a dispute which took place during the Spring Offensive in 1965 in the Chūbu Nihon Newspaper Company (Chūnichi), employing nearly 4,000 people.

It was 9:50 A.M. on May 19 when the union ordered its members to start striking from 10:00 A.M. onward. At the appointed time about twenty members in the second floor printing section surrounded two matrix rolling machines.

185

Then about one hundred members gathered around the two machines, at the same time blocking access to a full-page galley-proof press. Two union leaders explained the union's plan for the dispute to the assembled members, fifty or sixty of whom were singing union songs and shouting "Bargain with us!" and "The company must show its good faith!" The managing staff was unable to get near the machines.

Company officials repeatedly requested the union members to allow them to have access to the machines, but they refused to move. Work on the presses, scheduled to start at 11:00 A.M., could not go ahead because of obstruction by the union. Around 11:30 several foremen tried to close the door of the plant to keep the union members who were still outside from entering. The foremen were pushed back and both sides suffered injuries in the ensuing tussle.

Around 1:30 P.M. management gave written notice to the union to vacate the plant, but the union stood its ground. An hour later about 100 managerial people managed to push back some 200 union members who were surrounding the printing presses. Then they brought up a type-form on a cart and, after more pushing and shoving, succeeded in setting a lock-up on the press. After making some proof sheets, they withdrew. The jostling, however, resulted in injuries on both sides.

It was then approximately 3:00 P.M. The company reported the situation to the police who shortly thereafter arrived on the scene. The union members abandoned their position around the printing and proof presses and sat down along the inside walls of the plant. Management then operated the machines and finished work on the following day's morning edition amid hisses and boos from the surrounding union members.

About 6:00 A.M. of the next morning the company gave notice of a lock-out starting at 7:00 A.M. Right after this announcement the foremen and salespeople started to remove the striking union members, a procedure which caused still more injuries.

Later in the morning about 150 to 200 policemen entered

the printing section and by noon all the union members had been dispersed. Two union members were arrested on charges of trespassing, but both were released the next day and were cleared of all charges the following year.

The union continued the strike after the initial confrontation but the company managed to publish the paper with the assistance of non-union employees. At the suggestion of the Central Labor Relations Commission the company and the union started negotiations on May 28 and an agreement was reached on June 1, thirteen days after the start of the strike. As a consequence of this dispute, the union lost about 100 of its 600 members.[7]

In this case the union occupied the plant and, despite some casualties, did not leave until the police were brought in. The rationale for their action was simply that the printing work would be carried out by non-union employees and that there was no other way to effect a work stoppage. At that time there were two other unions in the company: a 200-member dissident offshoot of the larger union and a splinter group with about 40 members. In circumstances like these, when a union is breaking apart internally, a large number of workers refuse to go on strike. As a result, mass picketing and a sit-down strike within the plant are inevitable if the strike is to be effective. Six years later, when the commission finally handed down its decision concerning the status of the workers who had been dismissed as a result of the May 19 strike, the union that initiated it had been reduced to a mere 109 members.

The Japanese unions' frequent use of mass picketing and sit-ins is often explained and to some extent justified by the fact that it is easy for the company to recruit non-union labor since most unions are organized on an enterprise basis. According to some scholars, the existence of a relatively large number of unemployed workers in the society is a factor in the frequency of these tactics, although I do not believe this to be the case—at least in the recent past. It is also evident that the general public in Japan does not understand the meaning of a strike and that public opinion is frequently hostile toward unions that strike. In general, Japanese society does not look on strikebreaking as wrong.

The following well-known American anecdote could never happen in Japan. Upon being arrested and interrogated, a thief confesses to one charge after the other, but stubbornly denies the accusation that he is guilty of strikebreaking. He admits that he is indeed degenerate but not so wicked as to behave that shamelessly. It is true that Japanese are not as outraged by strikebreaking as Americans are, but nevertheless it is not an easy matter to recruit strikebreakers from outside an enterprise. First of all, outsiders are not usually prepared to perform routine tasks immediately. Furthermore, the supply of labor is not that abundant since, in recent years, the unemployment rate in Japan has never been as high as that of Western societies.[8]

In most cases where mass picketing or sit-ins cause trouble, a breakaway union forms if the union is not strong enough to control its members. In these circumstances, management is able to carry on business with the non-union labor force inside the company. Cases like those mentioned earlier, where management tried to ignore union demands and smash the union organization are exceptional and might even be considered vestiges of the past. However, even in large modernized companies, the use of force during a strike is becoming more frequent because simple strikes are becoming ineffective as disputes. Technological developments, which have decreased the number of workers on the production line, make replacement by non-union employees easier.

When union organizations are severely split or under great pressure from management, strikes cannot be effective without a sit-in or the occupation of the plant. But even if unions control an overwhelming majority of the employees and there is no breakaway union, they still tend to resort to sit-ins simply because their organization is enterprise based. An enterprise union's activities are limited to the confines of the company facilities, a situation underlined by the fact that union offices are always located in the company building. A union's activities would be severely hampered if it was prevented from using company facilities during a strike. When the group is enterprise based, abandoning the work place is equivalent to giving up the fight. Therefore, acts of dispute must always be carried out within the company facilities, whether or not strikebreakers are recruited and the business continues to operate.

c. Utilization of Gangsters: The general public's misconception of the reasons for strikes, especially its lack of respect for picket lines, is often cited as one of the reasons for mass picketing. During the disputes at the Mitsukoshi and Iwataya department stores, a large number of customers tried to break the picket lines in order to do their shopping.[9] While the former is one of the best stores in Japan, as is the latter in its area, there are numerous other stores close by that could have supplied the customers with daily necessities for the duration of the strike.

During several consecutive past spring offensives, when the unions of private as well as national railways went on strike, it became evident that passengers blamed union members for the inconveniences caused by the strike. In recent years, however, this attitude seems to be changing. During the 1972 Spring Offensive newspapers reported that people said they enjoyed the "sudden holiday" instead of complaining about the resulting hardships. One wonders whether people have begun to understand the meaning of strikes or whether they are becoming used to them and are tired of complaining. Still, one must admire some employees who are so loyal to their companies that they get up several hours earlier during a transportation strike in order to reach their place of work on time. Some persons even walk along the railway lines for miles to reach their companies.

A strike is a time when the loyalty of the company to people not directly connected to the enterprise comes to light. For instance, during the Mitsukoshi strike of 1941, the employees of some of Mitsukoshi subcontractors were sent to replace sales clerks in the retail store. They were remarkably cooperative and actively helped to break the strike. In the same way during the dispute at the Chūnichi Newspaper Company, the management, foremen, distributors and delivery personnel of newsstands worked very hard at removing the strikers from the plant. During a strike, employees of subsidiary companies or companies with trade connections are often as loyal or more loyal than the parent company's own employees. Perhaps, this is because a strike is a serious challenge to the enterprise family. All those connected with the main enterprise form a strong interest group and, when threatened, do not hesitate to act since they know that the repercussions might be more disastrous for them than for the parent company.

Japanese unions encounter another enemy during strikes. In the cases of the Kubo Shoten and the Chūnichi Newspaper Company disputes, the police intervened and sent men on the scene. However, unlike the pattern of the prewar period, the police nowadays are reluctant to get involved in labor disputes; it is no longer so easy for companies to get the police to act according to their wishes. Therefore, some employers hire special guards and sometimes even *bōryokudan* (Japanese-style gangsters, also called *yakuza*). One might be tempted to think that only unscrupulous companies would make use of gangsters to attack union workers. However, the following case, involving a broadcasting company, shows that the use of gangsters has become accepted in labor relations even by well-established concerns.

The broadcasting company had decided to transfer the vice-president and secretary general of the union from the main office of the company. The union demanded to bargain on this matter and then voted for a strike. Posters were distributed and pasted on the walls of the company buildings and union members carrying placards circled around the management offices protesting the company's decision. At this stage the company hired about 40 laborers as strong-arm men and ordered the union members to leave the workplace. Following this action, the company asked someone from one of its affiliates to put pressure on the union members and their families in an effort to destroy the union organization. The following excerpt is from the Labor Relations Commission report which details the company's alleged used of strong-arm tactics.

Two persons, one of whom was an employee of a business concern which had connections with the broadcasting company and the other an employee of the company, decided that they needed someone who had a strong will and enough push to persuade the union members to do whatever they said. Following up on this decision, one of them approached a person who was visiting Fukui City (the company's location) for the purpose of organizing a radical right-wing group there. They met with several others to decide what steps to take to force the retirement of the active union members.

Sometime after this consultation, several persons drove to the house of one of the union men. When the union member answered the knock on his door, one person caught him and held a handkerchief soaked in benzine to his face. They hit him on the head and tried to force him into their car but could not, and so one of them kicked the worker in the chest causing an injury that incapacitated him for ten days.

The two men who had originally approached the gangster did so at the suggestion of the auditor of the broadcasting company. Furthermore, documents intended to be used against the union were found on the company premises.[10]

The Commission ruled that the company's activities involved unfair labor practices. In this case it was the company that resorted to violence, but unions also commit violent acts.

d. Union Violence: The Kongō Seisakujo Company dispute started in March 1965 when the company announced its intention to cut down their manpower by 219 persons. The union disputed the decision and engaged in several acts of dispute including the refusal to work overtime and short-term strikes. Union members pasted posters on the walls and windows all around the plant. On these posters were statements like "Chief X! You shall die if you disturb us!" and "Mr. Y! If you destroy our posters or take pictures of us, we will kill you!" The company protested against such intimidation tactics and asked the union to remove the

191

posters. Meanwhile, partly because of interference by outsiders, including the local branch of the industrial federation, the confrontation between management and the union became more and more serious.

As often happens, the union was racked by internal dissension; one group of members was in favor of the union leaders and the other group against them. Those union members who disagreed with the union executives' policy had, as early as May 14, initiated a signature campaign against them and had collected no less than 207 signatures. After such a large number of members had expressed dissatisfaction with their leaders, the union executives became uneasy. At the same time relations between the company and the union had degenerated following an unsuccessful attempt to negotiate the dispute on May 17 and 19. On May 20 the two groups of union members confronted each other within the company facilities, shouting and jostling each other. This series of setbacks led the union leaders to desperate activities:

The confrontation between the union and the company got progressively more serious when a rumor spread that the union might occupy the plant. The rumor was given credence by the union's preparations to stay overnight at its offices and the prospective stay of the managerial staff at the technical center of the company. Groups supporting the union leaders entered the plant and pushed past the plant guards. These protestors, including quite a few outsiders, gathered around the technical center and created a disturbance from midnight on May 20 to May 24. The commotion was greatest on May 20 when the union learned which section of the plant was scheduled to be cut back and the names of the persons who were to be laid off. They held mass meetings demanding to meet with management and an explanation of the lay-off plans. During all that time, they pounded violently on drums, broke windows and shouted through loudspeakers which were held against the ears of the managerial staff. One of the directors of the company and the chief of personnel suffered ear trauma because of the noise and the latter received blows which left bruises on his back.[11]

Before the end of May 1965 a group of 324 workers had withdrawn from the main union and had started their own organization. Thereafter the parent union got smaller and smaller until it comprised only seventy workers, at which time the dispute was finally settled. In most of the cases where unions resort to violent actions, there exists a situation similar to that seen in the cases involving mass picketing and plant occupation. The common characteristics are that unions do not control a majority of the employees in the enterprise or that secondary unions are involved, putting the strikers in a desperate position. Furthermore, even unions which organize a majority of workers sometimes lose the support of their members and fall into a minority position because of the excessively militant attitudes of the union executives during disputes.

Union membership at the Keitei Gumi Seisakujo Company numbered twenty-seven out of fifty workers. Immediately after it was established, the union initiated a dispute to demand a year-end bonus and lost a few members in the process. In August of the following year, the union, consisting of less than half the number of the original employee membership, conducted a series of short-term strikes. They marched around with placards and held meetings in the plant where non-union employees were hard at work. One morning the union pasted about 400 posters inside the plant, and even on some of the machines. Protesting union members interfered when the president of the company, who happened to be a woman, tried to take these posters off. Several times she found herself surrounded by unionists who demanded that she negotiate with them. One day they followed her into the streets after she refused to negotiate under duress. They also pasted posters on the walls of her house. The company eventually dismissed the president of the union which, ironically enough, had only three members left, whereupon the union declared an "indefinite strike" protesting his dismissal.[12]

In both the cases of the Kongō Seisakujo Company and the Keitei Gumi Seisakujo Company, the Labor Relations Commission ruled in the final analysis that the employers had been guilty of unfair labor practices. In view of this ruling, it appears that the unions lost their members and fell to minority positions mainly because of the company interference. But even if the unions' rash actions were a result of management's attacks, they inevitably made the situation much worse for themselves by falling back on extreme and violent actions.

2. CAMPUS RIOTS AND LABOR DISPUTES

a. Bargaining without Dialogue: The attitude and behavior of students during the campus turmoil a few years ago had several features in common with unions in labor disputes. Students went on "strike" and demanded "collective bargaining." Students forced school presidents, deans and professors to attend their mass meetings and to accept their demands. If the professors did not comply, the meetings continued until they were completely exhausted and finally surrendered. Such "collective bargaining," which is often called "mass bargaining," occurred quite often during the period of disorder right after the Second World War, and now and then still crops up in industrial relations in Japan. Closing classrooms by constructing barricades is similar in nature to mass picketing and sit-down strikes. "Independent" lectures and seminars organized by students also have a strong similarity to union take-overs.

When the closing of a campus continues for a long time, students of anti-strike factions often try to remove the barricades, resulting in collisions with the student groups who insist that the closing should continue. This is almost the same situation one encounters whenever prolonged labor disputes bring about the creation of second unions or when workers try forcibly to cross picket lines, often with tragic consequences. During the campus troubles the university administration often employs guards, fierce dogs and summons mobile police units on the campus, much as the employers make use of *bōryokudan* or call the police to expel workers engaged in a sit-down strike. Even lockouts are frequently resorted to by university authorities in order to keep out troublesome students.

This similarity raises a fundamental problem, namely, whether the element of violence found in industrial relations and in the student movement may not be deeply rooted in the Japanese mentality. Yōnosuke Nagai, a political scientist, has some comments on this point:

> Groups of students stage so-called mass bargaining sessions not unlike mass trials during which they unilaterally criticize university authorities. In this type of bargaining, they take advantage of the anonymity of people in a group, a psychological phenomenon that allows free rein to savage and sadistic impulses which otherwise remain suppressed at the level of the subconscious. Emotional judgments are foisted on others in the form of one-sided, ready-made conclusions, a process which is almost unthinkable in Western society and is very oriental by nature.[13]

However, the use of "physical power" instead of dialogue is regarded as a pathological symptom of immature labor relations, a condition that will eventually be overcome. Indeed, cases of mass bargaining or violence, which used to be quite common during the postwar period, today tend to be thought of as oddities happening only in less-developed areas of labor-management relations like small enterprises or in cases involving anti-Yoyogi organizations. Even in the larger enterprises, however, once the relationship between a union and the employer deteriorates, similar violent incidents occur, as was shown in some of the cases cited above. Thus we have to examine whether or not violent incidents are exceptional and whether they are destined to gradually stop occurring in the future.

b. Physical Power and Maturity: The history of the labor movement shows that violence in labor disputes is far from a rare phenomenon, even in Western countries. Still, violence is hardly considered an intrinsic and essential factor in contemporary industrial relations. This is certainly the case in collective bargaining. The union's bargaining power depends on how many workers are organized in a particular labor market or a particular Japanese enterprise; the extent to which the union can hurt the employer's business when it goes on strike; and on how long the union can support the members who have to do without wages during a walkout. It also depends on whether or not the union can control members during a strike so that they will not break the strike under employer pressure. If a union has a large amount of this type of power and control, it needs to send only a single representative to meet with management, submit the union's demand and communicate the union's readiness to go on strike if not satisfied with management's response. It is not necessary to send large numbers of workers, threaten, shout and upbraid management to finally force management's surrender under duress. The same goes for strikes as well. If unions organize a majority of the workers in an enterprise and their control over them is sufficient to avoid strikebreaking, all they have to do is stop work and they need not even trouble about picketing *en masse*, sitting down or occupying the plant.

Violence in labor disputes is usually caused by weaknesses within the union organization. If the union's bargaining power increases, the phenomenon of "physical power" is destined to disappear. For unions which benefit from a strong organization and solid finances, violence is not only unnecessary but is actually harmful and destructive. The trend among West German unions to avoid striking is a good illustration of this process. Their reluctance to go on strike does not result from a wish to avoid a fight. Instead, they avoid strikes because their experience of more than a hundred years has taught them that striking is to no avail if they are weak and unnecessary if they are strong. From this viewpoint, it is nothing but adventurism for a weak Japanese union to drive its members to an unpromising strike, and to rely on "physical power" to compensate for weakness.

As long as the main purpose of the union movement is to maintain and improve the interests of the workers through bargaining with employers, unions should first of all organize as many workers as possible, and then promote loyalty among members, maintain discipline, improve union finances and increase their strike funds. Unions must avoid plunging into any risky ventures just to parade their militancy. In German industrial relations, as already described, employers are usually willing to make a quick compromise if the result of a strike vote shows a high rate of support among union members. The strike vote has, in fact, taken the place of the strike itself. This fact is a strong indication that the daily efforts expanded to strengthen the union organization are what contribute more to winning disputes than any hard work and heroic exertions during a strike.

This analysis is also valid for the student movement. If the purpose of the student movement is to have certain demands accepted by university authorities, it needs support from as many students as possible and these students must be willing to fight till the end. If the majority of students go on strike for a long time and, as a result, the university stops functioning, the university authorities cannot afford to neglect their demands. Student strikes, of course, do not generate as much pressure as those involving workers. But if students go on strike in order to have certain demands accepted, it is unreasonable for them to ignore the wishes of anti-strike students as well as of those (often a majority) who are simply not interested in the student movement. Neither is it wise on the part of striking students to prevent students from attending lectures and to deny them access to the campus by constructing barricades and using "Gewalt-clubs." Furthermore, shouting insults, threats of violence and confining professors for a long time until they are overcome by mental exhaustion contradict the very nature of bargaining or negotiation.

However, "mass bargaining" in the context of the student movement has a different purpose than collective bargaining has in industrial relations. Students seem to be not so much interested in getting their demands fulfilled as in causing trouble in order to keep their movement going. If this is so, their behavior makes sense. But why do Japanese trade unionists behave like students?

As already mentioned above, when one looks at the history of the union movement in Western countries, one finds a steady decline in the use of "physical power" in bargaining as the unions grow in maturity. In Japanese industrial relations too, the reliance on "physical power" has declined gradually. If, indeed, violence is only the result of weaknesses in union organization, it will eventually disappear with the development and expansion of union organization. Another reason for union violence is also pointed out, namely, the employers' hostility toward unions. This attitude is not restricted to Japan. However, it is evident that employers can afford to be hostile only when the unions are weak and that employers start to accept unions only after union organization becomes strong.

When we state that the organizational weakness of Japanese unions is the fundamental reason for their unreasonable behavior, we must keep in mind that this weakness resides in their inability to bargain collectively in the Western sense of the term. Perhaps the real problem is that Japanese unions are not only incapable of bargaining but, like the student movement, they are not very interested in bargaining itself. Radical organizations, including unions and student groups, often do not really intend to bargain and settle disputes. Rather, they wish to carry on a dispute for the dispute's own sake to continue fighting to keep their organization alive. In the case of cultural disputes, as opposed to economic disputes ("issue conflicts" to use Boulding's terminology),[14] both parties exhibit this tendency. In such cases, the rational way to reach a settlement based on the calculation of economic gains and losses does not work. Therefore, it becomes imperative at this point to see how the dispute settlement machinery is working in Japanese industrial relations.

NOTES

1. For example, see Odaka v. Japan, Supreme Court, Grand Bench, November 15, 1950, 4 SSKH 2257.

2. Misuzu Tōfu v. Misuzu Tōfu Union, Nagoya District Court, March 28, 1967, 18 RKMS 237.

3. Kaoru Ōta, *Rōdō Kumiai-ron*, p. 69.

4. Kubo Shoten Case, Tokyo Metropolitan Labor Relations Commission, July 28, 1970, 43 FRKM 126.

5. Tokyo Shoin Case, Tokyo Metropolitan Labor Relations Commission, December 10, 1968, 39 FRKM 126.

6. Yoyogi is the name of the place where the headquarters of the Japanese Communist Party is located.

7. Tokyo Chūbu Nihon Newspaper Co. Case, Tokyo Metropolitan Labor Relations Commission, February 16, 1971, 44 FRKM 100.

8. After 1960, when the Japanese economy had fully recovered from the Second World War, until 1975, the annual unemployment rate never went above 1.5%. After 1975, because of the recession caused by the oil crisis, it went up to 2%. See Bureau of Statistics, Office of the Prime Minister, *Rōdō Ryoku Chōsa* [Labor Force Survey], 1961–77.

9. See Part II, chapter 8, section 10.

10. Fukui Hōsō Company Case, Fukui Labor Relations Commission, March 5, 1971, 44 FRKM 607.

11. Kongō Seisakujo Company Case, Central Labor Relations Commission, July 1, 1970, 43 FRKM 607.

12. Keitei Gumi Seisakujo Case, Tokyo Metropolitan Labor Relations Commission, December 1, 1970, 43 FRKM 430.

13. Yōnosuke Nagai, *Jūkōzō Shakai to Bōryoku* [Soft-Structured Society and Violence] (Tokyo: Chūōkōronsha, 1971), p. 77.

14. Kenneth E. Boulding, "The Economics of Human Conflict," in *The Nature of Human Conflict*, ed. Elton B. McNeil (Englewood Cliffs, N.J.: Prentice-Hall, 1965), p. 172.

Part III

Dispute Settlement

10

THE ROLE
OF THE THIRD PARTY

1. "ADD BOTH SIDES AND DIVIDE BY TWO"

Conflict is not expected to occur in traditional Japanese society.
Even if dissatisfaction is expressed openly and conflict ensues, the
parties usually try to make concessions to each other in an attempt
to resolve the conflict in such a way that both parties are satisfied
and can resume their former harmonious relationship. The traditional way of dispute settlement is very well expressed by the idiom
arasoi o mizu ni nagasu (literally, let the dispute flow to the water).
This means, in effect, let's·forget the dispute and be friendly again.
Phrases such as *kenka ryō-seibai* (both disputants are penalized
equally) or *arasoi o maruku osameru* (to settle the dispute in a circle) also express traditional approaches to dispute settlement.
Sometimes both disputing parties find it impossible to reach an
amicable settlement by themselves. They may then agree to *arasoi
o azukeru* (to leave the dispute with someone), that is, to nominate
a third party to settle the dispute and to accept his suggestions
without argument. The third party then tries to conciliate the
dispute by appealing to the antagonists' goodwill and to the
friendly sentiments which form the basis of traditional personal
relationships. He never settles the case by imposing any external
norm or standard and usually avoids making any clear-cut, black-
and-white decision. He tries to persuade both parties to yield some-

thing in order for them to regain their mutual trust and enjoy amicable and peaceful relations in the future. The effectiveness of this method of dispute settlement depends upon the third party's prestige and the degree of trust which both disputants place in him. In these cases, both parties often say that though they are not satisfied with the solution, they will abide by the agreement in order "to save the face" of the third party.

In Japanese enterprises as well, great emphasis is placed on harmonious personal relations and disputes are not expected to arise. Any conflict or open expression of one's dissatisfaction is likely to cause distress to those concerned since it threatens the relationship.[1] The relationship between an enterprise union and management is not substantially different from interpersonal relationships. Established mature unions usually enjoy amicable relations with their employers. But even in a climate of harmonious labor relations, grievances can accumulate to the point that mutual understanding is destroyed and both parties engage in a struggle for power. At that point, the dispute may still be resolved by a third party, provided he has enough authority and influence with both parties. While in personal relations go-betweens are often private persons, in industrial relations the third party, with very few exceptions, is a representiative of a government organization.

There are two reasons for the dominant role played by government agencies in labor dispute settlement. First, the respect for government authority in Japanese society is so strong that conflicting parties tend to seek settlement from such authorities. Industrial disputes arise in a "social vacuum," and it would be very difficult to find a private person who could command enough power and prestige to be respected by both strongly antagonistic parties. The second reason is related to the problem of accessibility and availability of dispute-settlement institutions. In civil cases the law courts play an important role in solving cases by means of reconciliation,[2] but this is possible only after one of the parties has brought the case to litigation. However, ordinary Japanese people are more reluctant than Westerners to go to court for civil disputes.

This is because of the importance of maintaining amicable relationships which litigation is bound to destroy. We will come back to this point in connection with its implications in the functioning of law courts in labor disputes.

On the other hand, in the case of industrial relations disputes, another dispute-settlement institution is available in addition to the courts, namely the labor relations commission (LRC) system. The remarkable feature of this institution is that it is a tri-partite body. Each commission consists of an equal number of commissioners representing the public, labor and the employers. Thus disputing parties feel that access to this institution is easier than to the courts. Almost all important labor disputes are handled by the labor relations commissions, while the private arbitration system, which plays a very important role in settling labor disputes in the United States, is negligible in Japan.

One would naturally assume that since government institutions are entrusted with the settlement of labor disputes, their solutions would be based on legal norms and specific standards or policies. The Labor Relations Adjustment Law of 1946, together with the Trade Union Law of 1949, regulate the procedure of dispute settlement in the LRC system. Both these laws provide a Western-type of dispute-settlement procedure emphasizing conciliation, mediation and arbitration. There is also an emergency procedure to settle disputes in the public utilities sector. Therefore, if dispute settlement by the LRC is typically Western and relies on legal norms, why do conflicting parties familiar with the Japanese amicable way of dispute settlement prefer to appeal to the LRC rather than to a private go-between—however difficult it might be to find such a person? Certainly in many cases the parties are reluctant to seek settlement by the LRC and go to it only after their relationship and trust in each other have been so damaged that amicable settlement has become impossible. However, as already mentioned in connection with the Spring Offensive,[3] disputing parties tend to call upon the LRC to resolve their differences in order to avoid having to negotiate in good faith. This tendency suggests that dispute settlement by such a government agency as the LRC could have more in common with the traditional method of dispute settlement than with settlements based on universal standards.

In 1976 the total number of dispute-settlement cases handled by the LRC system amounted to 1,528. Out of this total 1,468 were conciliation cases; mediation and arbitration cases numbered only 52 and 8 respectively.[4] The fact that conciliation is the favorite type of settlement procedure while mediation and arbitration are not so popular is understandable. Conciliation is the most informal and closest to the traditional Japanese method of settlement by amicable mutual understanding, while arbitration is the farthest removed. In the case of mediation, the usual practice is for the LRC to submit its proposal only after both parties have reached an "understanding." This is also true in cases where the LRC makes a conciliation proposal. It is often pointed out that the parties rarely refuse to accept an LRC proposal, which would mean to destroy the "face" of the commissioners; similarly, the commissioners would not submit a proposal which might be rejected because they do not want to lose "face." In actual practice, it seems that the LRC system follows the tradition of amicable dispute settlement by an authority whom the parties respect and obey. In the following passage, Ōta describes his experience in dispute conciliation during a Spring Offensive. At the time, he was Labor Commissioner for the Central Labor Relations Commission, together with Employer Commissioner Hajime Maeda, then chairman of the *Nikkeiren* (Japanese Employers' Association).

My talk with Mr. Maeda was carried out completely without data. . . . On the day before the strike was scheduled, at the final stage, I gave him a figure which I had arrived at only by intuition. Mr. Maeda also quoted a figure which was based on his intuition, in the way horse traders bargain by touching fingers under their sleeves. The public member's role was only to present this result wrapped up in a neat package. . . .

I am always amazed at the delusion of Japanese unions

who believe that a theory of wages actually exists. If our negotiating tactics relied on the concept of the "market basket" scheme of wages,[5] no matter how strong we made the case for the workers' needs, we would never obtain a wage increase. Some union leaders work under the illusion they can get more money from employers with such theories. . . . If this theory could persuade employers to increase wages, we could pay one million yen per day to Professor Ōkōchi, an economist and an expert on wage problems, and let him bargain for us. Would employers accept wage increases according to this theory? Not a chance.[6]

In the light of my experience as public commissioner of the Tokyo Metropolitan LRC for more than ten years, I fully agree with Ōta's statement that dispute settlement at the LRC is never based on theory or statistics. Although public commissioners are appointed from among so-called men of knowledge and experience, when it comes to actual conciliation their understanding of the theory of wages and of industrial relations does not count. More important is whether both parties can trust the commissioner as a person, which depends perhaps less on his ability than on his personality.

Since the LRC proposals are not derived from the application of legal norms or universal standards, the commissioners' authority and ability to command respect from both parties reside in their status as representatives of a government agency. Yet, in view of the antagonism between unions and government, public commissioners need to maintain their independence from the government in order to allay the unions' suspicions. Not only their effectiveness but their position is at stake. The law requires that both labor and management commissioners agree on the appointment of the public commissioner. Therefore, those who have lost the confidence of either side will never be reappointed.

A sarcastic and commonly expressed view of conciliation by the LRC is that "they add both sides and divide by two." This means that the LRC decides the amount of a wage increase by adding the amount demanded and the amount offered, and dividing the sum by two to arrive at a compromise figure. This method of conciliation implies a rather casual approach to dispute settlement and one which is similar to the traditional principle of "*kenka ryō-seibai*" (both disputants are penalized equally). However, since dispute settlement by the LRC is not based on "theory," this approach is as valid as any.

We have been referring to the "authority" of the LRC. The reader should not conclude that commissioners are actually held in high esteem. In view of the fact that disputing parties often bring their case to the LRC without having made an effort to bargain in good faith, one can presume that the reliance upon the "authority" of the LRC is a means of passing the buck. In short, letting the LRC settle a dispute makes it possible for both sides to say, "We are not responsible for the settlement since the commission said such and such." Thus the LRC dispute-settlement procedure is a game which has for its object saving the "face" of all parties, especially the "face" of the leaders *vis-à-vis* their constituents, which include union officers and members; personnel managers and the directors; subsidiary companies and the parent company; as well as individual companies and the employers' organization.

2. RIGHTS VERSUS INTERESTS— THE ROLE OF THE COURTS

The labor relations commissions as well as the law courts have the jurisdiction to handle the legal problems concerning labor. The central and local labor relations commission settle disputes through conciliation, mediation and arbitration as mentioned in the previous sections. Besides these functions they also hear unfair labor practices cases. In this function the commissions play a semi-judicial role, namely, to investigate the charges against company management and issue orders.

A violation of an order of one of the commissions which has

been upheld in the courts is punishable by imprisonment of up to one year, or a fine not exceeding one hundred thousand yen, or both. Violation of an order which becomes final without challenge by the employer to the courts is also punishable by a fine not exceeding one hundred thousand yen. This function of the commissions is semi-judicial or adjudicatory in the sense that it finds facts based on the evidence and issues orders enforced by punishment for non-compliance. The number of the adjudication cases at the law courts and the commissions is not very large, as seen in Tables 12 and 13. However, in spite of the previously mentioned reluctance of the Japanese to go to court, the parties of industrial relations disputes are still taking trouble to utilize the legal institutions as one approach to dispute settlement.

Table 12
Number of Labor Cases in Court
(Not including criminal cases)

Year	No. of Cases Filed	No. of Cases Disposed of
1970	1,709	1,890
1971	1,869	1,606
1972	4,714	2,067
1973	1,721	2,266
1974	1,864	3,257
1975	2,297	3,115

Source: *Hōsō Jihō* [Journal of Lawyers' Association] 28, no. 7 (1976), p. 175.

Table 13
Number of Unfair Labor Practices Cases
(Filed at all the LRC)

Year	No. of Cases
1967	730
1968	591
1969	676
1970	1,483
1971	569
1972	928
1973	596
1974	714
1975	929
1976	730

Source: *Rōdō Iinkai Nenpō* [Annual Report of the Labor Relations Commission], no. 30 (1976), p. 75; see also no. 31 (1977), p. 2.

In Western European industrial relations the difference between "conflict of vested rights" (*Rechtsstreit*) and "conflict of interest" (*Interessenstreit*) is generally recognized.[7] The former is defined as a dispute concerning the vested rights and obligations of the parties, which are usually handled by the courts as a legal dispute. The latter is not related to vested rights but rather is a dispute to establish new rights and obligations. Thus a conflict of interest is not regarded as a legal dispute and is settled, as a rule, by negotiation between the parties. In Western society, when conflict of interest disputes are not settled by negotiations—whether or not acts of dispute have taken place—they are supposed to be settled by procedures such as conciliation, mediation or arbitration by a private or public agency, rather than by the courts.

This distinction is based on the premise that the conflict of interest is by its nature impossible to settle by applying legal norms. For example, let us suppose that a dispute arises over the interpretation of a wage agreement, individual or collective, which has already been concluded and is still in force. This is a conflict concerning the vested rights of workers to wages and the employer's obligation to pay based on a signed agreement. The court may render a legal opinion on the applicable rights and obligations and may interpret the law, contract or collective agreement. On the other hand, let us suppose that the workers demand wage increases because they are dissatisfied with the amount paid during a previous agreement, and a conflict arises because of the employer's refusal to grant the increase. This case is not a conflict concerning the existence or scope of vested rights and obligations. The problem is not how much the workers are entitled to, but how much of a wage increase is appropriate, which is not a matter of legal opinion. This kind of conflict is not to be disposed of by the courts, but must be settled by a third party, involving existing public dispute settlement machinery. The type of labor disputes which we have been discussing in the previous chapters of this book were, for the most part, conflicts of interest.

However, in Japanese industrial relations, the distinction between conflicts of vested rights and conflicts of interest has not been clearly made, except perhaps on a purely academic basis. This is due to the simple and obvious fact that Japanese industrial relations are not concerned with the exact definition of the rights and obligations of the parties in a dispute. In chapter two, I described a collective agreement where the court ruled that "the provision in question is so obscure, it is almost impossible . . . to ascertain what kind of practices existed in fact and which working conditions were agreed upon by the parties and were to be included in the contract when it was concluded."[8] The parties themselves find it very difficult to determine whether a conflict concerning the provisions of a collective agreement is a conflict of vested rights or a conflict of interest. Thus it is not unusual for the parties to negotiate before they can agree on the meaning of certain clauses in the collective agreement. In the course of such negotiations, should agreement appear unlikely, the dispute also may be brought to court. With only slight exaggeration, one might say that in Japanese industrial relations any problem or disagreement between labor and management can be dealt with either by formal collective bargaining or through the courts. These two approaches to dispute settlement are never clearly distinguished and can be pursued simultaneously.

The case below illustrates a typical "obscure provision" which led to a dispute. The case involves the Kōtsū (Transportation) Union of Kure City and Kure City. In this case both parties signed a memorandum agreeing "to regard the usual practice as a standard norm" for working conditions, if there were no specifically relevant provisions in the collective agreement. Soon thereafter, the union claimed that the rule stated in the memorandum should apply to the standards for operating hours and driving mileage of company buses. The union asked the company to negotiate on these matters. Meanwhile, management proceeded unilaterally to change bus routes, which resulted in changes in operating hours and mileage. The company interpreted the memorandum as not applicable to the recent changes. Due to the company's unilateral actions and refusal to negotiate, the union asked the court for two temporary injunctions: one to order the company to bargain with the union, and the other to order the company to stop changing bus routes until an agreement was reached in negotiations. The union also asked for collective bargaining when it asked for a legal opinion of the court on the issue of how to interpret the agreement embodied in the memorandum. In addition, it is worth pointing out that the union applied to the court for a temporary injunction to require bargaining.

In recent years there has been an increase in the number of cases in which unions have sought temporary injunctions to compel management to negotiate. Japanese courts also have been more inclined to grant such requests than in the past. Such temporary injunctions are unknown in other countries and, in Japan, lawyers have objected to them on the theoretical grounds that if the employer persists in refusing to negotiate, it is doubtful whether the injunction can be enforced. Bargaining in good faith, by its very nature, implies a willingness to bargain. Therefore, using legal power to enforce the obligation to bargain is a contradiction in terms. In civil law, temporary injunctions are regarded as appropriate only for rights which are concrete and exact, which is not the case for collective bargaining. Temporary injunctions should be to guarantee rights for which the protection given by the ordinary procedure might come too late, or safeguard rights guaranteed under a temporary injunction yet threatened by subsequent ordinary procedure.

The trend toward seeking such temporary injunctions is a result of the unions' increasing tendency to rely on the judiciary in their efforts to gain the constitutional right to bargain collectively—especially if the unions are not powerful enough on their own to compel the employer to recognize them and to bargain with them. This is another example of the Japanese unions' "excessive legalism," in the sense that they resort to legal proceedings as often as possible without paying much attention to the broader question of whether legal action is appropriate or not in the case in question. There is no doubt that unions are well aware that this method is not justifiable. They have no real intention of seeking further legal action once they have obtained a temporary injunction. Thus they are intentionally taking advantage of the legal system in order to gain their immediate goal, which is to force the employer to bargain with them.[9]

3. THE VERDICT IS EQUIVALENT TO THE EMPEROR'S SEAL

If the unions do not intend to enforce their claims by pursuing ordinary legal procedures, and if they do not care much about the validity of their right and its enforcement by legal means, why do they spend so much of their time, energy and money in bringing these cases to court? The unions' main (perhaps exclusive) intention here is to strengthen their position, whether they are engaged in bargaining or in an industrial dispute, by getting a government agency to acknowledge officially the unfairness of the employer. They need "*okami no osumitsuki*" (The Emperor's Seal), which certainly awes even the most impudent employer. For this reason, unions care little whether the injunction can be enforced or not. Neither do they consider instituting ordinary legal proceedings.

The following case is a good illustration of what leads a union to seek a temporary injunction:

> On March 15, 1965, the union asked for negotiations on five demands, including wage increases. After two sessions of joint consultation and three sessions of bargaining, the union established the right to strike on April 14 and refused to do overtime work after April 16. They held six short-term strikes between April 23 and May 22.
>
> Meanwhile, the company, one of the major motion picture producers in Japan, tried to remove from the plant some films, which were due for release, in order to put the final touches on them outside the plant. Union pickets prevented them. On the morning of May 22, the company succeeded in

taking the films out of the plant with the help of the police. The company then discharged the union's leaders for the reason that they had "obstructed business."

The union requested that the company bargain on three subjects: wage increases, rescinding the union leaders' discharge, and the company's responsibility for bringing the police into the plant. The company refused to bargain, stating that they would not meet with union representatives if the group included the dismissed leaders. Meanwhile some union members withdrew from the union and established a new union; thereafter, increasing numbers of union members joined this second union.

Under these desperate circumstances, the original union appealed to the court to issue an order to require the company to bargain with them.[10]

This entire process is characteristic of a large number of difficult disputes in Japanese industrial relations. The whole sequence of events, including failure of negotiations, reckless acts of dispute, bringing in police or gangsters, discharging union leaders and attempting to split the union, makes the union aware of the weakness of its position. Finding it impossible to win on its own, the union appeals to the courts for legal redress. The courts are the unions' last resort. Whenever unions seek an injunction, it is because there is no possible ground left for bargaining. Yet, injunctions are unlikely to create new grounds for bargaining.

4. PROLONGED ADJUDICATION

The refusal of an employer to bargain also could be taken to an LRC as an unfair labor practice. The cases brought to the LRCs are hardly different from those brought to the courts. The late Professor Mitsutoshi Azuma, who worked as a public commissioner for an LRC for more than twenty years, acquired a rather pessimistic view of the effectiveness of the LRCs:

The LRC and the courts are regarded by both disputing parties as institutions which will provide them with some rules of behavior which they are not able to set up by themselves.[11] The parties tend to fight to the finish regardless of the passing of time. Based on such ambitious expectations, they are deluded into thinking that the order of an LRC or the judgment of the courts is able to perform the function of rule-making a hundred percent effectively. The gap between this illusion and the reality of the unfair labor practice system makes the rapid disposition of cases difficult. In this situation, the reactions of the parties are largely inconsistent: they range from demanding an early solution to seeking a delay in the procedure. Industrial relations are conducted without established rules, governed by emotional elements, and developed amid treacherous antagonism and misunderstanding. This is mostly the case in small and medium-size enterprises, but larger enterprises present the same characteristics when disputes are allowed to grow unchecked. Thus Japanese industrial disputes have elements which do not make them capable of being solved by the unfair labor practice scheme. This system can be expected to function only when a set of effective rules of behavior allows it to dispose of cases rapidly.[12]

Not only in cases of refusal to bargain but also in unfair labor practice cases in general the slowness of legal procedures has often been pointed out as an important reason for the ineffectiveness of the remedies proposed by the LRCs. The time period for the entire procedure in unfair labor practice cases brought to a close by order or decision of a local LRC is surprisingly long, averaging 635 days in 1976.[13] In cases of refusal to bargain or interference in union administration, the employer usually has accomplished his aim long before the order is issued. Therefore, an LRC's order is not at all effective in rescuing the union from the damage caused by unfair labor practices. The same applies to cases where union leaders are dismissed because of their union activities. The LRC's order becomes pointless if, as it is often the case, it is issued more than a year after the union leader has been dismissed. "Even if the order to reinstate is issued and obeyed by the employer, when the union leader comes back to the working place, there is a good chance that he cannot cope with the antagonism of his fellow workers. He usually gets tired of being looked upon as a heretic and finally resigns from his job."[14]

A number of reasons account for the length of LRC procedures. First of all, in the course of its development over a period of nearly thirty years, the Japanese unfair labor practice system has borrowed more elements from civil court procedure than from its original model, the American system. Thus what was conceived as a simple and quick remedy has become a complicated and legally complex process, which requires the involvement of lawyers at every step. As a result, the procedure has come to resemble court procedure, and intervals between each hearing are more and more prolonged. These delays between sessions are partly due to the difficulty of setting up dates convenient for the public commissioners, most of whom are not full-time officers and are busy with their own work. It is also often pointed out that the employers delay the procedures intentionally. However, as Azuma has pointed out, both parties are unable to regulate their relationship in an orderly manner and they expect an LRC to set up the rules itself. Thus they tend to "fight to the finish regardless of the passing of time." As a result the unions are not particularly anxious to have the case solved rapidly, although they pretend to want an early solution. This apparent contradiction in union attitude stems from another aspect of the dispute-settlement process which will be examined in detail in the following section.

5. THE COURTROOM AS A STAGE FOR CHALLENGE

As we have seen before, once mutual trust is lost and amicable understanding has become impossible in an enterprise, the employer refuses to bargain and tries to split the union or destroy it by dismissing its leaders. This behavior on the part of employers is nothing but a desperate reaction to an impossible situation. Since they are accustomed (one might even say addicted) to the traditional pattern of amicable solution and mutual understanding, they are incapable of negotiating reasonably and logically. In such circumstances, the only way for the union to avoid being dragged into reckless, violent actions is to go either to an LRC or to the courts. In most cases, however, it is only after unions have already gotten into trouble that they seek legal remedy in an attempt to get out of a blind alley.

When the dispute is brought to the courts or to an LRC in such circumstances, these institutions are supposed to provide some kind of legal judgment, either to apply labor law in the case of the courts or, in the case of an LRC, to issue a policy decision which is determined by the spirit of the labor law. However, the principles of labor law are of a fundamentally Western nature, since the whole system of Japanese labor law has been borrowed piecemeal from British, German, French and American laws. Often these principles are quite different from the usual standards of behavior of the parties in Japanese industrial relations.

Generally speaking, legal norms are either norms of judgment, according to which an *ex post facto* settlement is to be made after a dispute has occurred, or they are norms of action, which the citizens should observe in their conduct. In Japanese industrial relations, the role of labor law as a norm of action is a minor one. As we have seen, both parties make use of the law to an extensive degree in order to attack the opposite party. At the same time they neglect the law by indulging in *amae* relationships, that is, relationships of mutual dependence, when it is convenient. In short, the law is never regarded as a guide by which to regulate their own behavior. Because the Japanese unions have been emphasizing the importance of the so-called fight for rights, the workers' concern for their legal rights has certainly been strengthened. However, the very fact that militant unions have felt the need to give greater importance to this fight underscores the fact

217

that labor law is not playing the role of a norm of action in daily Japanese industrial relations. Furthermore, as the so-called fight for rights of the union has many common features with their newly developed "concept of power relationship," it is very doubtful that this fight for rights will stimulate a consciousness of rights among workers.

In any case, settlement of a dispute by the institutions such as the courts is based in principle on universal norms, such as labor laws, which state clearly and exactly the rights and obligations of both parties. Since the function of the adjudication process is to settle the dispute by deciding which party's claim is right or wrong in accordance with a universal standard, it inevitably results in defining in clear and exact terms a relationship which, hitherto, had been allowed to remain undefined and fluid. However, as we have already seen, labor relations in Japanese enterprises are rooted in undefined and fluid personal relationships. To bring disputes to the court for settlement purposes means to destroy the amicable relationship by imposing a clear-cut solution. "For the traditional legal mind, litigation means an open challenge against another party, i.e., to pick a quarrel."[15] This is why, in the traditional judicial process, the ideal approach is always to settle the dispute according to the principle of *kenka ryō-seibai* (both disputants are penalized equally).

Since litigation is a challenge to amicable personal relationships, it is regarded by the union as an effective means to expand the dispute and to obtain a better settlement than would be possible within a normally harmonious relationship. Ironically enough, the function of litigation is similar to that of violent behavior and other extravagant actions often resorted to by unions to shock the employer and to destroy the normal climate of personal relationships in the enterprise. Thus it is no wonder that unions bring problems to court which are not by nature suitable to settlement by legal procedure, since they do not very much care whether the issue gets settled or not.

In this sense the purpose of litigation, like the purpose of strikes, is to enable a union to demonstrate its strength and determination.

Because a union needs to produce a dramatic showdown, they look upon the courtroom as a stage for confronting the employer. With this objective in mind, they mobilize large numbers of union members and their friends and invite them to watch the procedure. Union members attend the hearings wearing headbands and armbands, a practice which most courts prohibit and which sometimes causes trouble; others remain outside the courtroom waving red flags, holding meetings and shouting slogans against the "reactionary" judges. Even inside the courtroom or session room of an LRC, the observers behave improperly, shouting, cheering, clapping their hands, and ignoring the warnings of the judge or public commissioners. Union lawyers also tend to forget their legal responsibilities: they direct their speeches at the union observers and harass the employer's witnesses in cross-examination. In spite of their request for a speedy procedure, the unions call a large number of witnesses to talk at length about the "history of unscrupulous labor management" of the company and about the humiliations and bitterness they have experienced for many years.

According to experienced LRC public commissioners, such open expression of the employees' hostility to management serves as a a catharsis. Both parties are able to unburden themselves by releasing their long-accumulated indignations, thus allowing unpleasant feelings to fade away.[16] Sometimes, however, this outpouring may increase rather than decrease the antagonism. In most cases, it is hardly to be expected that the hitherto amicable (one might even say emotional) relationship will suddenly change into an exact rights-and-obligations relationship, or that such a challenge and showdown will help both parties to acquire reasonable and logical attitudes toward each other. Thus, even if the dispute is settled by the court or an LRC in accordance with universal standards, the relationship within the enterprise will remain as it was during the dispute. The challengers, even if their claims are sustained by the courts or LRC, will eventually be excluded from the harmonious interpersonal relationship prevailing in the enterprise, and will "get tired of being looked upon as heretics." The remedies provided by the courts and LRC cannot prevent such an outcome.

6. RECONCILIATION OF DIFFERENCES

At this stage of the discussion, it is possible to state that the courts, not to mention the LRCs, find it difficult to carry out their function as judicial institutions, namely, to ascertain the facts and find solutions based on legal norms. Japanese courts are called upon to perform the impossible task of rendering a legal judgment on issues where the parties' rights and obligations are so obscure and uncertain that it is almost impossible for the court to ascertain what they are. For instance, Japanese courts often have to decide on the reasonableness of reduction of a certain number of employees or the specific retirement age in a particular enterprise in order to decide whether a dismissal is valid. It is extremely doubtful whether such a judgment on the fairness of certain management decisions is legally possible for the courts and, even if it were possible, whether it is appropriate. Management representatives complain with some justification that, though the judges might be well trained for legal judgments, labor-management issues are outside the scope of legal judgments and, in any case, they (not the judges) are responsible for the conduct of the enterprise.

When the judges decide the reasonableness of certain management actions on the basis of "abuse of right," it certainly is a valid legal judgment. However, judgments on the basis of "abuse of right" rest in the final analysis on one's concept of "social justice." As already mentioned in connection with the problem of the "appropriateness" of an act of dispute,[17] social justice is hard to determine in the field of labor law, where the views of both parties are so divided. A brilliant Japanese labor law scholar, who has scrutinized the supporting arguments in labor cases in postwar Japan, commented on this point as follows:

> There are two important standards resorted to and cited in past legal cases in the field of labor, i.e., "reason" and "abuse of right," both of which are rather flexible "blank" norms. . . . Since the standards cited do not necessarily mean standards of judgment, this does not necessarily mean that the judg-

220

ment is subjective. However, judging from the statements of the legal decisions, Japanese court decisions in labor law cases tend to allow some kind of "qualitative" judgment, sometimes more or less subjective, depending on its legal construction. As a result, the substance of such judgments has the following characteristics: a) a soft-focused grasp of the issue; b) obscure legal construction; and c) ineffective judgment, especially in the case of provisional injunctions. Thus the legal decisions in labor cases incline strongly toward arbitration or reconciliation.[18]

The tendency of judges to settle cases by reconciliation rather than by ordinary trial is a natural one, if one takes into account the characteristics of Japanese industrial relations and the need to settle the dispute adequately. This tendency is strong among judges who have more or less specialized in labor cases. Some judges make no secret of their conviction in this matter.[19]

In Japanese society, dispute is generally regarded as a threat to harmonious personal relationships. Therefore, bringing a lawsuit against someone is equivalent to a direct attack on the relationship itself. After a trial has started, if the plaintiff persists in his suit and turns down suggestions for compromise, he is likely to be criticized for his cruelty and stubbornness. As a result, both parties are more or less mentally ready to accept compromise suggestions. According to Kawashima, from 50 to 56 percent of civil cases at the court of first instance usually finish in judicial compromise or withdrawal—withdrawal meaning that accommodation took place outside court procedure.[20] Table 14 shows that between 1972 and 1976 more than half of the labor cases were resolved either by compromise or withdrawal. This trend is more evident in the unfair labor practice cases submitted to the LRCs. For most of the same years, more than 70 percent of the cases were resolved by compromise or withdrawal (see Table 15).

It is not surprising that the tendency to compromise is greater in the LRC system than in the courts. While the courts are a purely judicial institution, the LRC is by its very nature an administrative

Table 14
Number of Civil and Injunction Cases on Labor at the District Courts According to the Type of Solution

Year	Litigation	Compromise	Withdrawal, etc.	Total
1972	558	331	395	1,284
1973	547	277	568	1,392
1974	642	272	358	1,272
1975	668	333	405	1,406
1976	695	385	431	1,511

Source: *Hōsō Jihō* [Journal of Lawyers' Association] 29, no. 7 (1977), p. 129.

Table 15
Number of Disposed Cases of Unfair Labor Practice at the Local Labor Relations Commissions According to the Type of Solution

Year	Order and Decision*	Compromise and Withdrawal	Total
1972	153	1,124	1,277
1973	120	676	796
1974	119	455	574
1975	164	521	685
1976	162	516	678

Source: *Rōdō Iinkai Nenpō* [Annual Report of the Labor Relations Commission], no. 31 (1977), Appendix, p. 2.

* Decision means that the LRC turned down the cases because of apparent lack of prerequisite for the claim, disqualification as party or a belated appeal, or because the facts, even if sustained, did not constitute unfair labor practice.

commission which plays a semi-judicial role in unfair labor practice cases. As an administrative commission, it has greater latitude and discretion in its judgments than do the courts. Some public commissioners are convinced that the LRCs should settle all cases by compromise and only when they are unable to do so should they issue orders. Unlike the courts, whose fundamental function is to render clear-cut judgments, the LRCs' function is to normalize the relationship between labor and management. However, at present, this opinion on the function of the LRCs is not accepted by the unions. They prefer to utilize the LRC hearings as a stage for confronting management, so they can fight their battle in the open rather than reaching a compromise in a more informal way.

NOTES

1. Dore, *British Factory—Japanese Factory*, p. 185.
2. For the role of the law courts in effecting reconciliation in civil cases rather than handling legal decisions, see Takeyoshi Kawashima, "Dispute Settlement in Contemporary Japan," in *Law in Japan*, p. 48.
3. See Part II, chapter 7, section 4.
4. Central Labor Relations Commission, *Rōdō Iinkai Nenpō* [Annual Report of the Labor Relations Commission], no. 31 (1977), p. 13.
5. The "market basket scheme" is a simple wage calculation based on the total price of goods necessary for daily life.
6. Kaoru Ōta, *Tatakai no Nakade* [In the Midst of Struggle], p. 301.
7. The distinction between conflicts of "rights" and of "interests" is admitted in theory in most Western industrialized countries, such as Germany, the United States, Sweden, Austria, as well as in Britian, Italy and France—although in the last three countries the distinction is less important in practice. For details, see K. W. Wedderburn, "Conflicts of 'Rights' and Conflicts of 'Interests' in Labor Disputes," in *Dispute Settlement Procedures in Five Western European Countries*, ed. Benjamin Aaron (Los Angeles: University of California Press, 1969), pp. 65–66. In Germany, this distinction is admitted to be essential and fundamental in the ordering of labor relations. It was introduced during the Weimar Republic, when special conciliation boards (*Schlichtungs*) were established and it was necessary to distinguish between their jurisdiction and that of labor courts. The classical concepts were established by Erwin Jacobi, one of the leading labor lawyers at that time. He characterized disputes over rights as those to be decided by "legal judgments" according to the legal order, while disputes over interests were to be settled by an adjustment or voluntary agreement corresponding to the interests of both parties. In case of failure, a legal decision was not possible. For details, see Thilo Ramm, "Labor Courts and Grievance Settlement in West Germany," in *Labor Courts and Grievance Settlement in Western Europe*, ed. Benjamin Aaron (Berkeley and Los Angeles: University of California Press, 1971), pp. 93–94.
8. See Part I, chapter 2, section 2a.
9. Judges complain about this trend and call it the "trend of temporary injunction which substitutes for the ordinary procedure," see Zadankai [Discussions], "Kari Shobun Seido Unyō no Kako, Genzai, Shōrai" [The Past, Present and Future Operation of the Temporary Injunction System], in *Hanrei Times*, no. 67 (1957), p. 42.
10. Daiei Trade Union v. Daiei Co., Tokyo District Court, July 9, 1965, 16 RKMS 566.
11. They do not expect the Labor Relations Commissions to give them the answers to specific problems so much as they expect that the LRCs will provide them with a kind of panacea which will solve all the problems they have in their impossible industrial relations.
12. Mitsutoshi Azuma, "Futō Rōdō-kōi ni Okeru Niritsu-haihan," [Antinomy in Unfair Labor Practices], p. 14.

13. Central Labor Relations Commission, *Rōdō Iinkai Nenpō*, no. 31(1977), p. 6.

14. Azuma, "Futō Rōdō-kōi," p. 14.

15. Takeyoshi Kawashima, *Nihonjin no Hō Ishiki* [Legal Rights Consciousness of the Japanese], p. 140.

16. Such a situation is not unique to Japanese society and is rather common in other non-Western societies. It is interesting to find a quite similar description by Laura Nader of Zapotec Indian court procedure in Mexico: "The *presidente*'s role is that of mediator, adjudicator and group therapist. His principal function seems to be to listen—often asking questions to clear up contradictions. He does not cross-examine, but rather allows the litigants to vent their spleen, and in this way he brings out the nature of the basis of the conflict," in "Styles of Court Procedure: To Make the Balance," *Law in Culture and Society*, ed. Laura Nader (Chicago: Aldine Publishing Co., 1969), p. 85.

17. See Part I, chapter 3, section 1.

18. Kōichirō Yamaguchi, "Rōdō Saiban no Kyakkan Sei" [The Objectiveness of Legal Judgment on Labor Cases], *Jurist*, no. 487 (1971), p. 29.

19. As an example among a number of such opinions, see *Rōdō Hanrei* [Labor Cases], nos. 151 and 164.

20. Kawashima, *Nihonjin no Hō Ishiki*, p. 150.

11

INTERNATIONAL
LABOR DISPUTE SETTLEMENT

1. PRINCIPLE OF AUTONOMY

The principle of autonomy assumes that industrial disputes should be settled by the parties themselves without any interference or help from governmental institutions. Generally speaking, this principle has been the basis of dispute settlement in Western industrialized countries although, in practice, it has suffered some alterations. For instance, the legally binding nature of collective agreements has been recognized by law in many Western European countries since early in the twentieth century. This means that when the provisions of a collective agreement are violated, the parties are entitled to ask the courts for remedy. Yet, even today, the principle of autonomy is repeatedly emphasized as a fundamental rule of industrial relations in most of these countries. One recalls, for instance, Germany's proud stress on their *Tarifautonomie* (autonomy in bargaining). Some departure from this principle occurred in the Anglo-American legal systems, notably in the United States, with the passage of unfair labor practice laws in 1935 (the Wagner Act). Even in Great Britain, where until recently this principle had been upheld consistently, a significant change took place with the Industrial Relations Act of 1972. It is still too early to draw any conclusions on the recent changes in British industrial relations, particularly since the act was repealed in 1975.

Nonetheless, the principle of autonomy has been the basis of industrial relations for many decades in most of the industrialized countries and, even today, government intervention is regarded as an exceptional action, suitable in cases of emergency situations only. There are a number of solid reasons, based on the specific nature of labor disputes, why government intervention should not be utilized. First of all, disputes are day-by-day occurrences in industrial relations. Their sheer number, for one thing, would make it hard (if not impossible) to depend on governmental agencies for their solution.

Second, industrial relations are by nature continuous relationships, and the parties must resume their relationship after the dispute has been settled. However, if the dispute has not been settled by the parties themselves but has been brought to the courts instead, it often results in the end of the relationship. This is not only true in Japanese society, where to engage in litigation means to pick a quarrel and to challenge an opponent to a fight but also in Western countries.[1] Thus if the parties wish to continue their relationship, they will prefer to reach a settlement by themselves or through private dispute settlement institutions rather than through a governmental agency, especially the courts. In industrial relations, continuing a relationship is often not just a matter of wish but of necessity. In most cases, even though the employer may want to do so, he is unable to destroy the union organization completely.

Third, in most countries, at least in the early stages of the trade union movement, unions do not trust the government because of its hostility toward them and since unions are suspicious of government intervention. This has been historically one of the most important factors for adherence to the principle of autonomy.

Fourth, most important labor disputes are really "conflicts of interest" and are not related to the rights and obligations of the parties. As shown in the previous chapter, "conflicts of interest," unlike "conflicts of vested rights," are not suitable for settlement by government dispute settlement agencies or the law courts.

In this sense, the principle of autonomous dispute settlement stems from the nature of labor disputes. However, this principle is

226

not absolute but can be amended to fit the needs of the system of industrial relations prevailing in each country at different times. First, this principle is based on the assumption that the autonomous settlement of disputes works well. As a result, when parties are unable to settle a dispute by themselves, government intervention is regarded as justified or even inevitable. As already mentioned, the possibility of autonomous dispute settlement in a certain society depends generally on the nature of unionism and industrial relations in that society. Autonomous settlement will play a dominant role in societies where business unionism prevails. This type of industrial relations makes it easier for the parties to economize and organize the dispute and, therefore, find solutions without government intervention. However, even in such industrial relations, there always emerge new kinds of disputes which have to be organized in a different ways, as the emergence of wildcat strikes in recent years suggests.

Second, society sometimes cannot afford the luxury of autonomous dispute settlement. The level of tolerance depends principally on a society's economic prosperity, the stage of economic development it has reached, and its economic and industrial structure. It also depends on the society's legal and political system, the degree of political stability and, last but not least, on the nature of industrial relations. At one extreme are countries which admit complete autonomy in all sectors of industrial relations and only prohibit strikes for military and police personnel, prison employees, etc. At the other extreme are countries which do not recognize workers' organizations at all. There is an unlimited number of variations between these two extremes. Nevertheless, in most industrialized countries, the general autonomy of the parties and the autonomous settlement of disputes are recognized in principle. The few exceptions concern restrictions on strikes by public employees—sometimes by limits set on their right to bargain—as well as regulations on strikes in public utilities.

Third, since the principle of autonomy originated in part with the attitudes of hostility and mistrust between government and the unions, it is not stressed as strongly where such attitudes do not exist. For instance, in such countries as Australia and New Zealand, if we limit ourselves to industrial democracies, governments friendly to the unions were in power in the early stages of union development. In such countries, arbitration procedures through government agencies, including compulsory arbitration, have played a very large role throughout the history of their industrial relations.

2. RECENT CHANGES IN WESTERN INDUSTRIAL SOCIETY

Nowadays the traditional principle of autonomy in industrial relations is being reconsidered and modified in most Western industrialized countries. The role of government in industrial relations is gradually increasing. This change is brought about by a complex set of factors. First of all, in West Germany and Great Britain, rapid economic development and full employment have improved the working conditions in individual enterprises so much that the standards established by collective agreements have become irrelevant. As a result, the process of horizontal standardization of industrial crafts by horizontally structured unions has lost importance. Because the unions have not had agents at the plant or enterprise level, there has been a decline in their formerly important function of regulating actual working conditions. In an attempt to reverse this trend, British unions have tried to change their organizations to include the shop stewards, who originally were representatives of the employees at the workshop level but did not formally belong to the union organization. In West Germany, too, unions have been trying to infiltrate the *Betriebsrate* (works councils) on the one hand and, at the same time, establish their own agents, called *Vertrauensleute* (trustmen or shop stewards), at the workshop level. So far such efforts have not been successful in either country. Leaders at the shop-floor level have resisted control by the unions and have led wildcat strikes to improve working conditions at the shop level. This phenomenon shows that the procedure of autonomous dispute settlement by the existing union organizations has not been functioning well in these countries.

The second factor is closely connected with autonomy. As a result of technological innovations and changes in the composition of the labor force, in particular the growing importance of technical and white-collar workers, the needs and problems of the workers have changed. In the past the main issues in industrial relations were minimum standards for wages, working hours and working conditions which could be uniformly determined on a regional or national basis within an industry or craft. Present issues are more complicated and include psychological needs and problems—such as a poor working environment, monotonous labor and mental fatigue—which need to be dealt with concretely and specifically on each shop floor. As far as autonomous dispute settlement is concerned, the difficulty is twofold. On the one hand, problems such as higher wages, shorter working hours, etc., which used to be handled by union management negotiations, now tend to be solved by forces outside the unions' sphere of activity, that is, by rapid economic growth and full employment. Thus the importance of union organization is undermined.[2] On the other hand, it is difficult to handle the new problems within a horizontal union organization, especially if unions, as in Great Britain and West Germany, do not have plant agents. In this sense too, the traditional autonomous dispute settlement, relying on the existing union organization, has not been working well in recent years.

Third, together with rapid economic expansion and full employment, the pursuit of higher wages by mammoth unions inevitably increases the threat of inflation by strengthening the vicious circle of wage and price increases. Certainly not everyone agrees on the real reasons for the inflation in contemporary industrial society. However, there is no doubt that government intervention in industrial relations stems, at least in part, from uncontrolled bargaining between giant corporations and mammoth unions, which has resulted in unfair income distribution. This is not the place to inquire into the meaning and effectiveness of the income policies implemented in most of the highly industrialized countries. Yet, it is worthwhile to note here that, in Western industrialized countries today, the inability to protect the interests of the non-organized workers and other groups in the society has been pointed out as the most fundamental defect of the collective bargaining system.[3]

In contemporary industrial society, social services including social security and social welfare, are considered essential functions of government. The social groups which need these services most are undoubtedly such non-organized groups as the unemployed—especially if they come from minority groups. A visitor to West Germany today can easily realize that those who should be protected are not those who are organized in powerful unions and enjoy privileged working conditions, but the foreign workers who work at dirty and tiring jobs in poor working conditions. The governments of several countries are about to regulate the process of autonomous bargaining in order to protect the welfare of these unorganized groups, whether or not their regulations meet with approval.

The principle of autonomy is suitable for certain specific types of industrial relations situations, but it cannot be an absolute rule to fit any circumstance. Therefore, its legal expression, including the right to organize, bargain and strike, is not an "eternal and inviolable right" as Japanese unionists and lawyers often fancy. The restriction of these "fundamental" rights of workers and state intervention should be examined from the viewpoint of effective dispute settlement.

3. THIRD PARTY SETTLEMENT

In every country, courts have functioned as parts of the existing dispute settlement machinery. However, since the adjudication process of the courts consists in applying legal norms, it is not suitable for settling labor disputes which are conflicts of interest. Therefore, most industrialized countries have set up another mechanism which specializes in settling conflict-of-interest disputes through conciliation. Such dispute settlement procedures are part of either the private or public institutions. In the countries where importance is attached to the principle of autonomy, labor dispute settlement by private institutions usually has priority, and the intervention by state agencies is regarded as exceptional.

In recent years, the role of the government in dispute settlement has been increasing and, at the same time, the nature of the dispute-settlement process also has been changing gradually. According to the traditional viewpoint of the principle of autonomy, the conciliation procedure in conflict-of-interest disputes is to serve as an auxiliary to the bargaining process. The function of conciliation consists in removing misunderstandings and easing the tensions which are caused mainly by matters of prestige or personal antagonism between the individuals who represent both sides, and often obstruct autonomous settlement. One can say that the most striking difference between the judicial and conciliatory procedures is that the conciliator, unlike the judge, is not concerned with the substance of a settlement.[4] In short, if conciliation is nothing but an aid to bargaining, then it is blind to the principles of justice or fairness and unable to assert legal principles of public policy against the will of both parties.

However, in actual cases, especially in recent years, conciliators tend to free themselves from the limits of being mere providers of assistance in the bargaining process. They do pay much attention to the substance of the settlement. Public conciliators, especially, have become more and more conscious of their role as agents of public policy, particularly when the governments intend to implement income policies and restrict wage increases through the public dispute settlement machinery. The use of public conciliators to press the government policy on the disputing parties has been regarded as unwarranted governmental interference with the principle of autonomy. Nevertheless, even if conciliation is confined to the role of merely helping the bargaining process, the conciliator should not be denied any initiative. The content of a recommendation in conciliation cases should be decided by the conciliator; this is also true for the proposal in mediation cases and the award in arbitration cases, although the binding effect on the disputing parties varies in all three cases. If a conciliator wants solely to be of assistance to the bargaining process, he still has to find a compromise between both parties and give advice by accepting parts from each party's claim. In this sense the Japanese approach mentioned earlier, "add both sides and divide by two," is similar to the traditional Western conciliation method. However, even the most traditional conciliator might ask one of the parties to concede if he thinks the other party's claim is proper or, if he finds both claims exceedingly improper, he might propose what he thinks is proper and try to persuade both sides.

Yet, in this case, there still exists a difference between the criteria of judges and conciliators. Conciliators base their decisions on what they deem to be proper or fair in industrial relations situations, while judges' decisions are based on legal norms. Folke Schmidt distinguishes between conciliation which only assists in bargaining and conciliation in which the conciliator makes a judicatory decision. He calls the latter "administration" and defines it as "the application of norms in the absence of vested rights."[5] The norms applied in the "administration" of labor disputes are not legal ones but refer to what is "fair." In more concrete terms, he includes among such norms the comparison of wages between closely connected groups of workers in terms of region or job, productivity standards, increases in the cost of living, changes in living standards and, finally, guidelines for income policy.

These norms sometimes contradict each other. For instance, a decision to allow a wage increase to a lower wage group for the sake of fairness might contradict the standard of productivity. Thus the conciliator has to choose which norm to apply from among numerous and sometimes contradictory norms. What then should be his criterion? This example differentiates "ad-

232

ministration" from adjudication, although both forms apply norms. Judges in adjudication are expected to examine past facts in the perspective of vested rights and obligations and then to apply legal norms. In "administration," on the other hand, the conciliators must decide the criteria, i.e., which of the many vague and often contradictory norms contribute to a resumption of harmonious labor relations in the future. As far as conflicts of vested rights are concerned, adjudication procedures in court are a suitable method of settling industrial relations disputes. However, even in Western society, the distinction between conflicts of vested rights and conflicts of interests has always been made more clearly in theory than in actual cases. For instance, a dispute concerning the interpretation of a provision of a collective agreement is theoretically a dispute of vested rights, but in such a case the workers are much more concerned with how the relevant provision will be interpreted in the future than with the way it has been practiced in the past. The actual dispute concerns the problems of the future, even though it takes the form of a dispute concerning an agreement concluded in the past.

Another shortcoming of adjudication arises from the fact that, insofar as its function is to settle disputes by applying legal norms, it inevitably leads to a kind of all-or-nothing settlement and renders clear-cut decisions on which party wins and which loses. For instance, in most Western countries, an employer has the legal right to dismiss a worker for a number of reasons. However, "there is a strange contrast between the common law of a country and generally recognized third party standards."[6] Particularly in industrial relations, unions often regard a number of management decisions as subject to bargaining, even when the law states that they are within the scope of management's prerogative. Thus in many of these countries, the courts have had to bend the legal principles and take a more flexible approach. If they did not, the disputing parties took their case out of court to be adjudicated by an independent body.[7] In every country in the world in fact, judges have acted as conciliators and have played a creative part in finding what is proper in labor relations and in interpreting the provisions of labor laws or collective agreements. The courts also resort to various "general clauses," such as public policy, social adequacy, or "general principles" such as tacit agreement, labor-management practice, autonomy of the parties, etc. Thus in actual practice, judges often play a role which is quite similar to that of the conciliator in conflicts of interests.[8]

Even though necessity has forced judges to function as conciliators, some questions have been raised concerning the appropriateness of this trend. Judges are professional lawyers, not necessarily experts in industrial relations. They are not trained to make judgments outside the field of law. In some countries such as West Germany and France, where specialized labor courts have been established, the judges usually specialize in the field of labor. Non-professional associates representing labor and the employers also participate in the courts. The judgments of these labor courts are expected to be based on the experience and knowledge of these experts. Because of their makeup, these courts are much more conducive to finding what is proper in labor relations than ordinary courts. However, as labor courts are still courts of law, they are not completely free from the criticism that "the judge is often directly adjusting the conflict of interests, just as the legislator does, but without feeling responsibility for the choice he makes."[9]

The courts can hardly be expected to chart the development of labor relations in the future as their function is basically to settle disputes *ex post facto* through the adjudication process. In this sense, if the conciliation machinery could perform the role of "administration," as the term is used by Folke Schmidt, it could apply flexible and dynamic norms, which might be called the principles of fairness. The benefit of this approach is that it takes into account the future development of the relationship between the parties and it settles matters in a way which is better suited to the nature of labor relations.

4. DISPUTE SETTLEMENT IN THE FUTURE

As was mentioned earlier, the effort to organize labor disputes and to treat them as economic disputes has not been completely effective in Western industrialized countries. Similarly, autonomous settlement by the bargaining process and conciliation as an assistance to bargaining have had limited success. On the other hand, the administration procedure, which was previously unknown or at least not consciously implemented, is beginning to attract attention and the functions of the courts are also experiencing certain transformations. In short, it is evident that collective bargaining can only play a limited role as an instrument for settling disputes and that the government's role in dispute settlement has become more important. This phenomenon is related to the often-made observation that the Western industrial relations system is being transformed from a bi-partite to a tri-partite system.

The limitations of the collective bargaining system are nothing more than the above-mentioned limitations of economic rationalism. Today's labor conflicts are taking place outside the traditional industrial relations system and surpass the union organizations' ability to solve them. No other powerful organization has yet emerged which would be able to respond to these new needs and to replace the union organizations. Furthermore, the nature of today's conflicts makes them unsuitable for adjudication. A new system of dispute settlement might need to be based on ideas and principles which are completely different from those on which the traditional industrial relations system is based. Whether "administration" as a new approach to dispute settlement could cope with the needs of the changing contemporary society is as yet unknown. However, if new approaches consist only in modifying the functions of existing machinery, such as the courts and private or public conciliation mechanisms, the results would be merely "putting new wine into old bottles." In the area of citizen protection, as well as in labor relations, the traditional Scandinavian ombudsman system has been put in operation as a substitute for the courts in several Western countries, including the United States.[10] In the field of industrial relations, workers' participation in management has become dominant as an alternative, or at least a supplement, for the present system centered around collective bargaining, especially in West Europe.

The emergence of the interests in shared management in European countries is caused by the growing awareness of the shortcomings of collective bargaining to deal with the contemporary problems of industrialized society such as its traditional antagonistic character, union representation of only a minority of the labor force, and the predominance of economic issues in the bargaining process.[11] The idea of participation, particularly the German system of works councils and workers' representation on company boards, has been accepted by other European countries recently[12] and is based on the recognition of common interests between management and labor regarding the importance of the problems unique to the individual enterprise and shop floor.

This book has tried to suggest different approaches to evaluate the rather puzzling phenomenon of Japanese industrial relations. Westerners regard Japanese labor relations as highly effective while the Japanese look at relations between company management and employee associations (particularly unions) as strained and antagonistic. The high estimate of Japanese labor by Westerners is partly the result of a misunderstanding and perhaps ignorance of the reality of the Japanese situation. I have tried to shed some light in this book on the trouble facing Japanese labor today. At the same time, I have attempted to evaluate the reasons for a low estimation of the present state of labor relations by the Japanese.

Japan has been much too concerned with the idea of "modernization," taking the Western model of development as an ideal. Since we are now very well aware of the troubles and difficulty of using the Western model for industrial relations, Japanese labor is now facing a real challenge to create a "Japanese model" for labor relations which will not take the Western model as its ideal. In this sense, Japan has been unable to find an alternative to the Western example. Japan no longer is content to "catch up" to the

West economically. And it is now time for us to explore a future model for labor relations without seeking it in the West.

The reality of Japanese industrial relations shows that the main difficulty and confusion comes from the incongruity between the modern industrial relations system, the traditional approach to dispute settlement, and the Japanese value system. It is ironic to note that the very advantages of the "Japanese way," such as the human and personal aspects of labor relations, the avoidance of clear-cut decisions, a preference for conciliation rather than adjudication and a better understanding of the continuity of labor relations are mostly based on traditional practices and values which we have been regarding as obstacles to modernization. Thus, Japan should become emancipated from her obsession of believing that a different approach to labor relations is not the sign of underdevelopment but rather is reflective of the real meaning and functions of industrial relations in a different social context.

Difficulties have been caused by friction between traditional practices and values and "Western" ideas, as we Japanese understood them, rather than with the Western system itself. As a result, our labor relations sytem has been modified in practice into a peculiar Japanese entity. The ideologies of modernization, rationalization and emphasis on legal rights have played an important role in this transformation. Such Western ideology represented "progress" in Japanese minds. Thus, traditional values have been neglected or denied and no serious effort has been made to challenge the defects and evils of industrialization. A remarkable inconsistency between the ideology and practice has developed in the sense that, on the ideological level, everything traditionally Japanese has been negatively estimated while everything Western has been highly esteemed. However, in practice, the traditional values have been playing a dominant role in labor relations, albeit behind the scenes. Modern legal notions really never have been accepted as the basis for a value system to rule the behavior of employers and unions. The courts have been utilized only to assert one party's position when there is a serious conflict which cannot be settled in accordance with traditional rules of behavior.

Modern institutions such as the courts or labor relations commissions became involved in dispute settlement when the unions became dissatisfied with their bargaining position. Yet the courts or LRCs never have worked in ways beneficial to adjudication. The actual solutions to labor disputes always have taken place in a traditional way, either through established institutions (the LRCs or courts) or outside of them (traditional amicable way of settlement). Thus, the role of modern ideas and systems in labor relations has been rather negative. The methods for dispute settlement have never become the basis for rules of labor relations; instead, they have been used as excuses for providing an emotional catharsis for both parties in a labor dispute.

The observation of the recent trends in Europe shows that more emphasis on the human nature of labor relations and more communication with the shop floor is urgently needed to cope with contemporary problems in a highly industrialized society. Westerners will find many advantages in the traditional Japanese approach to labor relations. At the same time, I have tried to analyze why the Japanese system has tended to become obsolete and inflexible since it was introduced after the Second World War. The diversity of the functions of Japanese institutions is one of the reasons for the dynamic nature of Japanese society. Our difficulty is that we have been too naive on an ideological level as to believe that we have to utilize the Western system in accordance with its original principles for resolving conflicts. If we admit the reality of borrowing from the Western system for our own purposes, we might link more efficiently the traditional values and rationale of the Western system for the purpose of promoting a forum for solving contemporary labor problems. Thus, the Japanese experience demonstrates to the West that different values can be valuable for solving labor problems and that, for developing nations, ideological commitment to a Western model of industrial relations without insight into national cultural and sociological realities will cause only trouble.

NOTES

1. For instance, Thilo Ramm points out, "Labor disputes can be efficiently settled only if the employee is not threatened with the loss of his job when submitting a grievance. Today the French and the German labor courts almost always decide disputes only after the contract of employment was terminated," in "The Structure and Function of Labor Courts," in *Dispute Settlement Procedures in Five Western European Countries*, p. 23. Also, Folke Schmidt states, "If once a merchant would happen to bring an action in court against another merchant, this ordinarily would be the end of the business relation between them," in "Conciliation, Adjudication and Administration: Three Methods of Decision Making in Labor Disputes," in *Dispute Settlement Procedures*, p. 59.

2. "What the technostructure gives to the union, it can also give without a union or avoid having a union. At a minimum the union shrinks in stature," John Kenneth Galbraith, *The New Industrial State*, p. 275.

3. *Future Industrial Relations and Implications for the ILO: An Interim Report*, International Institute for Labor Studies, Geneva (August 1971), p. 60.

4. Folke Schmidt, "Conciliation, Adjudication and Administration," p. 47.

5. Folke Schmidt submits three methods of reasoning applied by bodies dealing with labor disputes: conciliation, adjudication and administration. He confesses that "the term administration is much too broad and has been chosen much for the lack of a better term," ibid., p. 47.

6. Ibid., p. 57.

7. Ibid.

8. "In many such cases . . . negotiation within established practice will not be so different in fact from adjudication by a tribunal which applies an industrial jurisprudence and attempts to conciliate. Both processes pay attention to agreed rights . . . . The rhetoric will differ more than the substance," K. W. Wedderburn, "Conflicts of 'Rights' and Conflicts of 'Interests' in Labor Disputes," in *Dispute Settlement Procedures*, p. 88.

9. Julius Stone, *Legal Systems and Lawyers' Reasonings* (Stanford: Stanford University Press, 1964), p. 229. He cites the following words from P. Hech, *Interessenjurisprudenz* (1933): "Er kann wie Pilatus die Hände waschen und ruhig sagen; Ich bin nicht schuld, schuld sind die Begriffe" ["He can wash his hands as Pilate and calmly say: 'I am not responsible, the concepts are responsible' "].

10. For a discussion of the ombudsman system, see Walter Gellhorn, *Ombudsmen and Others* (Cambridge, Mass.: Harvard University Press, 1967) and *When Americans Complain* (Cambridge, Mass.: Harvard University Press, 1966).

11. Organization for Economic Co-operation and Development [O.E.C.D.], *Workers' Participation*, Final Report on an International Management Seminar Convened by the OECD, Versailles, 5 March to 8 March, 1975 (Paris: OECD, 1976), pp. 56–57.

12. See Johannes Schregle, "Workers' Participation in Decisions with Undertakings," *International Labour Review* 113, no. 1 (1976), pp. 4 ff.

BIBLIOGRAPHY

Works in English and German

Aaron, Benjamin. "Methods of Industrial Action: Courts, Administrative Agencies and Legislatures." In *Industrial Conflict*, edited by Benjamin Aaron and K. W. Wedderburn. New York: Crane Russak & Co., 1972.

Abegglen, James. *Management and Worker: The Japanese Solution.* Tokyo: Kodansha International, 1973.

————. *The Japanese Factory.* Glencoe, Ill.: The Free Press, 1958.

Atleson, J. B. "Work Group Behavior and Wildcat Strikes: The Causes and Functions of Industrial Civil Disobedience." *Ohio State Law Journal* 34 (1973): 751–816.

Ballon, Robert J., ed. *Doing Business in Japan.* Tokyo: Sophia University Press, 1967.

————. *The Japanese Employee.* Tokyo: Sophia University Press, 1969.

Ben-Dasan, Isaiah. *The Japanese and the Jews.* Translated by Richard L. Gage. Tokyo: John Weatherhill Co., 1972.

Boulding, Kenneth E. *Conflict and Defense: General Theory.* New York: Harper & Brothers, 1962.

————. "The Economics of Human Conflict." In *The Nature of Human Conflict*, edited by Elton B. McNeil. Englewood Cliffs, N.J.: Prentice-Hall, 1965.

Brooks, George W. *Sources of Vitality in the American Labor Movement.* New York State School of Industrial and Labor Relations, *Bulletin* 41. Ithaca: Cornell University Press, 1960.

Caudill, William. "Patterns of Emotion in Modern Japan." In *Japanese Culture—Its Development and Characteristics*, edited by Robert J.

Smith and Richard K. Beardsley. Chicago: Aldine Publishing Co., 1962.

Cole, Robert E. "Permanent Employment in Japan: Facts and Fantasies." *Industrial and Labor Relations Review* 26, no. 1 (1972): 615–30.

———. *Japanese Blue Collar—The Changing Tradition.* Berkeley and Los Angeles: University of California Press, 1973.

Commons, John R. *The Legal Foundations of Capitalism.* New York: MacMillan Co., 1957.

Coser, Lewis. *The Function of Social Conflict.* New York: The Free Press, 1956.

Dahrendorf, Ralf. *Class and Class Conflict in Industrial Society.* Stanford: Stanford University Press, 1959.

Doi, Takeo. *The Anatomy of Dependence.* Translated by John Bester Tokyo: Kodansha International, 1973.

Dore, Ronald P. *British Factory—Japanese Factory.* Berkeley and Los Angeles: University of California Press, 1973.

———. "Commitment—To What, by Whom and Why?" *The Social and Cultural Background of Labor Management Relations in Asian Countries: Proceedings of the 1971 Asian Regional Conference on Industrial Relations.* Tokyo: Japan Institute of Labor, 1971.

Dubin, Robert. "Industrial Conflict and Social Welfare." *The Journal of Conflict Resolution* 1 (1957): 179–99.

———. "Constructive Aspects of Industrial Conflict." In *Industrial Conflict,* edited by Arthur Kornhauser, Robert Dubin and Arthur M. Ross. New York: McGraw-Hill Book Co., 1954.

Dufty, Norman F. *Changes in Labour Management Relations in the Enterprises.* Paris: Organization for Economic Co-operation and Development, 1975.

England, Joseph. "Equilibrium and Change in an Industrial Relations System: The Hong Kong Case." *The Social and Cultural Background of Labor Management Relations in Asian Countries.* Tokyo: Japan Institute of Labor, 1972.

Evans, Robert, Jr. *The Labor Economies of Japan and the United States.* New York: Praeger Publishers, 1971.

Fox, A. and A. Flanders. "The Reform of Collective Bargaining: From Donovan to Durkheim." *British Journal of Industrial Relations* 7 (1969): 151–80.

Galbraith, John Kenneth. *The New Industrial State,* 2d rev. ed. Boston: Houghton Mifflin Co., 1971.

Giugni, Gino. "The Peace Obligation." In *Industrial Conflict—A Comparative Legal Study*, edited by Benjamin Aaron and K. W. Wedderburn. New York: Crane, Russak & Co., 1972.

Goldstein, Joseph. *Government of British Trade Unions*. London: Allen & Unwin, 1952.

Gulliver, P. H. "Case Studies of Law in Non-Western Societies" and "Dispute Settlement without Courts: The Ndendeuli of Southern Tanzania." In *Law in Culture and Society*, edited by Laura Nader. Chicago: Aldine Publishing Co., 1969.

Hanami, Tadashi. "Future Industrial Relations—Japan." *Bulletin of the International Institute for Labor Studies*, no. 10 (1972): 85–113.

———. "The Lifetime Employment System in Japan." *Atlanta Economic Review* 26, no. 3 (1976): 35–39.

Harari, Ehud. *The Politics of Labor Legislation in Japan—National-International Interaction*. Berkeley and Los Angeles: University of California Press, 1973.

Henderson, D. F. *Conciliation and Japanese Law—Tokugawa and Modern*, 2 vols. Tokyo: University of Tokyo Press, 1965.

Horke, Gertrude. *Arbeiter unter der roten Sonne—Japans Unternehemensgenwerkshaften*. Vienna: Europaverlag, 1976.

Hyman, Richard. *Strikes*. London: Fontana, 1972.

Inglehart, Ronald. "The Silent Revolution in Europe: Intergenerational Change in Post-Industrial Societies." *The American Political Science Review* 65 (1971): 991–1017.

Karsh, Bernard and Robert E. Cole. "Industrialization and the Convergence Hypothesis: Some Aspects of Contemporary Japan." *Journal of Social Issues* 24, no. 4 (1968): 45–64.

Kawashima, Takeyoshi. "Dispute Resolution in Contemporary Japan." In *Law in Japan*, edited by A. T. von Mehren. Cambridge, Mass.: Harvard University Press; Tokyo and Rutland, Vt.: Charles E. Tuttle Co., 1964.

Kerr, Clark. *Labor and Management in Industrial Society*. Garden City, N.Y.: Doubleday & Co., 1964.

———; J. T. Dunlop; F. Harbison; and C. A. Meyers. *Industrialism and Industrial Man*. New York: Oxford University Press, 1964.

Knowles, K. G. J. C. *Strikes—A Study in Industrial Conflict*. Oxford: Basil Blackwell, 1952.

Kornhauser, Arthur; Robert Dubin; and Arthur M. Ross. *Industrial Conflict*. New York: McGraw-Hill Co., 1954.

Lipset, Seymour Martin. "Political Sociology." In *Sociology Today*, edited by R. K. Merton et al. New York: Basic Books, 1959.

Lubman, Stanley. "Mao and Mediation: Politics and Dispute Resolution in Communist China." *California Law Review* 55 (1967): 1284–1359.

Macaulay, Stewart. "Non-Contractual Relations in Business: A Preliminary Study." *American Sociological Review* 28, no. 1 (1963): 55–67.

Nader, Laura, ed. "Introduction" and "Styles of Court Procedure: To Make the Balance." In *Law in Culture and Society*. Chicago: Aldine Publishing Co., 1969.

Nakane, Chie. *Japanese Society*. Berkeley and Los Angeles: University of California Press, 1972.

Park, Robert E. and Ernest W. Burgess. *Introduction to the Science for Society*. Chicago: University of Chicago Press, 1921.

Parsons, Talcott. *The Social System*. London: Tavistock Institute Publications, 1952.

Ramm, Thilo. "Labor Courts and Grievance Settlement in West Germany." In *Labor Courts and Grievance Settlement in Western Europe*, edited by Benjamin Aaron. Berkeley and Los Angeles: I University of California Press, 1971.

———. "The Structure and Function of Labor Courts," in *Dispute Settlement Procedures in Five Western European Countries*, edited by Benjamin Aaron. Los Angeles: Institute of Industrial Relations of the University of California, 1969.

Roberts, Ben C. "Die Zunahme in der Entwicklung Industrieller Unruhen seit 1945 und ihre Tendenzen." In *Arbeitskonflikte und Arbeitskampf*, edited by International Stiftung HUMANUM. Cologne: Peter Hanstein Verlag, 1973.

Rohlen, Thomas P. *For Harmony and Strength—Japanese White-Collar Organization in Anthropological Perspective*. Berkeley and Los Angeles: University of California Press, 1974.

Ross, Arthur M. and Paul T. Hartman. *Changing Patterns of Industrial Conflict*. New York: John Wiley Co., 1960.

Sayles, Leonard R. "Wildcat Strikes " *Harvard Business Review* 32, no. 6 (1954): 42–52.

———, and George Strauss. *The Local Union*. 2d rev. ed. New York: Harcourt, Brace and World, 1967.

Schmidt, Folke. "Industrial Action: The Role of Trade Unions and Employers' Associations." In *Industrial Conflict—A Comparative Legal Survey*, edited by Benjamin Aaron and K. W. Wedderburn.

New York: Crane, Russak & Co., 1972.

————. "Conciliation, Adjudication and Administration: Three Methods of Decision Making in Labor Disputes," in *Dispute Settlement Procedures in Five Western European Countries*, edited by Benjamin Aaron. Los Angeles: Institute of Industrial Relations of the University of California, 1969.

Schregle, Johannes. "Workers' Participation in Decisions with Undertakings." *International Labour Review* 113, no. 1 (1976): 1–15.

Siegel, Abraham J. "Method and Substance in Theorizing about Worker Protest." *Aspects of Labor Economics—A Conference of the Universities—National Bureau Committee for Economic Research*. Princeton: Princeton University Press, 1962.

Stagner, Ross. "The Psychology of Human Conflict." In *The Nature of Human Conflict*, edited by Elton B. McNeil. Englewood Cliffs, N. J.: Prentice-Hall, 1965.

Stone, Julius. *Legal Systems and Lawyers' Reasonings*. Stanford: Stanford University Press, 1964.

Taira, Koji. *Economic Development and the Labor Market in Japan*. New York: Columbia University Press, 1970.

Wedderburn, K. W. "Conflicts of 'Rights' and Conflicts of 'Interests' in Labor Disputes." In *Dispute Settlement Procedures in Five Western European Countries*, edited by Benjamin Aaron. Los Angeles: Institute of Industrial Relations of the University of California, 1969.

Works in Japanese

Azuma, Mitsutoshi. "Futō Rōdō-kōi ni Okeru Niritsu-haihan" [Antinomy in Unfair Labor Practices]. *Nihon Rōdō-hō Gakkai shi* 28 [Journal of Japanese Labor Law Association] (1966): 3–18.

Ben-Dasan, Isaiah. *Nihonkyō ni tsuite* [On Nihonism]. Tokyo: Bungei Shunjūsha, 1972.

Cole, Robert E. "America no Nihon Rōshi Kankei-kan to Genjitsu" [American Ideas on Japanese Industrial Relations and Reality]. *Nihon Rōdō Kyōkai Zasshi* 161 [Journal of Japan Institute of Labor] (1972): 27–33.

Fujita, Wakao. *Rōdō Kumiai Undō no Tenkan* [Conversion of Labor Union Movement] Tokyo: Nihon Hyōronsha, 1967.

Hosoya, Matsuta. *Nihon no Rōdō Kumiai Undō* [Labor Union Movement in Japan]. Tokyo: Shakai Shisō Kenkyūkai, 1958.

Ishida, Takeshi. "Nihon ni Okeru Hōteki Shikō no Hatten to Kihonteki Jinken." [Development of Legal Thinking and Fundamental Human Rights in Japan]. In *Kihonteki Jinken* [Fundamental Human Rights], Vol. 2. Tokyo: Tokyo Daigaku Shuppankai, 1968.

Ishiguro, Takuji. "Nishi Doitsu ni Okeru Dantai Kōshō" [Collective Bargaining in West Germany]. *Kikan Rōdō-hō* 39 [Institution Labor Law] (1961): 140–50.

Ishii, Teruhisa. "Rōdō Iinkai ni tsuite" [On the Labor Relations Commission]. *Chūrōi Jihō* 519 [Central Labor Relations Commission Journal] (1973): 6–8.

Kamizuma, Yoshiaki. *Rōdō Undō Nōto* [Notes on the Labor Movement]. Tokyo: Rōdai Shinsho, 1965.

Kawashima, Takeyoshi. *Nihonjin no Hō Ishiki* [Legal Rights Consciousness of the Japanese]. Tokyo: Iwanami Shoten, 1967.

Kimura, Bin. *Hito to Hito to no Aida* [Between Persons]. Tokyo: Kōbundō, 1972.

Kishima Tankō Rōdō Kumiai [Kishima Coal Mining Company Employees Union]. *Teki yori mo Ichinichi Nagaku* [One Day Longer than the Enemy]. Tokyo: Kishima Tankō Rōdō Kumiai, 1958.

Koike, Kazuo. *Nihon no Chingin Kōshō* [Wage Negotiations in Japan]. Tokyo: Tokyo Daigaku Shuppankai, 1962.

Kōshiro, Kazutoshi. "Dantai Kōshō to Sōgi" [Collective Bargaining and Dispute]. In *Nihon no Rōdō Kumiai* [Trade Unions in Japan], edited by Taishirō Shirai. Tokyo: Nihon Hyōronsha, 1967.

Maruyama, Masao. "Rekishi Ishiki no 'Kōsō' " [The "Old Stratum" Historical Concept]. In *Rekishi Shisō-shū: Nihon no Shisō*: 6 [An Anthology of Historical Thought: Japanese Thought]. Tokyo: Chikuma Shobō, 1972.

Mishima, Yukio. *Ranryō Ō* [King Ranryō]. Tokyo: Shinchōsha, 1971.

Mitsui Tankō Rōdō Kumiai [Mitsui Coal Mining Company Employees Union]. *Eiyū Naki 113 Nichi no Tatakai* [Fight for 113 Days Without a Hero]. Tokyo: Rōdō Hōritsu Junpō, 1954.

Morinaga, Eizaburō. "Seisan-kanri" [Production Control]. In *Shin Rōdō-hō Kōza* [New Lectures on Labor Law], Vol. 4, edited by the Japan Labor Law Association. Tokyo: Yūhikaku, 1967.

Nagai, Yōnosuke. *Jūkōzō Shakai to Bōryoku* [Soft-Structured Society and Violence]. Tokyo: Chūōkōronsha, 1971.

Ōta, Kaoru. *Gendai no Rōdō-undō* [Modern Labor Movement].

Tokyo: Rōdō Horitsu Junpōsha, 1970.

———. *Rōdō Kumiai-ron* [On Trade Unions]. Tokyo: Rōdō Keizaisha, 1961.

———. *Tatakai no Nakade* [In the Midst of Struggle]. Tokyo: Aoki Shoten, 1971.

———. *Watashi no Keiei-ron to Keieisha-ron* [My Views on Management and Managers]. Tokyo: Yuki Shobō, 1966.

Shiba, Ryōtarō and Donald Keene. *Nihonjin to Nihon Bunka* [The Japanese and Japanese Culture]. Tokyo: Chūōkōron, 1971.

Shirai, Taishirō. *Kigyōbetsu Kumiai* [Enterprise Unions]. Tokyo: Chūōkōron, 1968.

———. *Rōdō Kumiai no Zaisei* [Finances of Trade Unions]. Tokyo: Nihon Hyōronsha, 1964.

Suzuki, Mitsuo. *Funsō no Ronri to Nihonjin* [Logic of Conflict and the Japanese]. Chūōkōron 8 [Public Opinion] (1971): 294–311.

Yamaguchi, Kōichirō. "Rōdō Saiban no Kyakkan Sei" [The Objectiveness of Legal Judgment in Labor Cases]. *Jurist*, no. 487 (1971): 24–30.

Zadankai [Discussions]. "Kari Shobun Seido Unyō no Kako, Genzai, Shōrai" [The Past, Present and Future Operations of the Provisional Disposition System]. *Hanrei Times*, no. 67 (1957): 39–56.

LAW REPORTS

Bessatsu Rōdō Hōritsu Junpō [BRHJ—Journal of Labor Law]. Rōdō Hōritsu Junpōsha, 1949-current. Semi-monthly.

Futō Rōdō Kōi Jiken Meirei-shū [FRKM—Reports of the Orders on Unfair Labor Practices Cases]. Office of the Central Labor Relations Commission, 1949-current. Annually or bi-annually.

Hanrei Jihō [Case Journal]. Nihon Hyōron-sha, 1953-current. Tri-monthly.

Rōdō Hanrei [Labor Cases]. Sangyō Rōdō Chōsa-sho, 1966-current. Bi-monthly.

Rōdō Kankei Minji Saibanrei-shū [RKMS—Selected Reports of Judicial Precedents in Civil Labor Cases]. Office of the Supreme Court, 1950-current. Bi-monthly.

Saikō Saibansho Keiji Hanrei-shū [SSKH—Reports of Judicial Precedents of the Supreme Court in Criminal Cases]. Office of the Supreme Court, 1947-current. Ten to fifteen times a year.

Saikō Saibansho Minji Hanrei-shū [SSMH—Reports of Judicial Precedents of the Supreme Court in Civil Cases]. Office of the Supreme Court, 1947-current. Ten to fifteen times a year.

DOCUMENTS AND OFFICIAL PUBLICATIONS
WESTERN AND JAPANESE SOURCES

Bureau of Statistics, Office of the Prime Minister. *Rōdō Ryoku Chosa* [Labor Force Survey]. Annual.

Central Labor Relations Commission. *Rōdō Iinkai Nenpō* [Annual Report of the Labor Relations Commission]. Annual.

International Institute for Labor Studies. *Future Industrial Relations and Implications for the ILO: An Interim Report*. Geneva: International Institute for Labor Studies, 1971.

International Labor Organization (ILO). "Report of the Fact-Finding and Conciliation Commission on Freedom of Association Concerning Persons Employed in the Public Sector in Japan" (Dreyer Report). *Official Bulletin* 49:1 (January 1966).

Japan Institute of Labor. *Directory of Major Trade Unions in Japan* (1977). Tokyo: Japan Institute of Labor, 1977.

Ministry of Labor. *Rōdō Kumiai Kihon Chōsa* [Basic Survey of Trade Unions]. Annual.

———. *Rōdō Sōgi Tōkei Chōsa Nen Hōkoku* [Annual Report of Statistics and Survey of Labor Disputes], 1975. Tokyo: Ministry of Labor, 1976.

———. *Rōdō Tōkei Yōran* [Summary of Labor Statistics]. Tokyo: Ministry of Labor, 1977.

Seisansei Honbu [Japan Productivity Center]. *Katsuyō Rōdō Tōkei* [Practical Labor Statistics], 1977. Tokyo: Japan Productivity Center, 1977.

U.S. Department of Labor. *Manpower Report, Report of the President: Report on Manpower Requirements, Resources, Utilization and Training*. Washington, D.C.: Government Printing Office 1974.

INDEX

Note: Page numbers in boldface indicate the main reference.

249

Kimura, Bin, 50, 51, 62, 64
kinship, 56; consciousness, 48, 51, 57, 110, 111; group, 55
Kishima Coal Mining Co. Case, 63
Knowles, K. G. J. C., 149
Kōheiiinkai (Local Civil Service Commission), 102
Kokkōrōren (Joint Federation of National Service Employees), 91
Kokurō (National Railway Workers' Union), 91, 122, 176
Kongō Seisakujo Co. Case, **191–93**, 194
Kornhauser, Arthur, 118
Kōrōi (Public Corporation and National Enterprise Labor Relations Commission), 103
Kōshiro, Kazutoshi, 146
Kubo Shoten Case, 190
Kure City Case, 211

labor mobility, 32ff., 95
Labor Relations Adjustment Law, 101, 181
Labor Relations Commission, **205–8**, 214–16, 219, 221, 238
Labor Relations Adjustment Law, 101, 181
labor shortage, 32, 33, 35
Labor Standards Law, 25, 162, 168
labor surplus, 32, 35,
Liberal Democratic Party, 111, 142
lifetime employment, 24, **25–35**, 37, 89
Lipset, S. M., 116
lockout, 54, 81ff., 153, 195
loyalty (to the enterprise), 28, 43

Macaulay, Stewart, 32
Maeda, Hajime, 206
mediation, 206, 208, 210
mediator, 61
Meyers, C. A., 23
Mishima, Yukio, 142
Mitsui Coal Mining Co. Case, 62, 65, 133–35
miuchi. See kinship

Nader, Laura, 58, 59
Nagai, Yōnosuke, 195
Nakane, Chie, 137, 138
national confederation, 90, 92ff.
National Labor Relations Board (of the U.S.), 74
National Railways, 90, 102, 106, 130, 145
National Railways Workers' Union. *See Kokurō*
Nihon Steel Co. Case, 62, 100
Nikkeiren (Japanese Employers Association), 205
Nishi Nihon Newspaper Co. Case, 168, 170
nōkin-suto, 172ff.
nominated strike, 163, **165–69**, 172; *see also* designated strike
"no-strike" clause, 54
Northwest Airlines Case, 82, 83

Ōkōchi, Kazuo, 207
ombudsman, 235
one-person strike, 165–69
organizational conflict, 120ff.
Ōta, Kaoru, 62, 85, 99, 133, 135, 144, 145, 165, 183, 184, 206

Parsons, Talcott, 31, 45
partial strike, **163–65**, 169ff., 172
Penal Code, 75, 156, 182
permanent employment. *See*

251